Casual Yogi have helped me become a better person and leader. We all know the "what"—that yoga is good for us. For an engineer like me, I needed the "why" and the "how." This book illustrates that and helps create a road map to achieve balance between body, mind, and career success.

— **TUHIN HALDER,** Vice President of Finance and Operations, Comcast Corporation

In today's evolving business climate, we must be balanced and flexible. This book provides a practical and traditionally proven approach to personal and professional transformation from someone who actually lives it.

— **TOM BAKALY,** Chief Executive Officer, Beach Cities Health District

Vish is a true shaman in business clothes. He has provided me with invaluable wisdom over the years, and now he and Vishvketu have written a book that is perfect for our times. *The Business Casual Yogi* is an easily digestible guide to balancing the pressures of life through yoga. It is an essential read for today's executives.

— **JORDAN BERKE,** Founder, Tomorrow Retail, and Former Vice President, Walmart eCommerce

An absolute treasure! Vish delivers a powerfully eloquent and timely formula for today's business leaders to truly succeed. Utilizing age-old proven methodologies, which Vish articulates in an easy-to-understand manner, business leaders can now easily implement these simple yet profound strategies to design and live a life that provides fulfillment and achievement. This book is a must-have companion for every business professional who wants to experience the most from life, both professionally and personally!

— **HEIDI LaGUMINA,** Master Platinum Results Coach, Robbins Research International, Inc.

This book is a great innovative guide for self-improvement! I would recommend it to everybody who would like to get more balance in their life. Observing our inner state can give us more awareness, joy, and success. If you would like to improve your performance in life and work, this book is a great support to achieve this aim.

— **ÁGNES KOVÁCS,** Olympic Gold-Medalist Swimmer and Executive Coach

Words do not have the capacity to express my love and respect for Yogrishi Vishvketu and Vish Chatterji. They have the ability to bring the Heavens to the Earth, and the Earth to the Heavens. That Divine balance I have felt every time I have been in Yogrishi Vishvketu's class. His sense of humor and his prayerful skills as a yogi are unsurpassed. His gift of Seva to his school for children uplifts and inspires me to serve more.

— **GURMUKH KHALSA,** Cofounder and Director, Golden Bridge Yoga Center, Los Angeles, and Master of Kundalini Yoga

This is a very important read for those interested in merging their yoga practice and spiritual values with the business world. I highly recommend this as another look on how we can cope with the vastly changing landscape of the financial situation worldwide, and being able to apply yogic and ancient Ayurvedic understanding to the mix.

— **SRIDHAR SILBERFEIN,** Founder, Desert Essence; Founder and Executive Producer, Bhakti Fest; Director, Center for Spiritual Studies

The Business Casual Yogi is a perfect template for personal growth, leadership, and transformation. Yogrishi Vishvketu and Vish Chatterji have designed a program that will change your body, mind-set, and decision-making. This is a seamless integration of Vedic sciences for enlightened living. Kudos!

— **DR. SUHAS KSHIRSAGAR,** BAMS, MD (Ayurveda), faculty member at Chopra Center for Well-Being, and author of *The Hot Belly Diet* and *Change Your Schedule, Change Your Life*

PRAISE FOR *THE BUSINESS CASUAL YOGI*

As a successful executive from the business world, having under-gone extensive yogic training, Vish offers a very credible, artic-ulate, and thoughtful approach to improving the quality of our professional lives by appropriately leveraging the principle of yoga in a business context.

— KASH RANGAN, Managing Director, Bank of America

I loved this book and will read it again. The authors beautifully blend practical and spiritual advice on how to be our best, whole selves. This book is packed with wisdom and is a must-read for my teams.

— KAHLA BROUSSARD, Vice President of Retail Operations, Sephora

A few books and thought systems deeply shaped my career and personal choices. *The 4-Hour Workweek* helped me break some business school habits. *Crucial Confrontations* helped me navi-gate challenging personal and professional relationships. Ikkyu's poems taught me that spiritualism and fun are not mutually ex-clusive. *The Business Casual Yogi* connected all of these dots in a delightful and completely unexpected way. Vish and Vishvketu explain the Vedic knowledge system through relatable personal anecdotes and practical questions that force self-reflection and pierce the veil surrounding yoga as a practice. Read this book if you want to achieve greater balance in your life.

— OHAD ZEIRA, Vice President Fleet Ventures, Avis Budget Group

Yogrishi Vishvketu and Vish Chatterji have written an excellent book that makes the ancient wisdom tradition of Yoga acces-sible to a modern audience who may be engaged in the world of business and technology. They are ideally suited to write this book, given Vish has a background in business, technology en-trepreneurship, and executive coaching. Yogarishi is well-steeped in a traditional lineage of yoga teachers based out of Rishikesh, which I often think of as the world capital or Silicon Valley of yoga traditions. The result is this book, which takes an ancient, sophisticated, and very practical wisdom tradition and makes it relevant to a modern-day professional audience that is interested in incorporating different elements of the vast philosophy of yoga into their lives and find success, meaning, and fulfillment in their personal and professional lives.

— **GOPI KALLAYIL,** Chief Evangelist, Brand Marketing, Google, and author of *The Internet to the Inner-net* and *The Happy Human*

A thoroughly enjoyable read. As a business professional who has not had much experience in yoga, I was curious to learn the connection. Ultimately, *The Business Casual Yogi* delivers on its promise of helping one take charge of mind, body, and career. The frameworks practiced in the eight limbs of yoga were extraordinarily helpful in laying out a path for success in business and life!

— **ERIK MORENO,** Executive Vice President, Corporate Development and Mergers and Acquisitions, Sony Pictures Entertainment

This book is an invaluable guide for anyone seeking to strengthen their mind-body-soul connection in a hyperactive modern world. When I first met Vish, I was chronically fatigued, constantly stressed, and my mind couldn't shut off. After incorporating the principles and techniques into my daily practice, I saw radical improvements to my mental, emotional, and physical health and in my leadership performance. This book has empowered me to take control and live my life from a place of gratitude, grace, and authenticity.

— **ZEINA CHARARA,** Senior Vice President of Finance, FabFitFun

Vish has helped me become a better person and a leader, as our relationship matured from being classmates at Ross, to friends, to family friends, and now coach. The teachings of *The Business*

Eight years ago, when my wine brand was just a figment of my imagination, Vish facilitated a deeper dive into not just the brand but also my "existential thrive" within the brand. He is indeed a born teacher. This book is a *"udyam-veda"* (business treatise)—not a light read but a systematic and prolific insight into an ancient philosophy that can shape a dynamic future.

— **NEETA MITTAL,** Founder, LXV Wines

Somehow, my dear friend Vish has always been able to make sense of things, from the early days when we were trying to understand the nuances of strategic warfare between titans of the business world in the classrooms of the business school at the University of Michigan. As a business executive living an intensely busy life across multiple continents, I have struggled to make sense of my life, [my] work, and what I seek to achieve. As I read this book, I found a clarity that was both comforting and enlightening. I was able to connect with a holistic element of my being and purpose, using the teachings of ancient Indian philosophies articulated in the context of our modern world. I invite you to experience the book for yourselves, because as Vish and Vishvketu say, after reading this book "you'll seek to unlock your intuition so that you rely on your own inner teacher to make the right choices for you.

— **SHAILABH ATAL,** Director, Business Transformation, Verizon

For those professionals looking to take their business and their personal lives to the next level, Vish has provided all the necessary tools and ingredients for your journey. Truly a book that personally inspires through introspection, and one you will want to continually refer to.

— **JIM SCHLAGER,** Principal, Moss Adams Wealth Management

Thank goodness someone has made yoga philosophy accessible to everyone in the twentieth century. Some may think yoga philosophy is for people who live in caves without the worries most of us living in this mad world now have. On the contrary, we need yoga philosophy even more. *The Business Casual Yogi* beautifully translates yogic wisdom and practices into an easy-to-understand guide enabling us to shine our light as we negotiate our life and career in modern-day chaos.

— **ANANDI,** Founder, The Sleep Guru, and author of *Breathe Better, Sleep Better*

My research suggests that negotiation success is enhanced by mindfully aligning emotions and genuinely drawing on your leadership strengths across roles—being yourself in collaborative and competitive conversations at work. Vish Chatterji and Yogrishi Vishvketu share wisdom, experiences, and practices to help you tune into yourself and others so that you can be fully present, centered, and grounded in business.

— **SHIRLI KOPELMAN,** PhD, Professor of Management and Organizations, Ross School of Business, University of Michigan, and author of *Negotiating Genuinely: Being Yourself in Business*

This is a book for our times. Everyone today is "in business" by virtue of what we each have to navigate to succeed in this world. By integrating the wisdom of both yoga and Ayurveda, the authors have offered modern readers a tried-and-true path to success by living in harmony with nature. Ayurveda is the only established medical system that defines health as a balance of body, mind, and spirit, and yoga is far more powerful than what most people understand as physical postures. The relevance of these ancient teachings in the context of Vedic philosophy from thousands of years ago is being daily proven by modern science, and the contemporary perspectives and direct lineage teachings of these two successful businessmen/yogis are priceless. This is a resource to turn to again and again on the path to lasting health and true wealth.

— **DENISE BARACK,** Director of Program Innovation, Kripalu Center for Yoga & Health

The
BUSINESS
CASUAL
YOGI

The
BUSINESS
CASUAL
YOGI

Take Charge of Your
BODY, MIND, AND CAREER

VISH CHATTERJI, MBA *with* YOGRISHI VISHVKETU, PhD

MANDALA
PUBLISHING
San Rafael, California

MANDALA
PUBLISHING

An Imprint of MandalaEarth
PO Box 3088
San Rafael, CA 94912
www.MandalaEarth.com

Find us on Facebook: www.facebook.com/MandalaEarth
Follow us on Twitter: @MandalaEarth

Library of Congress Cataloging-in-Publication Data available.

ISBN: 978-1-68383-687-2

Our goal in publishing this book is to provide general education and information about yoga and wellness topics. Yoga provides numerous benefits and is a great way to improve health, but before participating in any diet or exercise program or using any diet or fitness products or services that may be described in this book, we strongly recommend that you consult with a physician or other healthcare provider.

The information provided in this book is strictly for reference only and is not in any manner a substitute for medical advice or direct guidance of a qualified instructor. Not all exercises and activities described in this book are suitable for all persons. Practicing under the direct supervision and guidance of a qualified instructor, in addition to the direction of your healthcare provider, can also help determine what exercises and activities are suitable for your particular case.

Publisher: Raoul Goff
Associate Publisher: Phillip Jones
Creative Director: Chrissy Kwasnik
Associate Editor: Tessa Murphy
Managing Editor: Lauren LePera
Senior Production Editor: Rachel Anderson
Senior Production Manager: Greg Steffen

Illustrations by Adam Raiti
Designed by TheBookDesigners

Insight Editions would like to thank Anna Eames for her careful and thorough copyediting and Megan Sinead Harris for her design contributions.

ROOTS of PEACE   REPLANTED PAPER

Mandala Publishing, in association with Roots of Peace, will plant two trees for each tree used in the manufacturing of this book. Roots of Peace is an internationally renowned humanitarian organization dedicated to eradicating land mines worldwide and converting war-torn lands into productive farms and wildlife habitats. Roots of Peace will plant two million fruit and nut trees in Afghanistan and provide farmers there with the skills and support necessary for sustainable land use.

Manufactured in India by Insight Editions

10 9 8 7 6 5 4 3 2 1

business casual noun

busi·ness ca·su·al | ˈbiz-nəs ˈkazh-wəl

: a style of outer dress for working professionals

yogi noun

yo·gi | ˈyō-gē

: one who seeks their fullest inner potential through yoga

CONTENTS

FOREWORD

I am honored to write the foreword for *The Business Casual Yogi*. I have known Vish Chatterji for over twenty years and have heard many a tale from his Himalayan journeys and meetings with saints and teachers, one of them being his friend and teacher Yogrishi Vishvketu. Coming from the generation before Vish, I was allowed a unique perch from which to watch a young man explore his Indian roots; learn the Vedic traditions; develop and apply sensitivities; climb and move mountains; endure ups and downs; and mature in spiritual growth. Reflecting back, I am proud to have had an influence on Vish's remarkable journey, as when I invited Vish and his wife to their first encounter with Deepak Chopra, a noted Indian-born American author and thought leader who I followed in my own spiritual journey. Vish later studied under Deepak at the Chopra Center in California, which had a great impact on his coaching style and areas of interest.

I recall a conversation with Vish many years ago as he wondered how he could make an impact with his life. I advised him to first produce a level of personal achievement, credibility, and respect, and the rest would be easy. And so he has, with a BS in engineering from Northwestern and a top-of-his-class finish in the University of Michigan MBA program. He then went on to a career of amazing depth, which included responsible engineering and business positions in the auto industry and a mind-numbing string of accomplishments at several companies and startups in the tech industry on the West Coast. He has now emerged as a prominent new-day business and personal coach to help individuals and corporations reach heightened performance.

Much of my career was spent in the auto industry. I was with Ford Motor Company for twenty years and was credited by Lee Iacocca, Ford's president at the time, with being the chief architect of the highly successful and iconic Ford Mustang. While we produced great commercial successes, I also witnessed top management chaos that precluded open dialogue, alignment of goals, and market innovation. I knew at a gut level that there was a better leadership dynamic that could have resulted in greater success. For example, when I pitched an innovative idea for a "mini" van, it couldn't flourish. Iacocca and I both left Ford as a result of this chaos, going to Chrysler, where Iacocca became CEO and chairman, and I became president.

We created an exceptional management team, acquiring over fifty executives from Ford and leveraging a horde of exceptional Chrysler, leaders, who together executed a remarkable turnaround from the brink of bankruptcy. We launched the industry's first compact and intermediate front-wheel-drive vehicles and created a game-changing new vehicle segment with the Chrysler, minivan. The result was an unheard-of 50 percent increase in market share and dramatically improved quality and profit levels.

When I look back on how we created success, I believe it took highly motivated, energized, and keenly attuned leaders to effect such dramatic results. We had a deep awareness of our customers' needs. We focused on the right product experience, anticipated shifting market needs, and collaborated toward a common vision. These "soft skills" and "emotional intelligence"—terms unknown to us in those days—are prized in leadership today. *The Business Casual Yogi* offers us a clear system through yoga to cultivate those very skills.

During my time at Chrysler, there was no book out there to guide us, and so we learned through gut instinct and trial by fire, but there were indeed casualties. Notwithstanding the great success produced, there were failures in business decisions, careers, personal lives, and personal health. This book presents a system to achieve even greater success with lower personal cost. It will be a powerful resource for professionals in business today who face many of the same pressures to balance personal and professional lives amid their leadership challenges.

In my days of retirement, I have deepened my learning of the ancient Vedic system of India, and in it, I have found wisdom that is directly relevant to what is often missing in leadership today. This practical philosophy focuses on leveraging the entirety of our human potential to improve our lives. Relevant to leadership, this systematic cultivation of soft skills improves our ability to understand our customer, find the optimal path to market leadership, establish shared goals to drive progress, and build interpersonal relationships based on respect, trust, and selfless cooperation.

This is the territory that Vish and Vishvketu dare to explore, using yoga as a tool in a way that has not been done before, as a framework for leadership based on self-awareness and a deeper trust in our truest selves.

Enjoy the book and the journey.

HAL SPERLICH
Member, Automotive Hall of Fame
Former President, Chrysler Corporation
Former Vice President, Ford Motor Company
Former Chairman, Delco Remy International Corporation
Former Chairman and CEO, Pulte Homes

For Uma, Chetan, Jaya, Tejasvi, and Dharma.
May you continue to spread our light.

PREFACE

Yogrishi Vishvketu and I met almost twenty years ago in Rishikesh, India, at the foothills of the Himalayas at the famed Yoga Niketan Ashram, where he was a senior yoga teacher. I had just finished college and was backpacking through India, exploring my roots before starting my first job. After a trekking accident deep in the Himalayas, I navigated to Rishikesh to recuperate and by chance checked into the Yoga Niketan Ashram. There I learned yoga from Vishvketu, and the teachings became a foundational pillar of my life. The practice and study of yoga has supported me through a successful business leadership career and ultimately became a central tenet of my executive coaching work. Throughout my career, yoga has given me tools for self-awareness, improving my day-to-day interactions with colleagues; sensitized me to my customers' needs; guided my focus and tenacity to deliver on projects and goals; and allowed me to step back, see the bigger picture, and orient my career in meaningful directions. It has given me the insight and courage to step way out of my comfort zone and create the life and career of my dreams, and it has tamed my once ferocious temperament and transformed my stress-filled existence into one of more serenity, presence, and flow.

On his own successful journey after his early days in the Yoga Niketan Ashram, Vishvketu has cultivated a worldwide following of students and teachers and established a global yoga teacher training school, eventually returning to Rishikesh and building the internationally renowned Anand Prakash Yoga Ashram. He also formed a charitable trust and built a school providing free education to over 250 underserved children in rural India. Managing an ashram, an international following of yoga students, a school, and a heavy travel schedule, Vishvketu leads a successful business operation, and he maintains a disciplined yoga practice to keep himself energized and effective in his work. After we mutually advised each other on life, yoga, and business over a span of twenty years, the yogi became a business owner, and the business executive became a yogi. Our teacher-student relationship is now converging at this intersection of business and yoga to bring a full yoga practice and all its benefits into the realm of business.

I the MBA and he the yoga PhD aim to combine our expertise in modern business management and ancient wisdom to give the reader a broad understanding of the Vedic spiritual tradition and apply it in a practical and relatable way for the modern businessperson.

We have strived to stay faithful to the authentic teachings of the enlightened yogic sages of ancient India while rendering them comprehensible and relevant to a modern Western life. Drawing from teachings of self-improvement from yoga, Ayurveda (mind-body medicine system of India), and Vedic philosophy (wisdom tradition of ancient India), we'll refer to this combined massive body of ancient wisdom as the Vedic knowledge system. We have parsed the teachings of this system in order to make them more accessible and relevant to modern professionals. We also connect knowledge across the different disciplines, as we have done in our own lives, in order to provide an integrated methodology for self-improvement. We try to use a simple and practical approach that is also fun to learn. We draw from modern research data where available, and in other cases, we expound on information from learned teachers we have studied under. This book also contains important teaching stories from our own experiences that are not only true but also have a deeper subtext of passing on wisdom from the rich tradition. We have changed the names of the people in the stories in order to protect their privacy.

You can read this book and draw from it what makes sense for you. Each tool is designed to help improve your physical, mental, and spiritual health and greatly enhance your life. You'll seek to unlock your own intuition so that you rely on your own inner teacher to make the right choices for you. As Vishvketu always says in his yoga classes, first listen to yourself, then secondly listen to us. You know yourself best.

We'll ask you to think through reflection questions at the end of each chapter to gently incorporate some of the philosophies of *The Business Casual Yogi* into your life. In leadership best practices, and specifically in high-performance executive coaching, taking time to reflect and plan is critical to effecting change. Actually writing out key insights and action steps ensures commitment and follow-through. To get the most benefit from the teachings in this book, try to find ten to fifteen minutes at the end of each chapter to reflect and write out your answers to the questions. Refer back to your answers over time, observe any changes in your perspective, and adjust your answers as you evolve.

Throughout the book, we use English terms to describe concepts of the Vedic knowledge system, but we also provide the Sanskrit terminology as a reference point for further research and to lend richer context and deeper connection to the original source of the system. We have included a Sanskrit pronunciation guide at the end of the book. You are, of course, free to skip over all the Sanskrit references in the book and just enjoy the English conceptual translations.

We encourage you to do what makes sense for you based on your needs, lifestyle, and viewpoints. The information in this book does not involve a religion and is not intended to subvert any of your belief systems. Instead, it should enhance every arena of your life. If you are uncomfortable with a concept, feel free to skip over it and return to it at a later time when it may make more sense. Though the Vedic knowledge system originated in India, it predates the formal formation of India and any of the known religions of India. Though many of India's religions, including Hinduism, Buddhism, Jainism, and more borrow from this Vedic knowledge system, the system itself is not a religious system; it's a scientific system of self-exploration. Religion asks us to have faith, whereas the Vedic knowledge system asks us to question everything. If it works for you, use it, and if it doesn't, move on. Vishvketu likes to say, "Be a yogi scientist." In other words, explore, learn, and use your intuition to do what makes sense for you. Enjoy your journey of self-transformation through the teachings of the Vedic knowledge system.

INTRODUCTION

Business and yoga may seem incompatible at first, but most working people are regularly searching for ways to improve themselves and their lives. For twenty years, I was a working professional, rising through the ranks to higher levels of income, responsibility, and mind-numbing stress. In the midst of that life, I found the physical and philosophical system of yoga—disciplines beyond just the poses—to be the most powerful set of practical tools to attain calm, focus, and career success in a balanced and healthy way. This book offers a systematic method to cultivate self-improvement in work, in relationships, and in life.

The idea for this book first came about when I, a recovering tech entrepreneur turned executive coach, was being asked by an ever-increasing number of businesspeople for a book recommendation on yoga. I consulted my longtime friend and Himalayan yogi, Yogrishi Vishvketu, and it turns out this was not an easy question to answer. Most of the yoga books on the market are either targeted at the "yoga crowd"—athletic and often spiritual people, mostly women—or they are drenched in esoteric philosophy that is overkill for someone just trying to get started. Neither approach seems interesting or relevant to the world's working professionals. So, we decided to put our heads together and create the book that fills that very gap: a simple, practical yoga book that helps a modern working professional get started on a home practice, on a journey toward more meaning, happiness, and success in both career and life. We intend this book to be an accessible guide to the complete, integrated system of yoga, Ayurvedic medicine, and Vedic wisdom, including the physical, mental, and spiritual aspects that aren't covered in a typical yoga class. If you've ever thought you're not flexible enough to do yoga or that yoga studios are intimidating, then this book is for you. We focus on using yoga, Ayurveda, and Vedic philosophy as an integrated approach to a more fulfilling life.

Yoga broadly, beyond its physical postures, is a methodology for humans to cultivate and manifest their fullest potential. A systematic approach to life management, yoga can be the primary tool to unlock a person's maximum creativity, innovation, leadership potential, and balanced health. Juggling tough commutes, long days at the office, lunches at the desk, emotionally draining meetings, overloaded email inboxes, relentless goals and demands from bosses, and rampant technology intrusion has become the new norm. It can be hard to rise through the clutter to manifest our best selves. Yoga, Ayurveda, and their overarching Vedic philosophy can help us rise above the mundane logistics of the day-to-day grind and realize our greater potential. For those of you who hold influential roles in organizations, leading teams or managing projects, your mental, physical, and spiritual health are the keys to providing value to yourself, your team, and society. For those of you who work more independently or are just starting out in a career, your holistic health affects your ability to excel and advance while trying to be present for your family, your friends, and yourself. Yoga can help you cultivate balance and presence in your life so you can better access the most potent aspects of yourself in all spheres of life. We hope you find this book to be a powerful guide on a path to a deeper understanding of your true nature, advancement in your career, and a life of joy.

There appears to be limited knowledge of the full offering of yoga and even less awareness of Ayurveda and Vedic wisdom: In combination, these form a broad framework that includes techniques for improving the mind and body, finding peace and clarity, and embarking on a journey to discover the very meaning of your life. The broader philosophy has implications for how to approach work and how to orient toward a life of more flow and success.

In my work as an executive coach, in offices around the world, I've learned that most people have heard of yoga and meditation, and at some point, most have found themselves (sometimes unwittingly) in a yoga class. But when I ask about their experiences, they fret that they weren't flexible enough or didn't fit in, or they focus on the workout element of the class. These interactions have led me to a few conclusions about how yoga is perceived today:

- Yoga is seen as a purely physical exercise.
- Yoga is perceived to be mainly for women.
- Yoga is thought to require flexibility.
- A certain look is required to do yoga.

Modern professionals seem to be searching for a deeper sense of existence, and even from fitness-oriented yoga classes, people are finding some of that meaning—but they are often not sure what that meaning is. That feel-good feeling after class intrigues them, and so they go more often. A multibillion-dollar industry is burgeoning based on just a taste of full, integrated practice because, even in a limited form, yoga's transformational effects are unmistakable. This book seeks to offer broader exposure to the potential of a complete practice.

We indulge in various outlets to cope with our accumulating daily stress and to process pain. Many turn to psychotherapy and pharmaceuticals to try to find more happiness and more balance, and these have value—forms of talk therapy and Western medicine can certainly fit into the yoga framework—but detached from the rest of the system, such approaches will not send you completely toward your fullest potential. Others indulge in excessive acquisition of material goods, poor-quality entertainment, or worse, substance abuse, food abuse, and unhealthy interpersonal relationships to cope with the stress of modern life. These paths can send us backward and create more pain and obstruct career success.

For self-improvement, the self-help literature and leadership paradigms typically offer partial solutions disconnected from the comprehensive framework of our lives. In the West, we tend to seek silver bullets. For exercise, we go to a personal trainer; for diet, we go to a nutritionist; for mental health, we go to a therapist; when we are sick, we go to the doctor. Within each discipline, we pick the "best" approach—perhaps a Paleo diet, a protein-only diet, or a gluten-free diet depending on which friends' advice we trust and what news stories we consume. In the corporate space, the relentless competition for better leaders and more productive workforces is leading companies to pay millions for executive coaching, leadership and innovation training, and assessments and analyses—each powerful tools but not integrated or connected to one another for a more synergistic effect. Only a cohesive approach that promotes understanding of our own unique nature can propel our success at work and bring our life into harmony. The broader framework of yoga, Ayurveda, and Vedic wisdom actually contains the answers to many of the innovation, leadership, and life management questions of our day.

The yoga system and Ayurvedic medicine are not silver bullets; they are more like an integrated series of silver pellets working in harmony to unite our whole being under a broad umbrella of wellness, which then lays a foundation to better perform our life's work. Yoga belongs squarely in the corporate sector, as a solution to stress, as a tonic for stiff joints and hunched spines, and as a path toward a more joyful work-life balance. Furthermore, with high-performing leaders, just as with high-performing athletes, there is an intrinsic link between lifestyle choices and performance, so we look at all the aspects of our life as the foundation and support for improving and propelling our careers.

In this book, Vishvketu and I will cover some of the Vedic philosophy of the broader yoga tradition along with practical techniques and paradigms from Ayurvedic medicine for improving your health, wellness, and success. We will give you practical tools and techniques to start or deepen your existing practice with a systematic approach to life and work that includes:

- Philosophy
- Goal setting and visioning
- Self-awareness tools
- Lifestyle
- Diet
- Breath work
- Physical exercise
- Stillness
- Mind work
- Sound work
- Energetic work

The synergy of these practices, even as you begin to incorporate them one by one, will help you cultivate more fulfillment in your work, career, relationships, and life. You will enjoy better health, reduced stress levels, increased happiness, and more resilience. It is a remarkable system of philosophy, techniques, healing, and guidance that can unlock great creativity, innovation, and leadership—all through an accessible practice that doesn't require spandex, studios, gymnastic abilities, or punch cards.

Yoga should not just be accessible to the people with the time and comfort level to visit a yoga studio. It is everyone's birthright to live a life of happiness, fulfillment, and meaning, and as such it is everyone's birthright to access a system of knowledge that helps unlock this happiness. So, to all those who strive toward joy and success, who are too busy to visit a yoga studio or feel out of place in one, this book is dedicated to you. Here is an opportunity to unlock more of who you are so that you can be fully present in your service to the world, with grace and a continual unfolding of joy, happiness, and success. We fully intend this book to change your life.

CHAPTER ONE
Life Out of Balance

D o you respond to the question, "How are you?" with "so busy" or "stressed out" or "tired" or "burnt out," or simply "good" so you don't have to get into it? We are so used to these answers that we rarely pause and think: How did this become the standard accepted response, even a response we're proud of? What if you could answer, "I am great," and *really* mean it?

Some years ago, deep into my corporate career, I took a break for a few days and volunteered to assist Yogrishi Vishvketu at a yoga festival where he was teaching. At lunch one day, we sat with a young man in orange robes with a big bushy beard who was from India but spoke clear and articulate English. He explained that he had come to the US from India for a monthlong visit and was volunteering his time at different places during his travels. I asked him what he did back in India (wondering what kind of job allows someone to take a month off!), and with a broad smile, he replied, "Nothing, sir!" This did not cut it for me. "But don't you work?" I said, my astonishment rising. "No," he casually responded. "Well, did you study?" I said, my discomfort frothing to the surface. He replied, "I have a bachelor's degree in computer science." I asked if he'd ever had a job, and he told me about being a software engineer in a company for several years. "So, what do you do now?" I asked, feeling I was getting somewhere. "Nothing, sir!"

Of course, my yogi friend Vishvketu was just observing this odd interaction with a knowing grin on his face. I was behaving as he would predict: This oval peg of a man was not fitting into my square worldview honed through years of engineering and business. "You must do something?" I tried another angle. "Tell me about a normal day. When you wake up in the morning, what do you do?" I thought I had him at this point. "Well, sir, I watch cartoons," he replied with a broad grin, "but right now I am here at this festival volunteering and cooking the food you are eating!" His responses to my questions just did not work for my logical mind. Why wasn't he busy like the rest of us? A young man, well educated, in the prime of his youth—and just watching cartoons? What a waste! Although my need for everyone to be doing something wasn't being satisfied, I sensed that this man had a serenity about him that I have rarely encountered. He may have been one of the most peaceful, at ease people I have ever met. Even to this day, I can clearly remember his broad, enchanting smile of joy, almost like I had met a saint. Vishvketu and I came to call him Cartoon Baba, the latter word used commonly in India to refer to learned wise men on a spiritual path.

Most of us in Western society are not only uncomfortable just *being*; we are also uncomfortable if others are just being and not doing. We signal to the world continuously that we are *doing*— we tell others how busy we are and express disbelief and exasperation when we meet someone living otherwise. How dare he not be busy? How can she get off the hamster wheel? How can they survive that way? It challenges the very foundation of what we believe makes for a good and happy life, since we believe busyness breeds success. To someone outside our busy culture, we must appear to live in complete dysfunction, yet we think there is no other way to live.

OVERWORKED, COMPETITIVE, AND DISTRACTED

As our civilization evolved, particularly post–Industrial Revolution, we innovated new technologies, harnessed their potential, and discovered our ability to transcend nature and time in the name of progress and efficiency. We created concentrated urban developments where we could cheat darkness and learned ways to prepare and consume food faster and artificially stimulate our energy levels. Today, we are truly untethered from the constraints of nature our ancestors faced.

As expectations climbed higher and higher, we found technologies and organizational structures that increased worker productivity—including corporations that specialized in extracting maximum human value. In this paradigm, companies benefited from paying hardworking employees well, and those well-paid employees could buy the nice homes, cars, and other luxury accouterments that provide respite from the work. More industrial growth ensued, creating the modern economic engine that stewarded the lifestyle improvements that we enjoy today.

Maintaining the nicer lifestyle we reward ourselves with creates the need for more income, so we work harder. But there are always others who will work even harder. So, a ferociously competitive cycle emerges. Always seeing room for improvement and wanting to prove ourselves to others, we compete for that better job, house, car, or gadget, and then we grow concerned that if we lose our job, we can't afford the lifestyle. We're trapped by a new source of stress: a constant sense of income insecurity.

When someone else is always nipping at our heels to take our job or our promotion, and our lifestyle and appearances are on the line, we'll work to the point of exhaustion. It's so difficult to slow down or downsize. We feel pressure from the media, our peers, our bosses, and our families to improve in visible, measurable ways. We put pressure on ourselves to wear nicer clothes, live in a nicer home in a more expensive neighborhood, host social events, or purchase the latest gadgets. We feel justified in bowing to this pressure since we think these things create better lives for ourselves and our families.

In addition to this income pressure, we feel pressure to compete for knowledge supremacy, devouring information to show competence and relevance. After all, someone with more up-to-date information might embarrass me, or even threaten my career, my income growth, and my lifestyle. The news industry feeds on and amplifies this need for information, studying what gets consumers most "amped up" and then sensationalizing content, to produce continual engagement in order to compete. Sensationalized media then desensitizes us to tragedy and scandal. "Breaking news!" is just another corruption story, sex scandal, or murder. This overstimulation has an effect on our health; it takes a toll on our psycho-emotional systems, since every "breaking story" prompts a hit of adrenaline from our fight-or-flight response. The information assault—and the working professional's pressure to keep up with it—can wear us down emotionally. And the worst part is that we're trapped: We can never really unplug or we might miss something that helps us advance our careers and keep "improving" our lifestyles.

But contrary to our goals, always being plugged in shatters our focus. Every notification or newsfeed item triggers a shot of dopamine, the same neurotransmitter affected by addictive drugs such as cocaine or amphetamines, which gives the system a moment of heightened pleasure.[1] These attention grabbers, along with the sensationalist news cycle and the pressure to keep up with information, create an addiction-like dependency to being plugged in.[2] Recent research shows that millennials checks their phones on average 150 times in a day.[3] We reach for them at work, during meals, or in bed—times when we want to be focusing on something else. We check for updates and watch the news. Friends, family, and colleagues expect that we're constantly reachable. Our phone use drives this addictive chemical reaction cycle in our brains and ingrains a pattern of multitasking and regular stimulation into our lives, which wears us down emotionally, cognitively, and physically.

Our multitasking pervades nearly every moment of the day. When Vishvketu first visited the US, he stayed in a friend's home, and when he asked to use the washroom he was surprised to see a stack of magazines and books—he thought he had stepped into a library! We watch TV while eating; we check Facebook or read while on the toilet. We are unable to just be present. All of this distracted behavior disturbs the body and its natural cycles and functions at a neurological level.

During the workday, this habit affects the strength and quality of our work. In the midst of constant distractions, it can be challenging to truly focus. Scattered focus drains us and saps the momentum to advance in our careers as well as we could. We forget how to truly be present and tune in to situations around us. Just being fully present during a business meeting has become severely challenged with our easy access to a quick and easy shot of information pleasure.

Then at night, our technological tether disturbs our rejuvenation time. In my coaching practice, many clients who complain of sleep trouble and exhaustion admit to tuning in to email and news right until the moment they try to fall asleep. The blue light from our phones simulates daylight and suppresses melatonin production, so this late-night phone snacking shortens the duration and quality of our sleep, causing more frequent wake-ups.[4] And since that final phone check often signals some to-do or obligation, our dreams are affected, and sleep quality and anxiety levels suffer even further. And worse, that very technology is our window to another source of stress and distraction: *options*.

TOO MANY CHOICES

The amount of choice we have is so overwhelming that, oftentimes, we can barely decide what to do. A famous Wharton marketing study proved people were ten times more likely to buy a jar of jam when they had just six choices versus when they had twenty-four choices. Faced with too much choice, consumers felt overloaded and froze. This result illustrates what we face every day in modern society—an overload of choice.[5] Choices between diet plans, exercise options, cars, food, clothing, experiences, information . . . Instead of leading to happiness, they lead to a constant worry that we chose the wrong thing. That we're missing out. With that feeling comes a constant search for happiness rather than restful contentment.

When Vishvketu first arrived in North America from India, on a snowy, cold Canadian morning, he bundled up and ventured out to a local bagel shop. Curious to try this North American oddity, he went to the counter and in his thick accent excitedly asked, "Can I have bagel, please?" His mouth was watering in anticipation.

The woman behind the counter then asked, "What kind of bagel?"

He replied, a bit confused, "There are different kinds?"

"Yes, there is sourdough bagel, sesame seed bagel, cheese bagel, jalapeño bagel, onion bagel, cinnamon bagel, poppy seed bagel, everything bagel—which one would you like?"

Vishvketu, feeling a bit overwhelmed, replied, "Do you have just plain bagel?"

"Okay, yes, we have a plain bagel. What kind of cream cheese would you like with that? Garden, onion, strawberry, honey, chive, sundried tomato . . ."

Amazed with the amount of customization available, he replied, "Umm, plain cheese please."

"Toasted or untoasted?" Wow, he thought. There are just so many choices!

To this visitor from India, just ordering a bagel was quite an exasperating experience, especially with the line growing behind him. I'm sure we can all relate: How many times have we deliberated over a dinner menu or stressed over a Starbucks order—and then regretted our choice? In Western culture, the choices can become overwhelming and unnecessarily confusing. How can we let go of analyzing options and just trust our intuition? One of the qualities of good leadership is decisiveness even when there is an asymmetry of information—knowing how to cut through the clutter of choices. It is by tuning in better that all of us can find choices easier, more efficient, and less stressful. The techniques and methodologies of yoga can offer us a systematic cultivation of better choice-making and inward tuning, while also addressing the stressors of modern life.

TOUGHENING UP AND TUNING OUT

All of these unnatural paradigms that we are synced into—income insecurity, competition, the twenty-four-hour sensationalist news cycle, technology overload, choice overload—put immense pressures on our nervous and hormonal systems. Trying to balance itself, our body struggles to compensate with the chaos and learns to handle and deflect the stress overloads. We even learn, psychologically, to congratulate ourselves on toughening up. "Yep, I am stressed out, but I can handle it," we say to ourselves. "When the going gets tough, the tough get going." But what are we losing as this compensatory system activates? In our toughness, we become continually less affected by sensationalist news and more resilient to the demands of the workplace. We assume a competitive, fighting stance as our regular approach in life—ready to attack. Wait till a telemarketer calls my house, or my internet stalls—the full fury of this competitive fighting stance will unleash over the phone!

This constant sensory overload makes our entire neurological system, hormonal system, physiological system, and emotional state start to suffer. With the onslaught of modern living and the toughening-up process to handle it, we lose touch with our body's subtle signals to rejuvenate, rest, detoxify, or otherwise make better choices for our well-being. In our efforts to tune out, we are no longer able to tune in, and this starts to affect both our health and our effectiveness in life. Our immune systems become compromised, and we might feel chronically fatigued and constantly get sick. Some may experience hormonal or emotional imbalances that they cannot explain, and often doctors cannot explain or fix either; while focusing on a cure, they don't often have the bandwidth to assess the full picture of the underlying lifestyle factors.

We can also lose our emotional sensitivity and the ability to connect to our intuition and instincts, which help us be more effective at work. In an overworked, exhausted, and desensitized state, we are too tired and overstimulated to read a room or sense people's emotions, and thus our leadership and relationship abilities suffer as well. If we can barely tune in to ourselves, how can we distinguish a person who intends to cheat us versus someone doing us a good deed, or read what's behind a charismatic smile? During the tumultuous days of our start-up, my cofounder would ask me to join critical investor meetings—he had the pitch nailed, but he wanted me to read the room, to figure out how they were reacting. When needed, I'd signal him with an offhand comment and he'd adjust the pitch in real time. Stone-faced investors can be hard to read, but I felt my yoga practice had helped me develop that ability.

We have devised ingenious ways to deal with our buried sensitivities and the pressures of our modern lifestyle. We read self-help books that focus on only one aspect of life, see therapists intermittently, take drugs, self-medicate with alcohol, eat a bucket of ice cream, lash out at our coworkers, take a vacation and end up more exhausted than we started. Some of these methods are self-destructive or destructive to those around us; some of them help only parts of our lives. A quick hit of relief here and there does not solve our problems. We consist of a complex system of organs, glands, hormones, and neural networks that are intrinsically connected to our mental states and energy levels. Yoga can be a comprehensive tool for daily balance, not only at a physical level but also at a mental and spiritual level, which can help more of our greatness show up in modern life.

MOVING SO FAST WE MISS WHAT'S RIGHT HERE

After a trip to visit our publisher, Vishvketu and I landed in Los Angeles in the evening, and as we drove out of the parking lot and approached the parking attendant booth, we noticed a massive full moon rising just behind the booth. After the sensory overload of the flight, airports, crowds, and travel logistics, this moon just entranced us for a moment. And here, the parking attendant, bathed in that very moonlight, sitting in a glass booth with this magnificent orb of a backdrop, was looking quite grumpy from a long shift.

"Forty-seven dollars, sir, cash or credit?"

We asked him, "Did you see the moon?"

"Huh, what?" He looked at us, puzzled and annoyed.

"The moon, the moon—look behind you!"

Now he was really annoyed. "Forty-seven dollars, sir, credit card?"

"No, turn around, look, the moon is out, the moon."

He begrudgingly turned around, and after seeing the large luminescent ball in the sky that was bathing his booth, he lit up with joy. "Ah yes, the moon, so beautiful, wow, thank you, sir, thank you!" Just from this glimpse, his demeanor changed; maybe he sensed that he was part of something greater than that glass booth. Many of us are so engrossed in our work that we rarely look up and see joyful things right in front of us.

This pace of life is so fast that we just keep on running with the herd, often without taking the time to assess whether we're going in the right direction. We can derive a lot of happiness from this pattern. After all, safety, stability, and healthy routine—all parts of existing in a herd—are important components of most adult lives. But these things can help disguise a deeper need. Sometimes, a major life event can wake us up to what we're missing. And sometimes, the pace catches up with us in a catastrophic way.

Before catastrophe hits, recognize that you can slow down and just observe and discover who you really are, and where you really want to go. You can rediscover yourself amid your hurried pace. You can live the life that you want—*your* life, created through your own choices. As Vishvketu often says in yoga class, "Make sure you are holding your own toes."

Even our most important relationships can become subservient to our jobs and other demands on our time. Some of us chase opportunities fiercely but end up separating from our families. We might not pay attention to building stronger bonds with our spouses and children or even notice the treasures that those relationships bring to our lives before it is too late. Parents lament that they missed the best years with their kids. Those kids grow up with a poor understanding of full, attentive relationships, and then the cycle continues as they mature, prioritizing productivity and material success over family values. We also neglect our relationship with our ancestors. We carry the DNA and character traits of generations of people before us; if we cultivated that relationship, we might avoid repeating the mistakes of those before us, or we might see hidden talents within us. A deep loneliness and sense of disconnect stem from these lost relationships, and so we start to long for deeper connection—and it may be right in front of us, and even within us.

But finding that deeper connection would require attention to another relationship: our relationship with ourselves. With our demanding and fast-paced lifestyle and the easy availability of electricity and light, we have become out of sync with nature and distracted from the more subtle needs of our bodies and minds. We have lost our innate sense of what is good for us and what is bad for us. Instead of winding down as the sun sets, we replace the darkness with bright lights and fluorescent screens that discourage our bodies from getting much-needed rest. We knowingly decouple from the sun's cycles, and we are often completely unaware of the moon's cycles and the effects they might have on us. Seasons come and go, and we eat the same food and work the same way for the same number of hours. We stay up way past darkness, we get up at odd hours, and we eat at strange times, all counter to our bodies' natural needs and cycles. It is like putting ourselves through jet lag every day, then wondering why we feel tired or why our appetites are so sporadic.

Even the way we eat has become very unnatural. In the typical modern pace of life, it is challenging to eat on a schedule that makes sense for our bodies or to pay attention to what our bodies might be asking of us. Deadlines, meeting schedules, corporate dinners, and commutes throw off our eating times—or we actually *forget* to eat. We also forget that food is not just a biological necessity but also a source of vitality and pleasure, with texture and experience. Through yoga we can learn to regularly have meals that become a mindful, joyful activity and subtly signal our digestive system to extract more positive nourishment from the food. We are often in such a rush that we wolf down our food, barely looking at it let alone appreciating and savoring its qualities, which increases our chances of poor health and digestive troubles.[6] I have had many a fancy meal in my corporate life—exquisite food prepared with meticulous detail by a world-class chef—where everyone is so engrossed in the business conversation that the beauty on our plates goes unnoticed. We eat lunches at our desks while frantically trying to finish assignments, and we eat fast-food meals while driving. Gone are the days of office mates taking a social hour to go out and share a lunch together. We treat food as we do fuel in our car: Fill 'er up and let's go.

Our discordant sleep and eating cycles, lack of sensitivity to our bodies, and chronic stress become seeds of ill health. Studies show that chronic stress weakens our immune system, reduces our wound-healing ability, and increases susceptibility to illnesses ranging from the common cold to gastrointestinal disorders, heart disease, cancer, and psychiatric disorders.[7] Some people think they have toughened up so much that they have actually been able to push disease away for the sake of their work. Many a colleague has proudly informed me that they never get sick. Indeed, they don't. But then they take a vacation and all of a sudden come down with a major illness. Or they retire and pass away soon after. Overworking our bodies will catch up with all of us.

YOGA AS THE ANTIDOTE TO MODERN LIFE

The system of yogic knowledge enhances our sensitivity and connection to the cycles of nature and tunes us in to our body's needs. It helps us rejuvenate from stress and brings us clarity of mind, both of which help us make better choices. It increases our physical and mental well-being and improves our energy levels. Yoga can enhance our awareness of ourselves and others so that we can better moderate our day-to-day existence while directing our lives in a more powerful and positive direction. We can learn to innately make happier and healthier choices and start on a path to living to our fullest potential, realizing deeper success in our bodies, minds, and careers. It seems to be the very specific antidote to the various disruptive cycles of our modern times.

With the teachings of the Vedic knowledge system, you can set new goals in life that serve you directly, based on internal rather than external influences. You can own your destiny and decouple from things that don't serve you well. You can develop the confidence to lead the life you really want and then focus relentlessly on creating it. By turning inward in a methodical way, you can find contentment and poise that decouple you from the income insecurity cycle. You can learn to trust yourself to make better choices and better filter the information around you to focus on the things that serve you and propel you forward. You can intuitively recognize what efforts will have the most impact so that you can more efficiently achieve your career goals without breaking down your body and relationships. Yoga can help you reframe your goals to more smartly align with your natural talents and resources. You can improve your interpersonal skills as well as your relationship with technology, your body, and your rejuvenation needs.

The ancient sages of India, who developed the yoga system, lived austere lives and focused their energies and explorations inward. Over generations of knowledge seekers, this civilization developed remarkable insights into human nature and developed an entire system for cultivating innate human intelligence and flourishing. Their understanding of human potential and how to cultivate it remains relevant. This ancient civilization wrote about the human yearning to seek *self-actualization*, or realization of one's full potential. Centuries later, behavioral psychologist Abraham Maslow's "hierarchy of needs" theory of motivation identified self-actualization as the highest human need—the need that we seek to fulfill after more basic needs are met. Maslow's theories are often leveraged in modern marketing and consumer behavior; if a marketer targets their messaging at this human yearning, we feel compelled to purchase in the hope of fulfilling the promise of self-actualization. Contemporary psychologists have gone further to revise Maslow's hierarchy, and they have placed transcendence as an even higher need, in a tacit acknowledgment of the spiritual dimension of human need. In the yoga tradition, transcendence is experienced when we self-actualize. The ancient sages developed methodical systems of self-improvement toward this self-actualization, helping us tune in to our bodies and minds, to others, and to nature. The goal of this is to extend the experience of self-actualization so it can sustain us longer than the things we can obtain through consumerism. These insights formed the basis of what we are calling the Vedic knowledge system, Vedic referring to the time period of those ancient seers. It is a system of lifestyle changes, techniques, medical knowledge, and philosophy centered around living to our fullest potential. This ancient wisdom has perhaps become even more applicable in our modern lives, given the onslaughts of technology and consumer marketing on our choice-making.

As an essential first step, we must learn to tune in to our inner senses and intuition rather than tuning out from them. By connecting with ourselves and our needs, we can find what is really right for us, better care for our health and leverage our energy, avoid and handle challenges, and find better well-being and balance. By honoring our body's natural cycle to get the most efficient periods of work, care, and play, we can deepen our intuitive ability to choose healthy food, activities, and relationships for our unique lifestyles. Through our own awareness—by learning to trust our gut—we can transcend the unnatural cycles of modern life and manifest a more powerful and resilient existence. We can focus more precisely on the things that serve us and our missions, leading to more personal success. Instead of looking to all kinds of outside sources that lack knowledge of our unique needs and experiences, we can instead find all the answers within *ourselves* through yoga.

You can make better choices and live a more balanced life through the holistic system of yoga. The techniques cover all elements of life, including the following:

- Understanding your purpose
- Keeping your physical body healthy
- Taming your mind
- Nourishing your spirit
- Improving your self-healing abilities
- Choosing the right foods for you
- Developing the right schedule for your unique needs
- Understanding your whole self better

This integration of psychology, physiology, lifestyle, diet, and human interaction—this approach to body-mind-spirit health—is perhaps the most comprehensive framework that exists in humanity. It addresses our entire being, helping us manifest the most of who we are in everything we do. Yoga can help you find the flexibility and inner strength to cultivate breakthrough success in yourself, regardless of what's happening in the world. In the following chapters, we will apply this ancient wisdom to modern life in a practical way, enabling you to live a happier, healthier, and more successful life.

NOTES

1. Daniel Ciccarone, "Stimulant Abuse: Pharmacology, Cocaine, Methamphetamine, Treatment, Attempts at Pharmacotherapy," *Primary Care: Clinics in Office Practice*, March 2011, 38(1), 41–58, https://doi.org/10.1016/j.pop.2010.11.004.

2. Susan Weinschenk, "Why We're All Addicted to Texts, Twitter and Google," *Psychology Today*, Sept. 11, 2012, https://www.psychologytoday.com/us/blog/brain-wise/201209/why-were-all-addicted-texts-twitter-and-google.

3. Alex Mayyasi, "Which Generation Is Most Distracted by Their Phones?," *Priceonomics*, Feb. 26, 2016, https://priceonomics.com/which-generation-is-most-distracted-by-their/.

4. A. Green, M. Cohen-Zion, A. Haim, and Y. Dagan, "Evening Light Exposure to Computer Screens Disrupts Human Sleep, Biologican Rhythms, and Attention Abilities," *Chronobiology Internatational*, 2017, 34(7), 855–865, http://doi.org:10.1080/07420528.2017.1324878.

5. Barry Schwartz, "More Isn't Always Better," *Harvard Business Review,* June 2006, https://hbr.org/2006/06/more-isnt-always-better.

6. Linda Wasmer Andrews, "5 Health Risks of Eating Too Fast," *Clean Eating Magazine*, Updated Feb. 23, 2017, https://www.cleaneatingmag.com/clean-diet/5-health-risks-of-eating-too-fast.

7. Jean-Philippe Gouin and Janice K. Kiecolt-Glaser, "The Impact of Psychological Stress on Wound Healing: Methods and Mechanisms," *Immunology and Allergy Clinics of North America*, Feb. 1, 2012, 31(1), 81–93, https://www.ncbi.nlm.nih.gov/pmc/articles/PMC3052954/; Sheldon Cohen, et al., "Chronic Stress, Glucocorticoid Receptor Resistance, Inflammation, and Disease Risk," *Proceedings of the National Academy of Sciences*, Apr. 17, 2012, 109(16), 5995–5999, https://doi.org/10.1073/pnas.1118355109; Salleh Mohd Razali, "Life Event, Stress and Illness," *The Malaysian Journal of Medical Sciences*, Oct. 2008, 15(4), 9–18, https://www.ncbi.nlm.nih.gov/pmc/articles/PMC3341916/.

8. "What Is Osteopathic Medicine? The Benefits of Yoga," American Osteopathic Association, https://osteopathic.org/what-is-osteopathic-medicine/benefits-of-yoga/; David Gomes, "The 7 Best Yoga Poses for Your Health," *Medical Daily*, July 17, 2016, https://www.medicaldaily.com/yoga-poses-health-benefits-392070.

SELF-REFLECTION QUESTIONS

1. Which of the imbalance cycles do you see in your own life? Be honest, dispassionate, and ruthless in identifying these, and try looking at your life like an outsider.

2. What are some easy changes for you to implement to reduce some of that imbalance?

3. What are examples of balance and imbalance in the lifestyles of your peers, colleagues, and friends, and what lessons do these carry for your own life?

CHAPTER TWO
Yoga Beyond the Mat

The word *yoga* comes from the same root as the English word *yoke*, meaning "to join or to form a union." As we practice yoga in its whole and balanced form, we synchronize and align the mind, body, and spirit for the purpose of manifesting our full potential. The system was originally intended to end the suffering of the body, mind, and spirit on a journey toward an existence of perfection—to quiet the fluctuations of the mind in order to find inner stillness and power. The fundamental tool in the system is meditation: the tool by which we gain deep insight and awareness into our fullest potential (and the means through which many of the insights of the system were developed). In order to purify and protect the body to allow deeper, more prolonged meditations, the full system of yoga came into being—including breath work, sound work, and lifestyle choices that support yoga on the mat. The yoga practice on the mat then tones the physical body, strengthens the immune system, removes excess weight and toxins, balances our hormones, improves sleep, keeps our organs healthy, and clears the energetic channels,[1] all preparing the body to go deeper in meditation and spiritual evolution. Yoga on the mat is extremely valuable on its own, but especially for modern professionals, the practices before the mat and after the mat maximize your potential benefit.

THE YOGIC SYSTEM FOR THE WORKING PROFESSIONAL

The stillness and inner strength that come from the yoga system can be applied in many ways—ways that you didn't even know you needed. While you may find benefits like more material success, forward motion on your spiritual journey, or progress coping with a mental illness, our main focus is applying the yoga system toward career success, including purpose, leadership, awareness, and decision-making. Operating from a more conscious and self-aware place not only improves our time management and resource-investment choices but also helps in our everyday interactions, from communicating with our families and spouses, to raising our kids in a more conscious way, to contributing to society in a more powerful and meaningful way.

My friend Steven owns a construction business and used to suffer from all sorts of aches and pains on top of stress and overwork. A client of his suggested he try yoga, so he went to a class. The class was filled with fit, flexible yogis, mostly women. As a burly construction guy, he felt out of place but stayed through the class—and got a little competitive trying to match pace. He ended up injuring his knee. Luckily he doesn't embarrass easily, so he kept attending classes but stopped pushing so hard physically. After a few weeks, his employees noticed a huge difference in his demeanor. He had gained a calmness and patience that improved his business. He said to me, "I don't know why more people in business don't go to yoga. My body feels so much younger and less painful, and my employees are always surprised that I am not yelling at them so much." The increased clarity also helped him realize that he was working too much, and he started spending more time with his family and doing activities he enjoyed. And while he worked less, his business improved; he started winning more bids with his calmer, more confident demeanor. He was surprised that what he'd originally started for physical aches and pains had affected such powerful mental, lifestyle, and business changes.

In the corporate realm, business "gurus" (a word borrowed from the yoga tradition) tout various approaches to unlock inner potential and live a life with more purpose. Modern business management teachers are talking about connecting to your deeper intuition, even teaching meditation as part of leadership development. And world-renowned business schools like the Haas School at the University of California, Berkeley, are teaching meditation to cultivate the ability to be more present in business.

Because yoga was developed to realize a human's fullest potential, it directly applies to manifesting one's fullest potential in the realm of business and leadership. It can be used to ground and center through difficult business challenges or cultivate intuition to improve interpersonal communication and interactions. A daily practice cleanses the mind, body, and spirit from the toxic interactions that happen regularly in corporate life while also tuning us in to the sensitivities of human nature. Yoga creates a calm and centering force in one's life, building the resilience needed to tackle the greatest of challenges. In addition, the cultivation of one's subtle senses or "gut" enables intuitive understanding of others and smoother interactions in relationships, both professional and personal.

In my product-development days, the awareness and presence of mind I was building through yoga helped me tune into true customer needs. I was able to develop and deliver products that delighted consumers and create strong revenue. Some colleagues called it my "golden touch" when every product my teams developed garnered five-star consumer reviews. But I wasn't doing anything that others couldn't do with the right tools: In conjunction with my daily integrated yoga practice, I simply spent time with consumers, tuned in to their unarticulated needs, and then relentlessly focused on delivering to that need. As I got to know myself better, I could get out of my own way to observe the needs of my customers and execute to the highest standards. Once, my team was developing a new artificial intelligence technology for remote controls, and we wanted to understand the frustrations consumers had with their existing devices. We were in the living room of a research participant and asked him to demonstrate how he programs his remote control to control various living room devices. When he got confused and his remote control stopped functioning, we were keen to observe. Here was a key consumer pain point, in the wild! But then, one of my engineers, eager to fix things, jumped to the rescue, grabbing the remote and proceeding to program it. He was wholly unaware of the importance of simply observing the stumbling block we'd just identified. I've spent a lot of time in my career trying to help engineers gain insight into their consumer (and their team members), and it always begins with helping them cultivate more mindfulness, awareness, and presence.

In business, we are always trying to maximize return on investment. If there is a way to get more benefit for lower effort, we are all ears. Yoga has this effect. Baba Premnath, Vishvketu's yoga guru (a spiritual guide) seemed to sense this relationship between business and yoga. He used to teach Vishvketu that one must become sensitive with the breath in order to use the minimum amount of energy to get the maximum amount of benefit, just like a good businessman. Maturity in yoga comes from exerting just the right amount of effort for maximal gain. The time investment required by yoga is minimal, and the intuition, awareness, and purposeful direction that result from it lead to greater efficiency and quicker resolutions with fewer meetings and less time in the office. Given how busy our working lives can be, these benefits are invaluable.

In my current work coaching high-performance executives at Fortune 100 companies, I have seen first-hand the pressures of leading a modern company and how the tools of yoga can help. In most industries, there is tremendous competition and pressure to outperform in the marketplace. Leaders often face extreme competitive pressures and are always looking for that extra edge, but they don't have a lot of time to invest in themselves. I was coaching at a leadership retreat for a financial services company and was told my audience was composed of the top performers in a top-performing company in a highly competitive industry. Any little "edge" would be welcomed. These were two hundred high-functioning executives who had been through numerous management trainings before. As I began teaching the group about pieces of the Vedic knowledge system, I was initially met with some healthy skepticism; it was very unlike the more traditional trainings financial services firms tend to go for. What does all this woo-woo stuff have to do with a multibillion-dollar financial services company? But they got really engaged when they saw the edge yoga offers: the whole-person, whole-life approach that, rather than just improving a skill or two or offering a coping mechanism for stress, could harness untapped capacity in themselves and their employees. The HR chief at the retreat called it the "edge on the edge," individual department heads wanted their teams trained, and the audience rated it as one of the best sessions they had ever had at an executive retreat.

As I went through my MBA studies, and various leadership and executive training programs, I found that much of what is being taught falls within the framework of the Vedic knowledge system. This system contains frameworks for assessing our unique mind-body constitution, much like many of the personality assessment tools used in business. It also focuses on setting clear goals based on our strengths and purpose, not unlike many business goal-setting and branding methodologies. And similar to trainings on active listening, the Vedic system teaches how to get out of our own thought cycles to be more present for others in our lives. However, the personality assessments, affirmations, and self-help methods perennially deployed in management circles seem to only scratch the surface, amplifying only one or two areas of our lives. The Vedic system cares for the entire support system for our existence, such as diet, exercise, schedule choices, and healthy relationships, which are all critical to our work performance. It also tailors approaches to opportunities and challenges based on your nature and temperament, addressing our whole being, not just our work personalities.

ANCIENT WISDOM FOR A HOLISTIC MODERN LIFE

Yoga is commonly thought to be a Hindu tradition, but in fact it dates back to a secular tradition from ancient India. It is part of a larger system of knowledge from ancient India, which includes Ayurveda (mind-body medicine system), meditation practices, Jyotish (the study of the alignment of the planets and stars and their influence on us), Vastu (the understanding of physical space, the precursor to feng shui), and Vedic wisdom (the philosophy of the nature of our existence). All of these disciplines combine to form a complete holistic system that we are referring to as the Vedic knowledge system. It is an elaborate, sophisticated, and interconnected system that touches every aspect of our existence as humans within our universe.

This Vedic system of knowledge is thought to have originated over five thousand years ago, in the foothills of the Himalayas, along the banks of a now vanished river in Western India bordering modern-day India, Pakistan, and Afghanistan. This river supported a thriving and enlightened civilization known as the Indus River Valley Civilization, which flourished about 3000 BCE. Excavations in the 1920s of their cities (Mohenjo-Daro and Harappa) have unearthed urban planning layouts consistent with modern North American cities, as well as sophisticated plumbing and monetary systems. Though it was an ancient time, the modern discoveries are confirming that the insights and technologies of these people were far advanced for their time.[2]

Beyond their material world innovations, they also innovated inward through deep meditation and contemplation. They pondered some of the deepest questions of human existence and collectively developed, debated, and advanced upon various insights. Discovering, sharing, iterating, and enhancing, generation after generation, they codified a deep understanding of our human existence. After several thousand years, these insights were finally recorded in written form as some of the earliest human writings known today.

In these texts, we can see how keenly attuned these people were to the workings of the human body and mind. They wrote about the nature of our soul and its needs and desires. They wrote about the human mind and its various contentions of ego and intellect, producing insights now relevant to modern psychology. Without modern X-ray or MRI machines, they accurately described the physiological workings of the human body and detailed our body's energetic system with wisdom that still eludes modern science. They also developed healing methods that include treatises on psychology, pediatric surgery, pharmacology, digestion, and other healing modalities that are being validated by contemporary research.[3] They also identified the positions of the stars and planets at different times of year and recorded correlations to various earthly events tied to those planetary influences. Through these observations, they created the system of Vedic astrology, which is the first known astrological system in the world. They outlined techniques that include body exercise, mind exercise, spiritual exercise, diet, breath work, sound work, and many other methods that are now proving to be some of the most integrated ways to leverage our human potential.

These writings became known as the Vedas, which form the original source of this Vedic knowledge system. These texts predate any known human religion, and many of the modern religions of Asia such as Hinduism, Buddhism, and Jainism derived their teachings from these writings. Though India as a formal nation-state did not exist at the time of the Indus River Valley, the culture and religions of India, so intertwined with the wisdom of the Vedas, give us a deeper context and understanding of the Vedic knowledge system. Maintained in the culture of hundreds of generations of Indians, yoga is gift to all of us no matter our heritage. A meditation teacher of mine once pointed out that just because Thomas Edison invented the light bulb does mean light bulbs are just for Americans. In the same way, yoga is universally available to all of humanity.

Although the remarkable knowledge of the Vedas has endured in many ways, many of the teachings became devalued in India in favor of Western viewpoints after centuries of British rule. Western medicine was much favored over what became dismissed as "village medicine." Well-to-do families sent their children to study Western sciences, and as they reached positions of influence, the Vedic tradition was further relegated to the backwaters of India and viewed as esoteric and impractical. Poor rural villages isolated from Westernization continued to practice many of the ancient philosophies, but in the mainstream, the Vedic tradition became suppressed and, in many cases, usurped and reinterpreted by religious and political elites to further their ends. In much of India, the Vedic knowledge system became seen as dubious and outmoded. Many of the teachers of the tradition in India also, after developing their powers of influence through yogic practices, then improperly preyed on unsuspecting seekers, further devaluing the tradition and teachings.

In recent times, however, there has been a resurgent interest in the Vedic knowledge system, particularly in the Western world, given our present cultural emphasis on self-improvement. And it is primarily Western teachers that are bringing back the practicality and relevance of the Vedic knowledge system. As was foretold in many prophecies of Indian gurus, the wisdom of the East has traveled west, the West is improving upon it, and it will be reimported to the East as it continues to evolve. With Westerners' emphasis on scientific proof, alongside the evolution of quantum physics theory, the body of scientific evidence behind many of these ancient teachings is growing. Every year, new studies are published pointing to the efficacy of the techniques and tools described by the ancient teachings of the East.

While Western science is deepening our knowledge of this system, the commercial yoga industry of the West has subverted the system. Though all of yoga's offerings are as applicable to the Western working professional as they are to a spiritual aspirant in India, in the Western world, yoga is primarily practiced as a physical exercise with a focus on flexibility. It is a mainstream fitness activity that supports a huge industry of classes, clothes, and mats rolled up in designer yoga bags. It has also become a female-focused industry, with the average class containing mostly women, with a man here and there. I once saw some rubber-sole sandals for sale with the female sizes labeled "yoga mat flip-flops" and the male sizes labeled "beer cozy flip-flops"! Furthermore, many studios today casually distort the purpose of the yogic system by offering themes such as "yin and juice yoga" or "vino after *vinyasa*" or even "goat yoga," complete with a goat perched on your back while you are in child pose.

Despite the limited scope of many Western yoga classes, its mainstream practice is a step in the right direction. It is symptomatic of our times that we are searching for more meaning in life, and yoga's popularity means that more and more people are seeking and moving toward a path of happiness. People are also questioning the take-a-pill-for-everything approach and investigating natural approaches to disease, alternative and less-invasive healing therapies, and preventative health practices such as organic foods and more thoughtful diets. The ancient healing modalities of yoga are now scientifically measurable, catapulting yoga further into the mainstream. Though it may show up in odd forms, the essence of yoga is actually revealing itself. As many people have experienced, even exercise-oriented yoga classes bring a certain feeling of peace and healing different from regular stretching or other exercise. The increase in yoga studios throughout the world and the integration of yoga into the workplace and into schools show that people perceive there is something more going on than physical stretching.

The current resurgence is also fitting considering our current medical crisis. Facing limited access to care and incredible expenses associated with medical treatment, people are shifting toward well-being and preventive health measures, which the Vedic system is specifically equipped to supply. It is and always has been simple, commonsense health and wellness for the masses. We as individuals can take charge of our own mental and physical health rather than letting ourselves become beholden to an overburdened and expensive system. In fact, in ancient India, physicians would be compensated at the end of the year if no one got sick. Today, we incentivize physicians and pharmaceutical companies to keep us sick.

THE EIGHT LIMBS OF YOGA

Yoga is a complete system designed to move you closer to who you truly are. Before we even begin to think about yoga as it is considered on a two-by-six-foot rubber mat, we must understand the intentional system of living that underpins the yoga practice itself. The foundations of yogic living guidelines, as well as some ancillary Vedic philosophy to help contextualize yoga in your life, are just as important as the physical practice. In fact, as we mentioned, yoga itself is a foundational practice for meditation. Additionally, we will weave in teachings from Ayurveda, the sister science of yoga, which focuses on understanding ourselves from a mind-body medicine point of view. All these foundational teachings will then prepare us to leverage the most return on investment from our time on the mat, which then allows us to get the most out of our meditation practice. Each of these methodologies can provide just as much value to your life as yoga's physical aspects, but the elements have the greatest impact when used in combination.

Yoga is often referred to as having eight branches or limbs, which together form the tree of yoga. The eight branches, known as *ashtanga*, when practiced and observed simultaneously, are what unlock the full power of yoga. The eight branches have a synergistic approach, supporting one another and creating fertile ground for an enriched existence. By observing all eight branches, we make yoga work in a more effective way. If we just focus on one area, such as the mat, we are missing out on the full richness that yoga has to offer us. The first two branches are about life behaviors, the next two are what you perform on a yoga mat, and the final four are the progressive steps in meditation. They are like tree limbs, where we have to climb one in order to reach the next. The eight limbs are:

1. Guidelines for interacting with others (*yama*)
2. Guidelines for interacting with yourself (*niyama*)
3. Physical postures and techniques (*asana*)
4. Breathing exercises and techniques (*pranayama*)
5. Giving your five senses a rest (*pratyahara*)
6. Focus and concentration on a single point (*dharana*)
7. Experience of meditation (*dhyana*)
8. Experience of your true nature (*samadhi*)

GUIDELINES FOR SOCIETAL INTERACTION (YAMAS)

The first foundational piece of the yoga system, the yamas, is a set of recommendations on how one should behave in society—a set of moral guidelines. Under these guidelines, it is believed that as you behave to others, so will others behave to you. If you spend your days creating social harmony, then your yoga practice and life journey will be harmoniously supported. Many of us were taught these common-sense guidelines as children, and most of them go without saying. But often in the business world, with our focus on profits and achievement, we can forget the larger impact of our actions. But when codified as a system, they take on a deeper purpose to help us in our lives and prevent us from being short-sighted. The guidelines are:

1. Minimizing violence (*ahimsa*)
2. Increasing truthfulness (*satya*)

3. Not stealing (*asteya*)
4. Positive use of sexual energies (*brahmacharya*)
5. Not being overly attached to things (*aparigraha*)

Minimizing violence (ahimsa)

Ahimsa tells us to set an intention to minimize harm to others—beyond physical violence—by considering how our words and actions affect others. If we can set an intention to be less aggressive and show more compassion, it will improve our stress levels and happiness. If all of society practiced these guidelines, what a different world we would live in. It is important to stand up for what is right and to tackle problems and issues, but we must try to separate the problem from the person. If we can do that, we can defuse tension and actually fix a problem while preserving a relationship for the next inevitable challenge.

In many texts, nonviolence also includes not harming animals, and it goes without saying that we should not be cruel to any living being. This extends to animals we don't see, like the ones we raise for meat. Not everyone is ready or able to adopt a vegetarian or vegan diet, but there are ways to more positively impact the world without significantly changing your lifestyle. For instance, you might eat a vegetarian meal once a week or consume only humanely raised animal products. Follow whatever works for your lifestyle, but try to be conscious about creating a net-positive force in the world. As my awareness and thinking around my eating choices developed, I started to ask myself, "Do I really need a meat protein in this meal, is there an alternative, and if I still want the meat, is it coming from a humane source?" This slight adjustment in awareness has led to not only better health (evidenced by my lower cholesterol numbers) but in a reduction in my overall violence to other living beings.

Increasing truthfulness (satya)

As children, we were all told to tell the truth. As we grew older, we discovered that was just so our parents could get to the bottom of things, and we began justifying lies now and then. But telling untruths actually harms us. We disturb our quest to understand reality if we are continuously distorting reality. Telling the truth is a healthy habit that helps us sleep better at night and also helps us be more truthful to ourselves. In addition, it harmonizes our interaction with those around us. We can also consider how we deliver that truth in conjunction with ahimsa—are we delivering truth in harmful way to someone or in a constructive way? Constructive criticism can be a gift to another, especially when it is delivered with a positive intention. You might help a colleague advance their career by kindly pointing out particular behavior that is holding them back. Especially as you integrate your yoga practice, you will develop the discernment to deliver useful feedback in a helpful and caring way.

Not stealing (asteya)

Not stealing goes along with truthfulness, and asteya indicates that we should strive to be fair in all our dealings. Even if no one is watching, the act of taking something that is not ours causes pain for someone else and likely guilt for ourselves. Asteya applies to physical objects as well as stealing credit for someone else's idea or achievement. Even in negotiations, if you aim for fairness for all parties, then likely all parties will honor the agreement and try their best to uphold it. When someone feels robbed, even if there is a legal contract in place, that party will eventually find a way to subvert it.

Positive use of sexual energies (brahmacharya)

Sexual energy is something that can get out of control and show up in perverse ways. Entire companies are taken down by improper use of sexual energy. Intimacy is a fundamental human need, same as the nourishment that comes from food and sleep. Sex is one of the things that can satisfy that need. But as with food and sleep, it must be practiced in a conscientious and moderate way. Too much or too little of food or sleep causes physiological and mental issues, and the same case is with sexual energy. It is important to find healthy sexual relationships and partners where both partners enjoy the other's sexual energy in a positive way. To use sexual energy to exert power or to use a position of power to coerce sex hurts all parties involved and contributes to a societal problem of power abuse. Using sexual energy non-consensually or not being aware of the sexual implications within a work-related power balance does harm to others and to yourself. This is an area that requires astute self-awareness and intelligent restraint.

Not being overly attached to things (aparigraha)

Attachment creates all sorts of drama. As we hold on to things in our lives, we take up space, preventing new opportunities from appearing. Whatever your possessions, titles, and accomplishments are, be proud of them and enjoy them, but don't be so attached to them that they cloud your perspective. More broadly, seek to release attachment to a particular way that your life is going. It is likely to change, and you can avoid much struggle and wasted time if you don't cling to the way things were. Be open to the changes that come, and you can flow more easily in life. Attachment also comes in the form of coveting things and obsessing over the acquisition of things. Notice how we devote so much energy to something we long for, like the latest smartphone, but after a while of having it we take it for granted and soon find ourselves craving the next new model.

The concept of aparigraha also applies to our work, particularly our attachment to the identity that is wrapped up in our work. It is good to be proud of our work, but it should not be the only thing that gives us a sense of identity. When I was in the corporate world, I was always chasing the next title and more responsibility. When I went to a social event, the first area of conversation would always center on what kind of work I or other person did. I was very wrapped up in that identity, as were the people around me. When I worked hard, I loved it because it gave me a powerful sense of meaning and pride. I defined myself by my achievements and titles, and when an HR executive, especially in the tech-industry culture, would say, "We don't care about titles around here," it would annoy me to no end. How can I live without that label! It took a lot of soul-wrestling for me to finally figure out that my path was actually in coaching, teaching, and writing. Letting go of that attachment to my corporate executive identity made room for a new identity that could make me happier and more fulfilled. Whether it is a role change, a promotion, a career change, a pivot in your business, or a new business, letting go of what does not serve us anymore is what clears the decks for new opportunities to show up for us.

When I first set out on the path of yoga, I couldn't imagine living an ascetic life like Vishvketu's. I was attached to my life of casual dating and steak dinners. Over time, though, just reading and knowing about the yamas helped set an intention in motion that has moved me little by little to a more harmonious existence. I don't recommend worrying about any drastic life change in order to meet all these guidelines (unless, of course, you know that your actions are currently causing harm to others). Adopt what makes sense for you. Then refer back to the list continually and see what else makes sense for you as you progress.

PERSONAL GUIDELINES (NIYAMAS)

The next set of guidelines, the niyamas, refer to your own personal conduct and behavior. These personal guidelines are good habits to cultivate and set a foundation for a successful and fulfilled life. They show up in many forms in different self-help frameworks, but within the yoga framework, they are comprehensive and integrated with the yoga practices themselves. As you take care of yourself within these personal guidelines, your yoga practice will flourish, as will life in general. They include:

1. Cleanliness (*saucha*)
2. Contentment (*santosha*)
3. Discipline (*tapas*)
4. Introspection (*svadhaya*)
5. Surrender to a higher power (*ishvar pranidhan*)

Cleanliness (saucha)

The first guideline centers on purity and cleanliness. The purity part refers to eating clean, healthy food, drinking clean water, and breathing clean air. It also describes surrounding yourself with positive people and experiences. The cleanliness part applies both to you and to your environments. Maintaining good personal hygiene and grooming is essential in the world of business, as appearances reveal a lot about a person. Hygiene includes everything from keeping your hair smart, bathing regularly, wearing deodorant, and trimming your nails to maintaining a tidy workplace and living space. A messy desk reflects a scattered mind—if not to you, then to others. I have worked with many brilliant people who perform exceptionally well despite a messy mountain of papers, files, and souvenir trinkets. But, with perhaps the rare exception, improving this would probably result in an improvement of mental clarity and less take-home stress. At a minimum, a tidy desk signals organization skills to your colleagues. At the end of each workday, plan some time to reposition the files, papers, and implements you were using so that you arrive the next morning with a fresh start.

When I worked in the auto industry, the most efficient car technicians were always the ones who methodically wiped down every tool and put it back carefully in its "living place" in their toolbox. Others might get a first repair done quickly but then have to constantly hunt for tools for the rest of the day. The methodical mechanic who carefully returns each tool to its home throughout the day accomplishes more and with a calmer demeanor. These are the mechanics that the engineers typically try to assign to their projects, since their visible organization skills suggest more dependability.

In my home and workspace, I strive to ensure that every item has its own living place that it returns to when it is done being used. If it does not have a home, then it is likely to float, get lost, and create a mess, both in the physical realm and in my head as I frantically search for it. If I find that there is no room to have a specific home for an item, then it is a sign I have too much stuff. If I can get rid of some of it and create a more orderly environment, I can function at a higher level of excellence. This is the concept behind the KonMari method, based in the Japanese Shinto tradition, which postulates that by tidying your space you can change your life. Its creator, Marie Kondo, claims that a tidy home makes you better at making decisions and embracing change and gives you more ease in life. My wife and I put the method into practice and ended up getting rid of almost fifty garbage bags' worth of stuff. When our friends came over, they thought we had remodeled. We now experience less daily frustration and more clarity in our lives.

Contentment (santosha)

Contentment is a tough concept in Western culture. We are always wanting more and envious of those who have more, but often that envy is a distraction from true contentment. Santosha is about becoming comfortable and happy with what we have. We can be grateful on a daily basis for all the wonderful things we have in life. For anything we complain about, there are often others grateful for that thing. When people in New York complain about rainy weather, people in California may celebrate. It is all a matter of perspective. When we practice looking at aspects of our lives more positively, positivity will naturally start to come our way. Research even shows that a consistent expression of gratitude leads to improved mental health, reduced rates of depression, and higher scores on happiness measures. Being grateful gives us a more positive outlook, and that positivity has a powerful effect on our well-being and health.[4]

We are often so busy striving to get the next big thing that we forget to appreciate and savor what we already have. Before we know it, as we keep striving for more and more, we end up with more than we can handle. My wife has always had a love of animals and wanted a pet. One day, while wandering through a bunny rescue, she found two adorable rabbits that she decided to bring home. My kids and I were delighted. They were lovely, sweet animals with twitching noses and deep, expressive eyes, and they brought a soothing energy to our home. I was enamored of these joyful creatures. I built them a bunny mansion—a two-story structure made out of lumber and wire complete with tunnels, ladders, sleeping quarters, and outdoor play areas. Our family bonded with those two bunnies, and we enjoyed looking after them, and they enjoyed their mansion. But it wasn't long before the novelty wore off, the kids helped take care of them less and less, and a desire for something more started to show up. One day, as my wife was buying fresh hay and bunny food at the rescue place, she caught sight of two cute newly rescued bunnies. With the kids egging her on, and with the thought of filling the big bunny mansion, she brought them home. I was delighted. They were oh so cute, even cuter than our existing bunnies. We put the new pair into the mansion, and within minutes, the bunnies were fighting—drawing blood! Bunny fur was everywhere; the kids were in tears. The bunny mansion has since been split into attached townhomes, and we have double the amount of work. More is not always better when it comes to contentment.

Discipline (tapas)

In the yogic sense, discipline is having the willpower and perseverance to realize your goals. Discipline also requires some solid daily routines, even if you prefer to move through most of your day intuitively. Waking up at a healthy time, eating at the right times, exercising, and holding a spiritual practice are all foundational to a good existence. In the yoga practice itself, the discipline and regularity of the practice is also what makes it a powerful force in our lives. A twenty-to-thirty-minute practice daily is much more beneficial than a one-to-two-hour practice once or twice a week. Sometimes, all I focus on is getting to my mat every morning. Once I am on the mat, the practice just happens.

Introspection (svadhaya)

Svadhaya is the process of reflecting on one's actions, seeing what consequences those actions have had, and understanding how to improve. A regular practice of self-reflection might involve journaling or just writing a few notes about what went well and what

could be improved. The idea is to observe the self to build awareness and self-knowledge so that we can improve on a continual basis. It even improves our sleep; often clients of mine have
trouble sleeping because they are processing the day's events and
ruminating over what they could have done better. I ask them to
write just a few lines in a journal at the end of each day, and it
helps reduce a lot of that nighttime disturbance.

Surrender to a higher power (ishvar pranidhan)
The final personal guideline revolves around some sort of devotion or consideration of a higher power. It is about learning to
surrender to larger forces at play, even if you think you are in
control of everything. The higher power may be your belief in a
god, or in divine inspiration, or even the unpredictability of the
universe (a tenet of quantum physics theory). If you have anything in particular you are devoted to, you should honor that on
a regular basis. Whatever your belief system, the important thing
is acknowledging that not everything is in your control and that
sometimes you have to let go and let things work themselves out.

PHYSICAL POSTURES AND TECHNIQUES (ASANAS)

As we move beyond these societal and personal guidelines, we
get into the technical parts of the yoga system. The third branch
of yoga describes the physical postures and techniques that yoga
is commonly known for. The ancient yogis believed that a flexible body creates a flexible mind, and so physical postures are
intended to help open up the joints of the body, tone the body,
drain the lymphatic system to process and eliminate toxins, exercise the organs, stimulate the glandular systems of the body, and
energize the body.[5] Yoga postures develop more flexibility than
would come from calisthenics and simple stretching.[6] The physical postures of yoga also strengthen the muscles and bones that

support our being.[7] They are also said to increase the body's resistance to disease and aging, keeping our body in shape to perform our life work and interact with others. We will go into detail around physical postures in Chapter 9 of this book.

BREATHING EXERCISES AND TECHNIQUES (PRANAYAMA)

Breathing techniques revitalize and detoxify the body. Proper breathing is also key to improved physical performance, accelerating the body's energizing process and shedding toxins through the respiratory system. Pranayama is also said to regulate the hormonal and emotional mechanisms of the body, so becoming familiar with your breath leads to better regulation of emotions and reactions. Breathing is directly connected to our emotional and mental states: Our breath varies as our emotions change, and conversely, we can modulate our breath to affect our emotions. Research from UCLA shows breathing can be used to alter our emotional states and be used to tackle anxiety, specifically crediting pranayama for relieving stress, depression, and anxiety.[8] Here again we see a convergence of yoga and business. A yogi would tell a tense person to take a deep breath, just as a corporate executive might tell everyone to take a breath to defuse a tense situation. Once during an intense argument with my VP on the pricing strategy for a new vehicle, I got so heated and emotional that I lost track of my arguments, and she eventually said to me, "Vish, stop and just take a breath." I thought, "Wow, the yogi just got called out!" She didn't need to be a yogi to know that breathing would help redirect our conversation from emotions back to logic. We will address breathing techniques in Chapter 8.

GIVING YOUR FIVE SENSES A REST (PRATYAHARA)

The previous four limbs are all preparation for the next four, which all center around the meditative aspect of yoga. People often think of yoga and meditation as separate things, but they are quite interconnected. We cannot meditate if our body is ailing or if we feel aches and pains while we sit for meditation. Though the good health that comes from the physical yoga practice is nice benefit, its core intention is as a foundation for meditation.

Meditation is one of the most powerful tools toward improved self-awareness, reduced stress, and better health. In the yoga tradition, meditation has several stages, beginning with a first step of a withdrawal from your five senses (pratyahara). The deepest states of meditation are accessed only when we disconnect from all of our five senses. Whenever any sensory inputs are being received by our faculties and channeled into our brain (such as a person's voice during a guided meditation), we process and synthesize these inputs, preventing the brain from entering deeper meditative states. To truly reboot, we want to bring the brain down to as calm a state as possible. When one withdraws from all five senses, the brain can reach a deep state of wakeful rest. Researchers have measured unique alpha waves being emitted during this state, in the range of eight to twelve hertz—a wave range that has been correlated with increased creativity and improved mental health.[9]

FOCUS AND CONCENTRATION ON A SINGLE POINT (DHARANA)

When you withdraw from all stimuli, you can truly concentrate your mental energies on a single point. Almost all meditation traditions prescribe some vehicle of focus as a way to quiet the mind. It might be a mantra, a visual image, the breath, or something else. This singular concentration is the sixth limb of yoga, dharana. Like all the limbs, dharana is a rung on a ladder to get to the next branch. But it also has value in and of itself. Practicing focus on a regular basis within meditation improves our ability to focus better in life. As you practice returning to a single point of concentration, you are training yourself to continually return to your goals or tasks.

Setting clear goals is one thing, but relentlessly focusing on them is a deeper challenge that this branch of yoga helps us train for.

EXPERIENCE OF MEDITATION (DHYANA)

When you have rested your sensory faculties and focused the mind on a single point, not only do you gain a deep psychic rest and improve your concentration and willpower, but you also enter a state of meditation (dhyana), the seventh limb of yoga. There are multiple techniques for reaching a deep meditative state, and with regular practice of sensory withdrawal and single-pointed focus, the seventh limb manifests consistently. This is a place where we experience deep rest simultaneously with deep awareness. Spending time in this state releases all the benefits of meditation, such as stress relief, mental clarity, improved immunity, increased resilience, and more.

THE EXPERIENCE OF YOUR TRUE NATURE (SAMADHI)

Spending regular time in meditation leads spontaneously to moments of pure connectedness with your inner potential. This is the experience of samadhi, the eighth limb of yoga. The yogis believe that our true potential for a life of success, grace, happiness, and harmony come from inside rather than outside. The Vedic knowledge system postulates that any answer we are looking for is within us rather than outside of us. Their very teachings were discovered through a journey inward, specifically in states of samadhi. As we experience this state, we connect more deeply to our inner answers. The more we cultivate this connection in our daily life, the more the insights from it appear to us on a regular basis. We have to diligently work through all the prior branches as preparatory steps toward the more frequent experience of this connectedness. As we achieve more connectedness and become more grounded, we become more fulfilled and more tuned in to our true nature, our talents, and our gifts. Then as we come to know ourselves better, we learn to know others better, and with this deeper awareness, we can find more success and peace in our relationships. These final four limbs are covered in greater detail, along with practical techniques, in Chapter 10.

As we incorporate the wisdom contained in the eight limbs of yoga into our lives, we grow into our fullest potential, becoming more attuned to opportunities around us, aware of risks and obstacles in our way, resilient in overcoming these obstacles, and ready to manifest our potential in a more aligned way toward success. As Vishvketu says, our true nature is often obscured from our own view through the pressures and challenges of our modern world. As we practice the teachings in this book, we will bring more of who we are into action and start to live from a higher place in ourselves in our everyday actions. Vishvketu often quotes the line, "yoga karmasu khaushalam," from the ancient Hindu text the Bhagavad Gita. It describes that through yoga, you can achieve perfection, unity, and wholeness in your everyday work by being more connected to your true nature.

NOTES

1. "What Is Osteopathic Medicine? The Benefits of Yoga," American Osteopathic Association, https://osteopathic.org/what-is-osteopathic -medicine/benefits-of-yoga/; David Gomes, "The 7 Best Yoga Poses for Your Health," *Medical Daily*, July 17, 2016, https://www.medicaldaily.com/ yoga-poses-health-benefits-392070.
2. Georg Feuerstein, *The Yoga Tradition: Its History, Literature, Philosophy and Practice* (Chino Valley, AZ: Hohm Press, 2001).
3. Carolyn Gregoire, "5 Ways Modern Science Is Embracing Ancient Indian Wisdom," *HuffPost*, Dec. 8, 2014, updated Dec. 6, 2017, https://www.huffingtonpost.com/2014/12/08/science-embraces-ancient -indian-wisdom_n_6250978.html.
4. Joel Wong and Joshua Brown, "How Gratitude Changes You and Your Brain," *Greater Good Magazine*, June 6, 2017, https://greatergood. berkeley.edu/article/item/how_gratitude_changes_you_and_your_brain.

5. S. R. Narahari, Madhur Guruprasad Aggithaya, Liselotte Thernoe, Kuthaje S. Bose, and Terence J. Ryan, "Yoga Protocol for Treatment of Breast Cancer–Related Lymphedema," *International Journal of Yoga*, July–Dec. 2016, 9(2): 145–155. doi: 10.4103/0973-6131.183713.

6. Paulo T. V. Farinatti, et al., "Flexibility of the Elderly after One-Year Practice of Yoga and Calisthenics," *International Journal of Yoga Therapy*, Sept. 2014, 24, 71–77, https://www.researchgate.net/publication/274723211_Flexibility_of_the_elderly_after_one-year_practice_of_yoga_and_calisthenics.

7. "Yoga: Another Way to Prevent Osteoporosis?," *Harvard Women's Health Watch*, May 2016, https://www.health.harvard.edu/womens-health/yoga-another-way-to-prevent-osteoporosis.

8. Stephan Kozub, "Take a Deep Breath—No Really, It Will Calm Your Brain," *The Verge*, March 30, 2017, https://www.theverge.com/2017/3/30/15109762/deep-breath-study-breathing-affects-brain-neurons-emotional-state.

9. Christopher Bergland, "Alpha Brain Waves Boost Creativity and Reduce Depression," *Psychology Today*, Apr. 17, 2015, https://www.psychologytoday.com/us/blog/the-athletes-way/201504/alpha-brain-waves-boost-creativity-and-reduce-depression; Lorenza S. Colzato, Ayca Ozturk, and Bernhard Hommel, "Meditate to Create: The Impact of Focused-Attention and Open-Monitoring Training on Convergent and Divergent Thinking," *Frontiers in Psychology*, Apr. 18, 2012, https://www.ncbi.nlm.nih.gov/pmc/articles/PMC3328799/.

SELF-REFLECTION QUESTIONS

1. Which of the guidelines within the yamas and niyamas are already second nature to you?

2. In which of the guidelines within the yamas and niyamas do you see challenges for yourself?

3. How do you anticipate your participation and impact on society would change if you were to adopt all the yamas and niyamas into your life?

CHAPTER THREE

Why Are We Here?
The Aims of Life

Companies spend millions of dollars every year defining and redefining their missions, brand values, and visions. As a founder, consultant, and manager in various industries, I observed a direct correlation between clarity of mission and successful results. A business that understands why it exists and communicates this well throughout the organization sets the guideposts within which to operate the business, helping motivate employees and focus everyone's efforts toward success. Similarly, if we are clear on our *personal* mission, we spend less time drifting without foundation, and we better persevere through challenges. Having a core understanding of ourselves—knowing our raison d'être—helps us put our options in perspective and then make the right choices. Just like a company branding guide helps designers choose colors and fonts to stay on brand easily and efficiently, so too do personal life guidelines help us choose the right actions in life.

But finding clarity of purpose first requires building a strong foundation of goals and learning to honor them in a balanced way. The ancient Vedic knowledge system developed such a framework, called the *purusharthas*, which outlines our primary responsibilities in life. This paradigm of Vedic philosophy helps contextualize all the things that we manage on a daily basis within our overall goals in order to help us find the right balance for our lives—something working professionals frequently struggle with. With these tools, we can put the right amount of energy into the right initiatives and also have much more impact on the things that matter. These primary responsibilities, when honored in a balanced way, can give us much happiness and fulfillment and create the platform we need in order to have more success in all areas of life. Much of this book builds on this foundational set of life goals; these are the building blocks to finding success in all areas of life.

These purusharthas describe that we have four main aims in life—four goals that are important to balance against one another. They are commonly referred to in Sanskrit as *dharma, artha, kama*, and *moksha*. Dharma contains the duties and responsibilities that one must observe in life, artha is the goal of earning income and having prosperity in life, kama is the goal of finding pleasure in life, and moksha is the pursuit of spiritual freedom. All four are important to keep in balance. If we overindex on any one of the goals at the expense of another, then we are not honoring our overall purpose in life, and we can quickly unravel into an unbalanced existence.

VEDIC GOALS OF LIFE

Dharma: duties and life purpose
Artha: income and prosperity
Kama: pleasure and fun
Moksha: spiritual freedom

We all know people who are overly obsessed with earning money at the expense of everything else, or others who are so deep into spiritual pursuits that they can't even afford next month's rent. Life is a balance of the four pursuits, and all of them need to be indulged in a strategic way. I often have clients in my coaching practice that are ready to give up their well-paying jobs to pursue their inner calling without realizing that the job itself provides the financial platform to indulge in and cultivate that inner passion. Often the solution is paring back the intensity of that primary-income job so that the true passion can be better indulged. Rather than switching one goal for another, it is balancing them that leads to a more sustainable and happier evolution in life.

DHARMA (DUTIES AND LIFE PURPOSE)

The first aim, dharma, is often summarized as honoring one's life purpose. This is correct, but honoring one's life purpose involves a range of responsibilities, from the mundane (such as eating right) to the more esoteric (such as finding a calling). Dharma in and of itself is the idea of doing things in life that feel natural and easy to you. If an activity intuitively does not make you happy, it is usually a misalignment of dharma. Doing things in line with your dharma gives you the sense that you are in flow, like rowing with the current instead of against it. It includes services that you provide to your personal and professional worlds and to society.

It is a balanced sense of duty that comes from a heartfelt place rather than from a forced place.

Within dharma are several types of dharma, the main ones being the duty to your body, the duty to take care of your family, and the duty to honor your inner purpose in contribution to humanity.

Health is everything. Without health, you cannot perform your duties, maintain your prosperity, or enjoy all that life has to offer. So the first dharma (*sharir dharma* in Sanskrit) is to recognize the gift of your body. Love it, understand its fullest potential, and nurture it such that it operates at its best. A vehicle takes us where we need to go, but if we neglect to change the oil, replace the tires, or put fuel in it, it will break down and leave us stranded. In the same way, we must pay attention to the maintenance of our body—with fuel, exercise, and alignment—in order for it to serve the ideas and proclivities of our mind. By honoring the duty to take care of our body through the right diet, exercise, and rest, we begin the foundational yogic existence. When we protect our body from disease and breakdown, we can then give other needs our maximum potential.

The next area of duty is our responsibilities to our family, called *pariwari dharma* in Sanskrit. This includes caring for our partners, our parents, our siblings, and our children and recognizing them as vehicles for our own learning. With our emphasis on the nuclear family in the West, we often get disconnected from our relatives and even our parents (and often our kids as they start their own nuclear families). For whatever reason, we were born into the families we were, and whether we like it or not, our families are an integral part of our journey through life. In Vedic tradition, your family is a deliverer of lessons to you. Sadhguru, a humorous spiritual teacher of mine, used to say, "If you want to understand your karma [your unique challenges], spend some time with your family." For instance, when I am with my siblings,

I feel like there's a bright spotlight shining on the things I need to work on! Whatever your challenges, your family will help you understand them. Therefore, you have a duty to care for them as your teachers. Part of our own growth and learning comes from providing support, nurturing, and healing to our family. Within this role, we learn the tools to support and nurture others in life and society.

We can use our family to understand ourselves better, grow, and provide healing and support back to them. As we understand ourselves better, we will understand them better. But some family relationships can be challenging, draining, and even destructive. When drama, heartache, or danger to your well-being arises in family relationships, remember that healing and supporting does not always need to take a direct form. When a family member is facing major challenges, sometimes it's best to heal and help ourselves first. Spend time with your children, enjoy your romantic partner, be there for your parents as they age, but know your boundaries and when to protect yourself. Maintaining your own vitality is essential to truly being there for others—and being there, in a balanced way, for everyone in your life who needs your love and support.

I have an elderly mother suffering from dementia, and as her health degraded, I found myself becoming so consumed in her care that it affected my work, my family, and my marriage. I became frustrated to the point that I was not able to show up for her and give her the love and affection that she needed in her time of suffering. I learned through this experience what many books on caregiving talk about: Take care of yourself first, otherwise you cannot take care of others. Sacrificing yourself for someone else is not a healthy practice. Think of a doctor: If a doctor gets sick, they are unable to help anyone. And if the doctor gets too caught up with trying to heal one patient, their capacity to heal others is compromised.

When there is so much emotional or psychological turmoil in a family dynamic that we need to stay away to keep out of harm's way, we can send support and love from a distance. One way to do this is to silently send the family member you're worried about an intention, simply bringing your awareness to a hope or blessing you hold for them. You can feel and show compassion for a family member from afar while protecting your personal boundaries. Just by virtue of embarking on this journey of self-discovery, you have reached a level of awareness that others may not share. Use that awareness to disentangle from the other person's drama and help them from a healthier place of detachment. You can extricate yourself, do your own work, then support the person from a place of empathy rather than pity or pain. By separating from the situation, we can help compassionately and with our full selves.

Show compassion even when it is difficult, and help your family, without losing your balance and without expectation of how they might treat you in return. Showing compassion not only helps their suffering but also makes us stronger. Through training with our family, we can understand that ultimately, we are responsible for our reactions to other people's behavior, and we can always find compassion. Misbehaving family members are often the triggers that can help us understand our reactions to other people, and that recognition is the first step to owning our emotions. When we realize this responsibility, we find power in handling any challenging person in life, and we can own the protection of our emotional well-being.

Building on the strong foundation of taking care of our bodies and our families, the next area of dharma—the area most commonly associated with the word—is our duty to connect to and understand our higher calling or higher purpose. This higher purpose is what connects you, through your inner talents and skills, to the rest of humankind. It is an activity of the heart that contributes to society, creates harmony for you and others, and inspires you in the process. Practicing this area of dharma means practicing activities that you feel inspired and called to do that also carry an intention of service to society. In Sanskrit, this is called *atma dharma*, or the dharma of your soul. This is the work that fills your soul, makes you feel in "flow," and connects you through service to society. Chapter 4 will go much deeper into this area of dharma to help you identify the unique gifts that you have to offer society and that you should honor on a regular basis.

Part of this area of dharma is a duty to yourself to be regularly inspired. Inspiration can come from your work but also through other means such as spending time in nature, practicing meditation, watching or reading inspiring things, or spending time with inspiring teachers. Such activities will help you recognize inspiration in yourself and orient you to the inner calling that truly inspires you: an overall direction in life, a personal mission that guides you through ups and downs and keeps you on your path. Vishvketu explains that swerving all over the place in life is a danger both to yourself and to others around you. Think of a time in your life when you might not have had a clear sense of direction. Maybe that's now! Lacking direction can make you feel listless. It's not only frustrating for you, but it also spills over to those around you who want to see you thrive. You might feel depressed or lash out. What's more, society is in need of each of our talents, and finding your direction helps you serve society and yourself.

All of these aspects of dharma need to be considered in balance. A friend of mine, Terry, who is a forest conservationist at heart, decided to live in the mountains after retiring from his career as a civil engineer. He hiked daily through the woods, enjoying and taking in nature. It not only brought him great joy but also kept his body healthy. When he discovered that some of the forest areas that he regularly hiked were being sold by the county to be built into subdivisions, he took up the cause to preserve the forest. Terry found dedicated federal government funds budgeted for forest preservation, researched the types of habitats that would be destroyed, and engaged the applicable federal conservation agencies to help prepare an application to save the land. He formed a citizens committee around his kitchen table, and after numerous meetings, calls, and applications, he was able to engage the federal government, the national forest service, the developer, and the county to have the forest service buy up the land and designate it as protected national forest. After this success, he continued on with similar efforts in the mountain region he lives in, and to date he has successfully conserved over twenty thousand acres of land in the San Bernardino mountains of California.

A couple of years later, I ran into Terry during a hike in that very forest, on the trails that he had painstakingly carved out (as a "reward," the forest service gave him permission to create and maintain the trails in that area). I hadn't seen him for months. I remembered how much I'd missed his twinkling eyes and rugged mountain hardiness. It turns out that he'd recently become very ill and had been unable to continue his work for several months. He explained that, instead of spending time hiking in the woods he loved, he was continually at his computer or on the phone or traveling to meetings, and he'd completely neglected his body. He was so sick that he could no longer do his conservation work, nor hike. It was mentally and emotionally devastating for him, and his recovery took many months.

Terry's inner calling is around the preservation of nature for generations to enjoy, and he honored that duty well. But without honoring his duty to take care of his body, his life went so out of balance that he was unable to honor his inner calling for months. During that time, funding at the government level got tighter and tighter, and numerous acres were lost to development in those mountains. He is continuing his conservation efforts now, though in a much more balanced way.

ARTHA (INCOME AND PROSPERITY)

The second main aim of life, artha, is the concept of having enough material prosperity to be comfortable in life. Kabir, the Sufi mystic poet from the fifteenth century, wrote, "May God give me that much that my family and I have enough to eat, and if a person comes to my home, we can offer them food so that I won't be hungry and my visitor won't be hungry." The yogis understood that without having means, one cannot acquire the things in life that are needed in order to take care of your body, support your family, and pursue the other aims of life. Wealth and earning are not seen as inherently bad. Money is also what gives us choice and the freedom to pursue our soul dharma, leveraging our skills and talents.

But money must be earned honestly, used for the right purpose, and pursued in balance with the other duties of life. When the pursuit of earning entraps us, we become imbalanced and our relationships and other duties suffer. It is therefore important that we are conscious about budgeting and living well within our means. It is good to spend time each month reviewing our expenses and assessing wants versus needs. The key is to not stretch our budget so far that if we lose our job, our world would crumble. The business-school concept of "golden handcuffs" has stuck with me throughout my career: It describes the dilemma of earning good income and enjoying a nice lifestyle but therefore being tethered to that job; the golden handcuffs, though beautiful to look at, trap you. I took heed of this lesson throughout my career, living well below my means and keeping a healthy financial cushion so that in case I lost my job, or had to walk away from it, I would not have to worry. This freedom helped me be firm and confident in taking risks to build new and innovative businesses. I could take a sustainable and successful long-term view in decision-making, instead of caving to pressure to create short-term profits.

My conservative spending habits also gave me negotiating power with those in more senior positions. One sales executive petitioned my boss to let me go if I didn't shortcut my development timeline for a consumer electronics product in order to please a powerful and demanding retail customer. I stood firm to some very angry executives, took the risk in letting that customer walk away from our product, and meanwhile methodically focused on building the quality I believed was necessary for a long-term success. When we launched, the product was so well received by the market that we won lucrative deals with multiple other accounts, created a $100 million annual revenue division out of it, and even won back that original customer. Had we taken the shortcut, the product would have likely failed despite the short-term win. My resolve came from having the financial backing to follow my business instincts without putting myself and my family at risk.

This lesson continued to serve me well, right until my own freedom was tested. Much later in my career, I was called into the CEO's office and complimented for my leadership in helping to drive historic growth in the company. I was applauded for my initiative and creative thinking and told that I was being considered for a major promotion. But there was something that I needed to work on. Salivating at the opportunity for a bigger title and even more compensation, I was ready to change whatever needed changing, and maybe even put on some golden handcuffs! I was told that I needed to stop asking such challenging questions during our executive meetings. My "out-of-the-box thinking" was unnecessarily making some folks look bad (him in particular), and given how well the company was doing now, we could ease up a bit—maybe stay in the box a little more. In essence, I was being asked to say yes more often. This stirred something deeply and fundamentally against my ethos. I just could not stomach being a yes-man, though it was all that was standing between me and my coveted promotion.

It was a dilemma I had inadvertently been planning for with over two decades of careful budgeting. Within a couple of months, I tendered my resignation. On my last day, the CFO called me into his office and said, "I knew you were up to something, Vish!" He'd noticed that I was one of the few executives who wasn't wearing a Rolex, driving a fancy sports car, and buying a golf club membership. He knew I lived in a lower-priced neighborhood than the other executives and didn't have an expensive wine cellar. He'd noticed that while my income had increased, my lifestyle had not changed much. Therefore, I could walk away from a situation that didn't serve me anymore—a situation that would have caused imbalance in my life aims by chasing higher earnings at the cost of honoring my talents and creativity.

But many working professionals get so caught up in an imbalance of earning and spending that they can't imagine a time when money isn't coming in, and they lose the discipline to save. A neighbor of mine works in the commercial real estate industry. He'd told me that sales agents will make 2 or 3 percent commission on a commercial deal in the hundreds of millions of dollars and immediately go buy a yacht or yet another vacation home. He received a few requests from agents asking if the company could withhold part of their commissions. It turned out that quite a few agents, year after year, had no funds to pay taxes when they were due, and they were not able to put a savings structure in place themselves. Each year, they would have to liquidate some property, at a loss, just to be able to make the payments. Without financial discipline, these individuals were completely trapped in the golden handcuffs. For people in this situation, if a boss were to request something unethical or uncomfortable—or excessive over-time away from family—they would feel as if they have no choice. If they were to lose their job, their entire financial house of cards would come tumbling down, just as it did every tax season—but in this case, without a backup plan.

A good rule of thumb is to save up at least four to six months of living expenses so that if you are ever faced with a poor choice, you can easily walk away instead of doing something unethical or unbecoming. If you hold a more senior position in an organi-zation, where job opportunities are fewer and far between, and finding a new position usually takes longer, then you should plan on eight to ten months of buffer. I have maintained this financial strategy for most of my career and therefore was able to make sound choices in my work without ever feeling my hand was forced by someone with hiring-firing power over me. You will enjoy clear-headed freedom that helps support balance and lets your greater potential show up in your work.

Artha also involves taking a conscious approach to finance, in terms of both expenses and income. Consciousness in income comes from charging the right price for something. Whether you are selling a product in the market or selling your services, it is important to charge a price that is commensurate with the mar-ket. When it comes to products, the market usually sets the price for you. But small business owners who offer services, depend-ing on their in-built biases and personality quirks, can sometimes undervalue or even overvalue themselves. It is part of our duty to charge a fair price—to not take advantage of our customers or employers and to ensure we are compensated fairly for our work.

The particular imbalance of undercharging often comes up with people who offer services aligned with their higher calling—often something they would do for free—especially those in healing professions. However, we must evaluate our training and experience alongside the market and then charge accordingly. I once coached a yoga studio owner, Christine, who was so big-hearted and passionate about her job that she'd sent her business into the red by giving away memberships. She lamented that she felt guilty charging people, but I asked her how she could fulfill this inner calling to help heal people through yoga if the studio closed down. By charging a fair price to all members, she may lose a few people, but she would help lots more the future. She made the tough decision to charge all customers, offering a discount only for military service members, the customer group she cared the most deeply about helping. Thus she was able to maintain her business while honoring her inner purpose.

Using artha as a platform to help others can sometimes be confused with charity. We may feel that if we give money to charitable causes, we are not required to give our own service to society through dharma, so we work for income rather than for impact. Charity is enhanced when we also contribute our talents to help others in a way that inspires us. In the yoga definition, contributing to society within dharma must be linked to your unique talents and gifts. If philanthropy happens to be that higher purpose, then that should be indulged, but for most people that higher purpose comes from a service to the world. Some of the money you might give to charity could be used to serve you and society by helping you cultivate a talent that the world needs so that you can provide a meaningful service. Your money could also buy you time to contemplate and explore your meaningful contribution to society.

Often, I work with clients who are extremely frustrated with their jobs and want to switch careers to find more fulfillment. When they see the interrelationship of dharma and artha, they often have some deep revelations toward understanding the place of their job in their life. They start to see how the job can provide the financing for their true passion. Not everyone is so lucky that the work they do is exactly in line with their higher calling. For some, dharma and artha converge. But they don't have to. As long as we balance the work of earning with the work of our inner calling, life can be harmonious. I worked for many years as a corporate executive with compensation that opened up many choices for me. But I was quite imbalanced toward artha, and so I didn't slow down enough to understand my higher calling until much later in my career. If I were to do it over, I might have indulged in my passion projects on the side, so that dharma and artha could have been in more balance.

KAMA (PLEASURE AND FUN)

The next goal area of life in the Vedic tradition is to have fun— who would have thought, life is about having fun! Kama is the enjoyment of pleasure. I used to think of yogis as ascetics who lived in caves and meditated in austere conditions, depriving themselves of food and societal contact. While this is the path for some, for the rest of us, the yogic texts teach that we can live in balance, in harmony, and in an enlightened way right here within society. To do that, we must balance the aims of life, and one of those balancing forces comes from enjoying mundane pleasures. Pleasure can come from many sources: It can be creative pleasure through art or song or dance, it can come from cooking a nice meal or enjoying fine dining at a restaurant you love, or it can be relaxing and socializing with friends. Kama includes the pleasure that can come from a hike in the forest, a swim in a lake, or the thrill of a mountain bike ride. Of course, the word *kama* conjures up the Kama Sutra, which is a Vedic manual of sexual pleasure. Sexual pleasure in moderation and in a healthy way is one of life's enjoyments and a natural part of a balanced life.

All of this enjoyment, laughter, and merrymaking is part of a healthy and balanced life, and we should indulge in pleasurable activities on a regular basis. As with the other aims, balance is key. Just as some people work too much, others may become overly hedonistic. People who are imbalanced toward kama can barely hold down a job or relationship and do no service to humanity or to themselves. They might be afraid to face their true path, which can involve challenges and hardships, and overindulge in kama to hide from the truth. Kama is important in balance and in the context of understanding the purpose of your life. Many times, the cause of addictions is related to imbalances in the four aims of life.

Kama also involves connection to other human beings. We need social interaction and deep connection with others to feel alive. Just attend a sporting event and see how satisfying it is to cheer on a team with thousands of other fans. Sports are a primary outlet for some people, especially men, to connect with others. Human connection is so deeply needed that others will pay for it. Vishvketu once told me a story of a man who used to visit a sex worker every week. He would pay her for her time but then just talk to her. When she asked why, he explained that he was missing connection in his life, and she listened to him, intently and without judgment. Of course, her other clients who came for sex were looking for connection as well, but in such context these outlets are limited in their ability to fulfill our need for connection. We must actively cultivate human connection as part of kama—enjoyment—so that we don't seek them in destructive ways.

It is important to evaluate what is fun and pleasurable in your life and make sure to indulge in that pleasure in a balanced way. It is a natural part of life that you should have fun, be joyful, smile, and laugh. It even helps us perform better in our work—and not snap at our colleagues. I sometimes ask clients to make a list of ten things that they love doing. This list is not an exciting, travel-the-world-and-bungee-jump type list. This is a list of everyday pleasures such as watching a guilty-pleasure reality TV show, playing catch with a son or daughter, eating a home-cooked candlelit dinner with a partner, walking along a nature trail, or playing an instrument. For me it includes wandering the aisles at Costco, tinkering with home repairs, reading bedtime stories to my girls, and bicycling with my son down to the neighborhood juice shop. Once you create this list, try to do at least two or three of the items every week. As mundane as they may seem, we find pleasure in them. So once we plan the activity, we look forward to it, savor it, and then create a happy memory. Then, when we are in a challenging part of our week, we can remember that mundane moment of pleasure and look forward to the next one. This simple adjustment can help us through many a challenge with a bit more of a smile.

My client Frank is a senior director of sales at a large medical device company, and he was struggling with his marriage. As we evaluated his life situation, it became clear that all he did was work, shuttle his kids around to after-school activities, and then argue with his wife at the end of the day. This was clearly evidenced in Frank's affect, which displayed a lot of sadness and heaviness (not ideal for someone in a sales role). He was deeply concerned about his work performance, and to counter his sagging sales, he just worked harder and longer. When I asked him what he did for fun, he said he had no time for any personal activities, not even the gym. Work was all-consuming. I asked Frank to make the list of ten mundane pleasures, and after struggling for a few minutes, he could not list one. It had been so long since he had indulged in life's simple pleasures. Since he mentioned the gym, I asked if that could count on the list, and he agreed, so we got one! As I asked him to recount happy moments in his life, Frank's list started to grow, adding in long-forgotten poker nights with his buddies over cigars, reruns of crime dramas on TV, and bedtime stories with his daughter. In the ensuing weeks, as he honored his homework to do a few things from the list on a regular basis, his disposition became more cheerful, and it seemed some of the load on his shoulders lightened. When his wife filed for divorce not long after, Frank continued his relaxation process during that difficult time. Though he had been struggling with depression before, he managed to keep his spirits up and even improve his work performance. Finding joy in life, outside of work and obligations, is key to finding balance and showing up better in every situation.

MOKSHA (SPIRITUAL FREEDOM)

Finally, the fourth aim of life is moksha, or spiritual freedom and an awareness of your spiritual journey. Many people ignore their spiritual needs until some major calamity brings them to their knees, and all of a sudden, they realize that there is indeed something else going on in their life. Whether your spiritual practice is attending church or synagogue or temple or mosque, practicing meditation or yoga, studying sacred texts, doing selfless work, or walking in nature, it is important to acknowledge the higher forces that exist around us. There is a poster some people have at their desks with an image of our galaxy and a little dot with an arrow pointing to it saying, "You are here." Moksha helps us remember that, with all our problems, as big as they seem, we are part of a much greater existence. This sense can come from worship of a god or exploration of science. But whichever way you define the higher workings of the universe—atheist, agnostic, religious, or spiritual—it is important to connect to some understanding of the forces beyond our control on a regular basis.

It is also important that this spiritual pursuit does not rule your life at the expense of the other aims. For example, becoming a devotee of a guru and giving up everything in your life—health, family, and other duties coming second to that guru—is moksha out of balance. Do not be so busy sweeping the temple in your obedience to its god that you ignore your duties to your partner or child—or worse, become a slave to that guru instead of following your own path. These examples are extreme, but the important lesson is that we pursue our spiritual journey in a balanced way, without abandoning our other goals of earning, duties, and fun.

Vishvketu describes moksha as something that just happens automatically as a result of adhering to the other three aims of life. If you pursue your life's work diligently, fulfill your responsibilities and duties, earn to support yourself and your needs, and enjoy life, you will find spiritual fulfillment. There is a sense of freedom from the ups and downs of life that comes from just doing good work, taking care of yourself, and enjoying life. Nothing else is needed; the feeling of freedom just happens. He explains that when all the pieces of your life are in sync, a blissful, playful, fearless, and expansive existence result. That is moksha. It is the freedom that saints talk about, a sense of continual bliss and detachment from suffering. Moksha is not about running away from society to live in a cave to find liberation. While that may be a path for some, the framework of yoga talks about the concept of *jivanmukta*, which is finding spiritual liberation within the context of a normal life with everyday responsibilities. Moksha enables us to be fully present, not bombarded by external influences, free from material trappings and the opinions of others. We can make choices that serve us holistically, with the freedom to do things in our own unique and creative way, in flow with the universe and without attachment to the trials and tribulations of life. Life does what it does, and we navigate through both the calm and the stormy waters with grace. That more deeply connected way of life can be found within the context of an everyday existence.

One of my clients, Diane, loves to meditate. She would meditate two to three hours a day and was constantly looking for meditation retreats to meditate even longer. She told me it just felt so peaceful to her; she didn't have to think or interact with anyone. People around her had too many issues, and she was tired of dealing with them. She was a retired school counselor and volunteered at a local high school, helping at-risk teenage girls, but she was considering giving that up so that she could meditate more. In our coaching sessions, she often appeared "spaced out" and not fully present. In her zeal for meditation, she was disconnecting from her life and other people. Practiced in excess, this escape through moksha was taking her away from her dharma responsibilities. Her challenge was to find spiritual happiness in connection to the world, i.e., balancing moksha and dharma. We clarified her inner purpose, codified it on paper, and cut down her meditation time. She started to get much more grounded, and within a couple of weeks she realized how much joy her work brought her and actually increased her volunteer hours.

To be successful on our spiritual journey, we should also not judge others on their journeys. We are all doing our best to find a joyful existence. We have different beliefs, different levels of awareness, and different challenges. Judging other people's approaches only holds us back. Do your own work, do not judge others for being in a different place, and life will feel freer.

Happiness and success come from balance among these four aims of life. The workaholic with no time for family, the spiritual devotee who neglects their spouse, and the activist who neglects their body will all find misery one day. As a foundation for your journey, it is important to evaluate where you can find more balance, ensuring a healthy foundation for a life of meaning. As we figure out a strong purpose in the next chapter, the other aims will propel that purpose forward.

SELF-REFLECTION QUESTIONS

1. How balanced is your life across the four aims?

2. What is out of balance, and how could you improve this?

3. How balanced are you among the areas of dharma: your responsibility to your health, others in your life, and your inner calling? How could you improve this?

4. What is your list of ten mundane life pleasures—things that you can enjoy on a weekly basis? How will you incorporate them into your routine?

CHAPTER FOUR

Your Purpose:

Where Are You Headed?

The yoga tradition teaches that happiness begins with knowing why you are here—what your purpose is—and honoring that daily. As we learned in the previous chapter, this concept is known as dharma, which is similar to the business concept of a mission statement. We know that a solid mission can tap into an organization's latent power by coalescing the team's energy around a common vision and purpose. Your personal life purpose, or mission statement, relates to the higher calling described within the dharma section of the purusharthas discussed in Chapter 3. Just as a company with a clear mission statement is able to align disparate microdecisions into a collective intention that drives success, so too can we align our personal microdecisions around a clear intention to drive us toward a more powerful and directed existence. We each require our own clarity of mission in order to live to our fullest potential. Understanding your dharma creates an important foundation of alignment for the other integrated parts of yoga.

What is shocking, however, is that fewer than 20 percent of business leaders have a strong sense of personal purpose, according to a *Harvard Business Review* study from 2014.[1] Unsurprisingly, corporate leaders are some of the unhappiest, unhealthiest, most stressed people in our society. Trickling down from that type of leadership are miserable organizations and frustrated employees. And the consequences are truly life and death: A longitudinal study in psychological science found that having a purpose in life "acts as a buffer to mortality," and specifically, people with a strong sense of life purpose had a 15 percent lower risk of an early death.[2] In Dan Buettner's work with *National Geographic* researching the longest-living, happiest populations on the planet (dubbed the Blue Zones), *purpose* is one of the nine common denominators for happiness and longevity; in other words, statistically speaking, if you know why you wake up in the morning, you'll live longer.[3] (Other core principles of Blue Zones involve diet, social activity, exercise, meditation, and relaxation—aligned with the system of yoga!)

The ancient practitioners of yoga knew innately that a clear sense of purpose is central to good health and success. As discussed in Chapter 3, dharma is a broader concept than purpose and has been understood differently in different Eastern traditions. From a yogic point of view, it loosely translates as "right action in line with your purpose, toward your full potential"—in other words, knowing why you exist on this planet and continually taking action to manifest that purpose. Dharma is about serving humanity in a specific way that leverages our innate talents and gifts, and by doing so, brings us joy and fulfillment. Purpose aligns your work, actions, relationships, and life toward a happier and more fulfilled existence. By sharing our true talents and using them in service to society, we can find more collective success along with more personal success and fulfillment, both spiritual and material. Specifically, when the challenges along the way serve a greater purpose, we gain a special key to longevity and success: resilience.

At the core of any story of human perseverance, you will likely find a clear sense of purpose. Such is the case in Viktor Frankl's *Man's Search for Meaning*, where he hypothesizes that resistance to fatal illness or insanity in the Nazi concentration camps was improved by finding purpose in one's existence. He explains, "Everyone has his own specific vocation or mission in life to carry out a concrete assignment which demands fulfillment. Therein he cannot be replaced, nor can his life be repeated. Thus, everyone's task is as unique as is his specific opportunity to implement it." He observed in his fellow inmates that those who lost their sense of purpose were more likely to start to decline mentally and physically, and he hypothesized "their body fell victim to illness, without a *why* to live." With the power of purpose, humans are able to tap into their higher power to overcome the toughest of challenges. As Nietzsche said, "He who has a *why* to live can bear almost any *how*."[4]

In my volunteer work with former military leaders, I see the practice of dharma play out in an extraordinary way. Soldiers face intense physical, mental, and emotional hardship. They see human suffering on a scale many of us can barely imagine. But if you ask a soldier how their day was, they'll often give you a more positive answer than an office worker who had a few bad meetings. An important difference is that the soldier often feels a higher purpose. On a macro and micro level, this inspiration energizes their entire being and unlocks potential. On any given day, they know exactly where they stand and what they need to work toward and improve. This clarity creates incredible resilience.

So it makes sense that after returning to civilian life, many soldiers have a hard time adjusting to the loss of mission; those

I work with feel lost and adrift, and often suffer from PTSD, anxiety, and depression. In coaching soldiers, I find that when they identify a new personal mission, they can cultivate their success and happiness. Once they find it, they become master manifesters of that mission and also take more active steps in healing their pain and trauma, since they are able to look at their emotional health as a tool toward that mission. Former military leaders become some of our finest corporate leaders when they are able to take their extensive skills and experience and deploy them toward a personal mission that energizes, inspires, and heals them. Firmly rooted in purpose once more, they also start to rely less on unhealthy coping mechanisms to deal with past traumas.

Charles, a former Marine Corps officer, was feeling listless about what direction to take his career. He was gravitating toward a prestigious technology company that offered the highest pay, but he wasn't inspired by the work. When I asked him about his purpose during his combat tours, he was very clear. But when I asked him about his life purpose, he stared at me blankly. "I never really thought about that." So after some hours of discussion and whiteboarding, we found some clarity: He wanted to be a technically competent engineering leader in military defense technologies. Right away, he started to reach out to companies with positions that supported his personal mission. He started networking with more intention and less fear—and he *hated* networking. Within two months, Charles had several job offers in line with where he wanted to go in the future. He ended up taking a role in an engineering leadership training program at a Fortune 100 company for less pay than his previous offer but with much more excitement. He would not only learn the technical skills that he needed for his desired competency but also start on the path to his broader leadership ambitions. I could see a renewed enthusiasm for life in his eyes. Setting a strong vision helped him organize his energies and intentions and align his life toward that vision. It helped align choices with long-term happiness and fulfillment rather than short-term considerations. A happy, fulfilled person in turn attracts success.

As a business leader, I experienced firsthand the power of mission in organizing intentions, focusing energy, and aligning decision-making. I worked at a technology company with brilliant engineers making brilliant technology, but the technology lacked a clear application in the market. Part of my personal purpose at that time was to build technologies that solved real consumer needs. Driven by that purpose, I went head-to-head with the CEO to divert some R&D funding toward understanding the consumer need better. He insisted consumer research would not tell us anything he didn't know from personal experience. At one point, after a heated argument, he slammed my office door so hard it almost shattered the glass panel. But with my mission clear (and a financial safety net secure, of course!), I stood my ground. After some intense consumer observation and research, we discovered a market need that our technology could be the first to solve. I set a clear mission for myself and the team for what the technology needed to solve based on that market need. Though many initially protested that I was leaving a bunch of cool features behind, the single mission soon became a team rallying cry. Amazing innovation followed around the core use case (purpose), which was then easily communicated to customers, who gravitated to the solution. By aligning my personal mission with the team's mission in context of a market need, we experienced a five-fold increase in the stock price of the company within two years. A clear mission had aligned disparate efforts to create personal and collective success (and brought me back into good favor with the CEO).

Successful start-ups have a leader who is connected to a deep inner calling to solve a problem. Founders who are focused only on the money might enjoy a few successes here and there but eventually face a reckoning. In fact, this is part of conventional investor wisdom: Savvy investors use questioning, observation, and intuition to determine the founders' true motivation and avoid putting money behind a misaligned vision.

But how do we know our dharma? How can you identify your personal purpose in life right now? It is easier to identify purpose in a military unit protecting its country or a start-up solving a market problem than it is to identify a personal purpose. But we also have disparate motivations, resources, talents, experiences, perspectives, and backgrounds, and it is equally important for us to align them. The first step is letting go of our constructed beliefs and frameworks so that we can even notice our dharma when it shows up. Then we identify purpose. Then we apply that purpose with intention by deploying our skills, networks, education, training, and finances in a supercharged way.

From childhood, we've been conditioned by parents, teachers, and society to perceive certain parameters on what we can and should be in life. Internal and external forces pressure us to take certain jobs, pursue certain activities, and associate with certain people. Often, money and appearances are factors. As a coach, I tend to see the despondency that comes from following a manufactured identity—the desire for a life of more meaning. There are some signs of a cultural shift—for example, millennials are known for prioritizing happiness over money. But we still must do our own work to release ourselves from attachments and expectations.

I thought I was happy and fulfilled in my identity as a senior corporate executive. I held a senior position at a technology company with great pay, an excellent team, and several major successes under my belt. My regular yoga and meditation practice helped balance the stress, and everything seemed just fine—I was so used to my frenetic pace that I was unaware that, deep down, it didn't feel right. Since I was being rewarded by societal indicators of success, and my parents were satisfied, I never really slowed down to reflect if my direction was actually right for *me*. Someone else had to point it out to me.

One evening, Vishvketu and I went to dinner with a longtime friend of his, Gurmukh Khalsa, a teacher of the Kundalini yoga style to the likes of Madonna and Michael Jackson. She immediately asked me where I teach. I looked at her completely puzzled and replied, "Who, me, teach?" I told her I am not a teacher but just a student of Vishvketu's. Nervous, I stumbled over my words. "I do business, I am a businessman, I run companies, I create technology products; I am a student, not a teacher." In that moment, it was like she was staring into my core and seeing a different image than the construct I had built. She replied with a compassionately wagging finger, "You have so many gifts and so much wisdom and experience to offer this world. You must not die just a student in this life." She continued on to another helping of food while I felt I had just had my soul chiropractically adjusted. Without skipping a beat, Vishvketu with a broad smile then asked if I would teach at his next yoga retreat. But it took a long time for this event to fully sink in for me. I was too deep in my curated identity to immediately grasp what was obvious to these highly attuned people.

I grew up in Hong Kong, a world center of business and commerce, where utmost respect was given to wealthy, powerful businessmen. Though he was the son of a teacher, my father himself was a businessman, and he was enamored of business tycoons. Incubated amid the hustle and bustle of the identically dressed businesspeople of Hong Kong, I oriented my own life on the same path. I envisioned a jet-setting career, visiting factories around the globe and ordering people around. So, I earned my MBA, worked hard, traveled the world, and yes, visited factories and ordered people around. But while I may have had more awareness and balance than many colleagues because of my yoga studies, I was on a path toward family trouble, poor health, and an imbalanced focus on career growth. It wasn't until my forties, some time after doing my core purpose reflection work, and my Gurmukh encounter, that I started to really discover why I was here on this planet. I let go of my attachment to an identity I was conditioned to want and learned to embrace my true calling.

This moment of "waking up," so to speak, is known in yoga as *samvega*, a realization of the true meaning of your existence and a lifting of a veil of illusion. For some it is gradual, for some abrupt, but it is always a connection to your truth and the courage to live it. It was the moment when Prince Siddhartha decided he would find a way to end suffering and emerged as the Buddha. In the Japanese tradition, it is known as *kensho*: the insight that you have recognized reality for what it really is. As I shifted toward teaching and coaching, my old friends and the mystics in my life didn't share my surprise at this new path. It turns out that I had naturally been doing the work of my inner calling all along, helping others get through tough challenges; I just wasn't recognizing it, embracing it, and manifesting it fully. Even if you think you're already doing what you love, having an *active* realization and daily pursuit of your purpose helps put you in complete alignment toward your greatest potential. This is also where seemingly serendipitous events start to happen that propel that purpose forward. Not long after I actively set my intention to coach instead of continuing the start-up, I got a call from a recently promoted friend asking if I could sign on as her executive coach.

Continuous reevaluation of dharma and how it shows up in your life is part of waking up and staying awake, especially

when we all have external and internal expectations to decon-
struct. Vishvketu realized his dharma in childhood. He ran away
from home at age six looking for a spiritual abode, steeped himself in learning of the yoga tradition, schooled at a traditional
gurukul (a forest-based yoga academy), studied at one of India's
most prestigious universities, and achieved a doctoral degree in
yoga philosophy. But there was a twist. As he journeyed deeper
and deeper into his spiritual practice and performed austerities
and intense study deep in the Himalayas under his guru Baba
Premnath, he decided that his dharma was to go even deeper
into his practice and isolate himself from the temptations and
distractions of society. He was ready to spend the rest of his
life meditating in a cave alone on his own spiritual quest. But
Baba Premnath said to him, "You will be a teacher of teachers."
Similar to my reaction when I was unmasked, Vishvketu was
dumbfounded. He was very attached to his identity as a solitary spiritual seeker. He learned to let go of that attachment and
manifest his true calling, eventually becoming a teacher of teachers on a global level and founding his own yoga ashram. Rather
than hiding away in a cave seeking enlightenment, Vishvketu
took the more dharma-aligned path of honoring his talents and
serving the world by training thousands of yoga teachers. He
is happiest and most in flow when he is training yoga teachers,
following the central tenet of his life work and dharma.

Many of us spend our lives trying to compete in an area that
we are not very talented in. It might be what our parents or peers
thought was important, or we might have run into circumstances
that put us in a role of responsibility that we were not ready for.
And we might not see the misalignment of talent because we are
also taught in the West that life is a struggle and you have to
work hard to rise up. So we gladly fight our way through life.
The concept of dharma offers us a different view: What if we

recognized our innate gifts and talents, cultivated them, and used them to serve others in a positive way? Life could be much less of a struggle. When you listen to your own inner voice, you will navigate life with more ease and flow. Through deeper dharmic awareness, we then also see expanded opportunities for us to flourish. As you practice this awareness and intuitive choice making, you develop muscle memory that reminds you what moving in the right direction feels like.

When I moved to Southern California, I took up surfing. Exercise, ocean, and networking—it's the golf of the tech world. I noticed experienced surfers expending so much less energy than I was. Eventually I realized that before they started, they would sit on shore observing the ocean and connecting to the patterns, whereas I would jump straight in. Then, in the water, they would synchronize their timing with a wave and naturally ride in to shore. When I stopped struggling and started observing, I too started to notice the right waves to catch and how to efficiently flow with them. It is this way with living our life purpose: Slow down, observe, connect, then let the wave carry you forward. Forget your preexisting notions of how it should work, how you should paddle, how you should stand (or, if you're a golfer, how hard you should swing). No matter how hard you try, working in harmony with your dharma will always be more efficient than trying to overengineer an outcome.

INVENTORY AND IDENTIFY YOUR GIFTS

After detaching yourself from conditioning and external pressures, the next step to finding your purpose—unless of course you happen to have a prophetic encounter with a mystic, and even then—is to carefully inventory all your gifts, talents, and inclinations. Then, trusting your intuition, you will identify within those the clues to your dharma. Finally, you will draft a purpose statement that leverages those key gifts in the service of others. (Remember, dharma is always connected to serving others; you have gifts for the purpose of bringing something to society.) Craft your purpose statement, however rough, and refine it continually. As we walk through this process, you will learn to do this alongside a solid spiritual practice to help cultivate your intuition and refine it in the right direction, ultimately manifesting your dharma in a meaningful and powerful way.

First, look for the types of activities in your life that you have a knack for. Set aside a couple of hours one weekend, and reflect back on your entire life. This is a recapitulation exercise and also a form of contemplative meditation. Start from your earliest memories, and replay the major events and milestones of your life story: hometown, friends, home life, teenage years, high school education, college years, relationships, activities and hobbies, vehicles, marriage, children, work, career. Reflect on these memories, both good and bad. What experiences strengthened you, and what propelled you to become who you are now? Start to think about what you did really well at, projects that were successful, roles where you performed extraordinarily. Think of things you felt passionate about. As you do this, write or draw out a visual timeline of your life, chronicling what you were naturally drawn toward, most proud of, and naturally good at. You can make a collage of photographs, magazine clippings, and other mementos, or you can sketch out a timeline.

Enjoy this exercise as you reflect on your entire journey through life. Pay attention to themes that recur across chapters in your life. If you have them, read through and reflect on your old report cards and performance reviews. For once, don't focus on the negative parts, only the really positive parts. After your initial effort, ask some of your close friends, colleagues, and partners what they see as your gifts and talents. Add these things to your timeline. Then, after perhaps a week's wait, sit down again. This time, start to think through your present life and make a list of activities you currently enjoy—that you find a sense of wholeness in and that you would naturally gravitate toward if you had all the time in the world. These activities could include things like problem-solving, writing or translating things, teaching, or physical exercise. This process can be healing, and along the way, you will become clearer on your life purpose and inner calling.

Now look at your entire inventory for common themes—the skills and activities that reoccur in your myriad roles, activities, projects, and reviews. These are your innate talents and passions: the clues to the core of who you are. You should aim for a list of ten to twenty verbs and sentence fragments that comprise your talents, nature, values, and passions. Some examples might include:

Gaining trust	Cheering	Mediating
Leading	Innovating	Teaching
Problem-solving	Connecting	Creating
Making change	Defining	Competing
Organizing	Unlocking	Collaborating
Visioning	Opening	Caring
Investigating	Entertaining	Energizing
Fixing	Performing	Counseling
Sorting	Supporting	Brainstorming
Building	Researching	Generating Ideas
Making	Calculating	Helping
Defining	Analyzing	Writing
Motivating	Facilitating	Standing up for

(You can tack on a noun to any of these, e.g., Helping—children.)

Next, look at your list and identify two categories of items. Assign an *A* to the phrases that you look at and think, "Wow, that is absolutely me," and a *B* to the phrases that you look at and think, "Yes, I do that well, but only when I have to." The *B* should also be assigned to things that you think you are supposed to enjoy but that don't truly feel as satisfying as the *A* items.

Now, brace yourself, this part can be emotional: Cross out all the *B* items. They do not serve you at your core, and they distract from your core purpose and evolutionary journey. I have had multiple clients in tears realizing they have spent their entire lives doing things that they were expected to and convinced that they had to. These things might fulfill your obligations, or maybe you're sort of good at them, or they are sort of interesting and fun, but overall, they are energetically draining. Be honest with yourself and cross them out—as many or as few as apply.

Now take a good hard look at what survived, and start to feel intuitively what stands out among the remaining items. Circle the things you naturally gravitate toward, that you could never give up, that seem to feed your soul, that bring you true happiness. When you are doing them, you lose track of time—of where you are—and power and competency emanate from you. You are more energized afterward than you were before you started. People close to you know you are naturally gifted at these things. When you do these things, you feel "in the zone" or "in flow." Psychologist Mihaly Csikszentmihalyi describes flow as a state of mind where you feel energized, fully involved, and joyful—completely absorbed in the activity you are doing without regard for things around you and without any sense of your own ego. He explains that this state is when we are at our happiest, and the more time we spend in flow, the happier a life we live. In the Vedic tradition, Csikszentmihalyi's flow correlates to the fulfillment and happiness that naturally comes from honoring your dharma on a regular basis. Both perspectives seek to communicate that, in doing such activities, you are manifesting a higher power. And the best part? The items you circled are giveaway clues to your true purpose. There is no specific quantity of items you should have at this stage; every selection should feel natural and true.

For many, the hardest part comes next: I want you to narrow down your circled items to three to five top priorities. You can start by ranking them, or just feel which ones really stand out for you. If your top-priority list is quite large, then you are likely to feel pulled into lots of different directions in your life, so be patient with this step. As you identify your top three to five list items, the key to your true purpose and inner calling will start to be revealed.

You are welcome to use other techniques to get to this point—perhaps you have spent time with an enlightened person, a great mentor, or a coach or discovered your calling through deep meditation, yoga practice, or therapy. The goal is to arrive at a list of three to five key words or phrases that describe your innate gifts, talents, values, and passions so that you can write a purpose statement around them. (One useful tool that I use with clients is a set of *Calling Cards: Uncover Your Calling* created by Richard Leider of Inventure—The Purpose Company, where you physically sort talents and skills into piles; the structure of tools like this can help if you're struggling to think of words.)

In my case, at the top of my list were:

Analyzing things
Solving problems
Fixing things
Getting to the root of things
Building stuff

This top list should feel deeply "you." When you look over it, you might almost feel giddy with excitement. Don't get caught up on whether you actively do these things or not or what job might incorporate these tasks. Let go of planning for a moment and just enjoy this shortlist of what you love.

PURPOSE STATEMENT

With this powerfully curated list, you can start to piece together a purpose statement. Look at your top items and understand that these make up your core gifts and talents—and that these talents can be used to serve others. Part of living with purpose is expressing your gifts by serving other people and improving their lives in a meaningful way. Think about how you have used the top items in your list to help others, and start to write a statement using the ideas and concepts expressed in your top choices. Your goal is to answer the question: "How can I serve others by using my passions, talents, gifts, and knowledge?" As best as you can at this stage, also identify whom you would focus on. It may be children, adults, soldiers, businesspeople, women, men, economically disadvantaged people, or animals. You might start with something simple, such as, "My purpose in life is to [insert verb] [insert whom you want to help] by using my gifts of x, y, and z." Approach from a gut level, and try to let your ideas flow without your constructed beliefs getting in the way. If you have a mind-centering practice, such as a calming breathing technique or meditation, employ it here. Do whatever you need to do to reach the needed mental equanimity. Don't worry about using the exact words from your top list, but do make sure that your key gifts and talents are expressed and that there is some connection to helping others. At first, your statement may be clunky, and that is okay. Write it down (or type it), no matter how unpolished it sounds. It has to get out of your head and into the world, and it is just a starting point from which you will refine further—a rough cut.

Now, put your draft statement aside. Sleep on it, so to speak. Revisit it in a few days and start to refine it: See if it still resonates and what needs tweaking. Trust your instincts. From this point, you should visit your statement weekly and keep adjusting and refining it until it starts to flow naturally and you feel comfortable sharing it with others in your life. You will know you have it when you say it out loud and it energetically and intuitively feels right to you—when you can say it with conviction. This statement will become a living entity that you revisit, refine, adjust, and use as a guidepost. Once it gets to a stronger and more resonant place, you will be amazed at how your purpose starts to manifest.

You will refine and adjust this statement until it sounds right, and it also may change over time as different aspects of your life journey take root or become priorities. Depending on where you are in understanding your overall life journey, you may prioritize it more around family; or it may be more about work. It might be about starting a business, it might be about finding love, and at another time it may be more spiritually focused in nature. The important thing is to understand what it is relevant for you and resonating with you right now. Refine the statement as best you can without spending too much time on it or overthinking it. Even if you just end up crafting a mission statement for a specific area of importance in your life, it can be a powerful tool to drive clarity and focus.

Years ago, deep into my business identity, where I was not open to a broader dharma path, I would craft mission statements specific to my business goals (since that was what I focused on), but they were tied to my personal gifts and talents. I had statements like "Use my understanding of consumer insights to create new technologies that make life at home more convenient." At another time, in a more senior role, it was, "Create a $100 million business division by creating mobile device accessories that delight our target consumer." These exercises did have a powerful effect in helping me create successful business outcomes, but without doing the exercise at a broader dharma level, you can see how I got lost in accomplishing these missions at the expense of reflecting more deeply on my true calling.

I first came across the idea of formalizing a life purpose statement at my local health district, of all places! Based on compelling Blue Zones data, they believed community well-being could be improved through holding free life purpose workshops. I signed up for one, and through a process similar to what I just described, I crafted a broader life purpose statement: "to bring out potential in businesspeople by getting to the heart of matters and solving problems on the inside to fix things on the outside." (See how this develops from my top five list.) It resonated with me deeply but seemed tangential to the executive work I was involved with at the time. I wrote it down and revisited and refined it over the ensuing months and years. It had the effect of putting my business mission statements into a broader life context. As I revised and honed the higher dharma statement, it simplified powerfully into "helping people find their way." I believe this exercise in clarity, supported with my yoga practice, had a powerful organizing effect on my life direction. As you can see, our purpose statements can and should evolve along the way, and years later, after several career adventures, I am living a clearer purpose.

MANIFESTING YOUR PURPOSE

Once you have a purpose statement you feel strongly connected to, you will find that things in your life seem to serve it. It's like when you learn a new word, and all of a sudden it shows up everywhere. You will automatically start paying more attention, both on a mental level and on a deeper intuitive level, to opportunities in your life that align with that purpose. The right people show up, the right conversations materialize, and the right opportunities present themselves, not out of magic but because you're paying attention and pursuing the right path. You also gain a conviction to follow your purpose more diligently and fearlessly. They say that luck is nothing but the preparation for opportunity, and identifying your purpose is the best way to prepare.

The concept of *sankalpa shakti* in yoga is the power of intention to manifest what you seek; I'm sure this concept will sound familiar to you. As Stephen Covey, author of the highly celebrated *The 7 Habits of Highly Effective People*, says, "Begin with the end in mind." High-performance athletes can attest to this phenomenon: You can't win if you don't envision yourself winning. My coaching colleague, Heidi, is an Olympic gold medalist in swimming. In her competitive days, she tells me, having a clear intention to win was as important as her innate swimming talent and her relentless training. Align your intention with your inner nature, resources, and drive, and your spirit will energize to manifest that intention.

Manifesting your purpose is a proactive practice, and it will look different for everyone. Incorporate your purpose into your lifestyle, finding ways to honor it on a regular basis. This will help you learn what it feels like to be in flow and connected to your inner purpose on a more consistent basis. Maybe you can orient your work responsibilities to honor more of your gifts and talents, or you might find hobbies, organizations, or meet-ups that let you exercise your purpose more consistently. However you do it, practice indulging in your highest desires on a regular basis. The longer you avoid it, the more your stress will grow, and society will suffer from missing out on your true contribution. The more you indulge in it, the more life will start to flow with ease and happiness. A Western-culture analogy is David Allen's concept of the fifty-thousand-foot view. Allen's methodology involves grouping all your projects under areas of responsibility that feed up to a two-to-three-year vision, then five-year goals, up to an overall purpose. In his book *Getting Things Done*, he explains these steps as different altitudes of view: the fifty-thousand-foot view of why you exist, incrementally down to a ten-thousand-foot view of a project, and eventually down to daily tasks at a runway level. You might be like me and find value in breaking down your purpose into parts and plans (*Getting Things Done* is a personal bible for me), or you might trust the natural, intuitive alignment that comes from a deep understanding and daily awareness of your fifty-thousand-foot view. Either way, that purpose ensures that you focus on the right daily minutiae and purpose-aligned activities. As your muscle memory builds, a purpose-driven life will start to happen naturally, and purpose-adverse activities will naturally fall away. You're on your way to a less stressful, more meaningful life, which those attuned to you will start to notice.

After I got deeper into my coaching and teaching path, I arrived at one of Vishvketu's yoga retreats. As I drove up to the forested retreat center, I was greeted by a beaming Vishvketu, with proud, sparkling eyes. "Wow, Vishwajeet!" he said, using my Indian name. "After many years, it now appears that you are rowing your boat *with* the current instead of against!"

LETTING GO INTO FLOW

As you follow the steps I've just outlined, you may find yourself developing an attachment to making your purpose a reality. Relentless focus on the goal is a good thing, right? Not necessarily. Obsessing over your purpose can impede your progress by creating preconceptions and closing you off to possibilities. Set your vision, have an intention, but remain open to the different ways you might manifest your purpose. Think about finding love; someone who is looking for the perfect partner may start specifying characteristics—brown hair, athletic, a certain height. But what if we brush shoulders with a blonde who is not athletic and the wrong height, and because we have our mind set on a specific image of our goal, we don't tune in? There is a difference between visualizing a clear intention and attaching to a specific image. Your purpose is a mental intention that forms a backdrop for your life. But day-to-day, you must let things unfold naturally and be open to opportunities without attaching to a specific version of your vision and closing yourself off to the broader forces at work. You have probably come across the concept of "marketing myopia," where a company is so focused on a narrow part of their vision that they miss the broader forces at play: A company might make the best buggy whip, but carriages are about to be replaced by automobiles. You may set a strong intention around getting a job at a fast-growing technology start-up, so when a recruiter from a consumer-goods company contacts you, you decline, not considering whether there might be an internal start-up within that company that fits your purpose.

Avoiding attachment to our purpose also involves being grounded and present for our immediate work and life. Vishvketu once told me a story of a villager who earned his money walking from his village with a clay pot on his head, filling it with water from a remote well and walking back to the village to sell the water. One day, as he was returning from the well with a full pot of water on his head, he started to imagine how much more money he could make if the pot were filled with butter. He could save up to buy a cow, milk the cow, churn the milk. Then the cow would have a baby, and he'd have more milk and more butter. In the middle of his daydream, he tripped over a large stone and dropped the water pot, destroying it. Now he had no water to sell and no pot to carry it in. We have to balance our big, audacious goals with our day-to-day existence. Remember the four aims in life, the purusharthas: dharma, artha, kama, and moksha. Balancing all of them is important, even and especially in pursuit of our purpose.

As you practice building your life purpose into your daily awareness, incorporating a complete yoga practice will help further clarify your intention and pave the way for you to better fulfill it. Yoga (including the accompanying Ayurvedic health and healing practices) is a framework of techniques and philosophy to purify body, mind, and spirit with the specific purpose to manifest one's dharma more fully. As your personal dharma becomes clearer to you, it will in turn set a stronger intention for your yoga practice, and also help you create more balance and success in life. This happier state then further improves your dharma awareness, enabling you to make the right connections and find the right opportunities with a minimal of obstacles and turbulence.

NOTES

1. Nick Craig and Scott A. Snook, "Managing Yourself: From Purpose to Impact," *Harvard Business Review*, May 2014, https://hbr.org/2014/05/from-purpose-to-impact.
2. Patrick L. Hill and Nicholas A. Turiano, "Purpose in Life as a Predictor of Mortality Across Adulthood," *Psychological Science*, 2014, 25(7): 1482–1486, https://pdfs.semanticscholar.org/59c5/bbc19423a3fecd64167f70d3a53086404618.pdf.
3. Dan Buettner, "The Secrets of Long Life," *Blue Zones*, https://bluezones.com/wp-content/uploads/2015/01/Nat_Geo_LongevityF.pdf.
4. Viktor E. Frankl, *Man's Search for Meaning* (New York: Washington Square Press, 1985), p. 131.

SELF-REFLECTION QUESTIONS

1. What are the top three to five gifts you identified in this chapter?

2. What is your draft purpose statement?

3. What in your life to date has distracted you from honoring your purpose statement?

4. How will you honor your purpose on a regular basis in your life?

5. Are there any specific areas of your life that would benefit from their own mission statements? How do these areas support your life purpose?

CHAPTER FIVE

Your Nature: Who Are You?

Ayurveda, the health and healing tradition used alongside yoga, emphasizes balance. In order to truly support our long-term health, happiness, and success, balance must apply to *all* areas of our life, from our work to our lifestyle to our diet. Seeking balance in every area supports more sustainable, long-term success in our careers. Just as an athlete's performance depends on proper food, rest, and exercise, so too can you as a high-functioning leader support and improve your performance through an optimized approach to your lifestyle.

Ayurveda recognizes that we all go about our work and life in a unique and individualized way. Therefore, balance is unique to each of us: What feels balanced for one person may not for another; there is no one-size-fits-all approach here. As we start to contemplate and develop our overall approach to life from the work we've done in previous chapters, we start to realize how unique our individual journeys are. We each have our own unique set of responsibilities, challenges, careers, and families, and of course, our unique life purpose. The Vedic knowledge system recognizes that we are all unique individuals with different outlooks, mentalities, and physical constitutions. In short, part of finding balance is learning who you are—as a unique mind-body combination.

Ayurveda helps direct us on this path. From the Sanskrit words *ayus* ("life") and *veda* ("knowledge")—or "knowledge of life"—Ayurveda is a body of knowledge that helps us identify our unique mental and physical natures and then apply *personalized* lifestyle principles specific to those natures. It helps us understand the optimum type of foods, exercises, and daily routines to support our optimum, balanced health.

Yoga and Ayurveda go hand in hand. As yoga is the system of techniques and philosophies for the body and mind to unlock our potential, Ayurveda is the foundational system of healing and nutrition that takes care of the body and mind to maintain health or heal from illness. Ayurveda teaches that good health comes from a holistic balance of physical, mental, and spiritual energies. It begins with understanding how each of us is unique and therefore needs distinct lifestyle and diet practices to maintain optimum health. Unlike Western nutrition approaches, the Vedic system teaches that what is nutritionally beneficial for one person may not be for another. Ayurveda helps us learn what to eat, when to eat, and other lifestyle directions, building a foundation for basic living that is in tune with your individual nature. Yoga builds on this with a system of philosophies and techniques to harness your fullest potential from your nature-synced living. In ancient India, students often learned Ayurveda first to bring the body into balance before studying yoga, thus deriving deeper and quicker benefits from yoga.

I first came to understand Ayurveda during a particularly stressful time in my career. I was creating a new division at a consumer-electronics company and under pressure to deliver huge returns. I relentlessly drove the team to execute at a high level. During my performance review, my boss was happy with the results but told me we had a people problem: My yelling and screaming was leaving people in tears at the end of meetings. In my typical authoritative style of those days, I retorted, "Oh, so you want me to hit impossible numbers and have everyone kumbayaing at the same time?" I took it as an insult to my work. I was delivering; so what if there were a few tears along the way? People need to shape up or ship out! I complained to my wife, and she tactfully corroborated that I did have a quick temper when under stress, and it was indeed something I needed to work on.

A bit peeved by this response, in typical fashion, I poured myself a tall whiskey and wandered over to my bookshelf, and a dusty, unread book on Ayurveda popped out at me (*The Book of Ayurveda: A Holistic Approach to Health and Longevity* by Judith Morrison). Perhaps aware that I needed some guidance, I sank into my favorite armchair, book and whiskey in hand, and started thumbing through. It was that evening that I discovered that I was a "pitta" constitution, or, simply translated, a fire type. Much like a Myers-Briggs inventory, this categorization of personalities was something I was used to from management trainings. *When a pitta type is out of balance, they get critical, angry, judgmental.* That's me! *Task-oriented, achievement-oriented, hates interruptions, tends to burn the village down when out of balance.* Oh yes! Then I got into the diet part: *Avoid red meat, oily foods, red wine, hard liquor—especially of a dark color.* At that point, I put down my drink. My lifestyle of anger, overwork, excess red meat, excess alcohol, and constant stress was putting me on a clear path to a heart attack (a condition that Ayurveda relates to chronic pitta imbalances). Then I connected the dots: Two of the bosses that I had admired the most in my career had suffered heart attacks. I admired them for their take-no-names, get-things-done mind-sets, without considering the health effects of the attitudes and lifestyles we shared.

The next day, I started to adopt the book's recommendations for calming the aggravating factors for my type of constitution. I cut down red meat, switched to white wine, cut out hard liquor, ate more cooling foods, and started swimming, cycling, and gardening (all pitta cooling activities). It did not take long: Within weeks my wife and colleagues were commenting on a noticeable change in my demeanor. At my next review, there were no complaints of employees in tears, and I still delivered on my goals. Now, in times of extreme stress, knowing my constitution, I make some of these adjustments to my lifestyle. In times of less stress, I relax a little more around lifestyle and diet. Ayurveda is all about balancing based on what is going on at a particular time in your life. As I have deepened my studies of Ayurveda and taught it in business coaching, I have found that it can significantly enhance career performance for all constitution types. Our unique constitution relates to our unique work style, how we respond to stress, what causes imbalance, and what antidotes could rebalance us.

Ayurveda is a powerful tool for self-awareness. Through this awareness, we can find not only balance and stress reduction but also more enlightened ways of relating to our work and colleagues and a better understanding of people around us and why they manage things differently than we do.

Similar to the DISC assessment or Myers-Briggs inventory used in leadership development, Ayurveda has a categorization system to help us understand ourselves better. These groupings are referred to as *doshas*, and there are three main doshas, or basic types of constitutions. All three doshas influence each of us, but typically we primarily tend toward one or two. Your choices, lifestyle, and environment all factor in. By understanding your nature and the influences of the world on *you* (including how you handle work and stress), you can make better choices to stay in balance, harness your strengths, and improve on your weaknesses. Though we are usually born with our dosha combination, it can change and take on different challenges as we age, so we must pay attention to ourselves over time. The word *dosha* itself means "imbalance"; it refers to our most likely source of imbalance. Too much of one dosha showing up in our lives leads to blockages in thinking and in health. So, if you are naturally predisposed to a certain dosha and you're increasing that same dosha because of the nature of your work, your performance will suffer. If left unattended over a period of time, Ayurveda suggests that we will start to experience health disorders related to that dosha category. When we know which dosha or doshas we naturally tend toward, we can proactively monitor if we are heading for imbalance and regain balance with food, diet, exercise, and other lifestyle choices. By understanding this system and its triggers and balancing mechanisms, you will be less blindsided by your own behavior and more perceptive of people around you and their unique reactions to life and work situations.

Doshas are, in essence, groupings of qualities or characteristics. The three doshas are *vata*, *pitta*, and *kapha*. They help categorize people and their mental and physical temperaments based on how the elements of nature show up within them. Vata is associated with air and space, pitta with fire and water, and kapha with earth and water. The dosha system rests on a foundational understanding of the five elements of nature, which show up in many ancient traditions as the building blocks of our universe and our physiology. Different words can be used to describe the elements, but at a basic level they are space (sometimes called ether, describing the concept of potential), air (sometimes called wind, describing the concept of movement), fire (transformation), water (protection and lubrication), and earth (solidity and structure).

Ayurveda correlates these elements to our various biological components. Space is the medium within which all of our being exists and the potential in which we create thoughts and make the sounds of verbal communication. It is also the space in any cavity of our body, such as our lungs and digestive passage. Air is the movement in our body: the movement of food through the digestive system, the transport mechanisms of oxygen and waste, and the movement of our muscles and synapses. Fire is the transformative action in our body. It is all the cellular destruction and creation, the homeostasis of our body temperature, the breakdown and absorption of nutrients, and the growth of body tissues. Water, as a protecting and lubricating element, is found in all the fluids of our body, from our circulatory system to our spinal fluid to the fluid in our cells and in our hormonal system. Finally, the earth element of solidity shows up in our bones, muscular structure, and cell walls. Because these five elements come together to create our very nature, understanding and balancing them leads to better understanding of ourselves and our strengths and weaknesses.

The elements also correlate with mind principles. For instant, space relates to our potential for new insights, air is our creativity, fire is our ability to focus and execute, water is our emotions and feelings, and earth is our grounding and calm. When these different elements stay in balance, we perform in a balanced and effective way. But with too much of one element, we fall out of balance; for example, we might lead only with the heart, or only with the head.

Element	Concept	Body	Mind
Space	Potentiality	Lungs and gastrointestinal system	Potential for new insights
Air	Movement	Respiratory and circulatory systems	Creativity
Fire	Transformation	Digestion	Focus and execution
Water	Protection	Circulatory systems	Emotions and feelings
Earth	Structure	Bones and muscles	Grounding and calm

These characteristics manifest everywhere in nature. Some things are airy and changeable, some are wet, some are hot, some are stable, and others have an ethereal, spacey quality. Some people have a fiery characteristic, perhaps in their body temperature or disposition. Those heavier with the water element might be easily moved to tears or prone to sweating. Some people are airy, with a lot of bubbly enthusiasm and changing ideas, while others might be earthy—grounded and less reactive to change. Objects, people, food, animals, colors, smells, almost anything can be described as some combination of the elements. Look around at this very moment and see if you can identify the five elements around you. Usually you will see some representation of at least earth, air, fire, and water. (I will give you a hint: The electricity around you is connected to the fire element.) Understanding how these basic elements influence us is the science of life that is Ayurveda. It is a tool for deeper insight into how the constant changes of life affect us and how to manage that change better.

Doshas and Elements of Nature

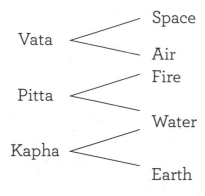

Each dosha, in addition to its physiological qualities, is associated with descriptive qualities. Vata is the combination of space and air and governs movement and potentiality, which might show up as out-of-the-box thinking. Pitta is the combination of fire and water and governs transformation, like acid that can powerfully clean, burn, or otherwise transform. Kapha is the combination of water and earth and governs the principle of protection and structure; like mud, it can solidify or produce inertia. Look at the list below for more descriptive terms for each dosha.

Vata— Space & Air	Pitta— Fire & Water	Kapha— Water & Earth
Cold	Hot	Cold
Light	Sharp	Heavy
Airy	Intense	Solid
Changeable	Fierce	Stable
Rough	Acidic	Smooth
Dry	Oily	Wet
Irregular	Pungent	Enduring
Quick	Penetrating	Slow

We'll all see people we know in these lists. People who favor vata (air and space elements) typically have a lighter and thinner frame, delicate digestive systems and sleep patterns, dryer skin, and finer hair. Their extremities tend to run cold, and they are usually asking for the heat to be turned up and/or are wearing extra layers at the office. They also tend to talk and move quickly and are usually very creative, lively, and enthusiastic. They don't like routine and are constantly changing things up. While they are great multitaskers, they often have several projects scattered about in various states of incompletion. At a networking event, they'll talk to everyone, flitting from subject to subject and person to person. They handle interruptions smoothly but are also easily distracted. They can be very flexible and adaptable but tend to have lower stamina and burn out quickly. A vata résumé often shows frequent job changes. In summary, vatas resemble the wind, always moving and changing.

Pitta types (fire and water elements) usually run hot; they're the ones taking off layers of clothing at the office. They might even have a pinkish or reddish glow to their skin. They have a medium frame, a solid, regular sleep schedule, and strong digestion—they can eat almost anything and burn it up. They enjoy routines and schedules and are good at getting things done. They don't handle interruptions well, preferring to focus on one task at a time. They show up on time to meetings and get frustrated when frantic vatas show up late. Pittas are direct and precise in their communication, often sharp-witted, and very linear, logical and decisive in their thinking. They are also usually very warm and friendly when in balance. They are typically quick to action, though they can suffer from too much haste or intensity. A pitta résumé is usually packed with responsibilities and accomplishments in different areas, each job role showing success in multiple arenas. This is your quintessential type A personality—fiery and driven.

Kaphas are the solid, dependable types (earth and water elements). They tend to easily gain weight and have a larger overall frame. They have smooth skin and lustrous hair and are usually very laid-back and easygoing. They sleep very deeply and often have trouble getting up early. They are very methodical and thoughtful and will carefully analyze before making a decision. They have the stamina and perseverance to work until the job is done, though they may be hard to motivate initially. They have strong attention to detail. Usually very good listeners, they are loyal and supportive. They speak in a measured and calm way. They make very faithful and dependable friends and also tend toward being homebodies. A kapha résumé would have longer stints at a few jobs, as they are not usually comfortable changing up their work a lot. In summary, kaphas are grounded and earthy.

Each of the doshas also reacts to stress and trauma differently. A vata tends to become fearful, anxious, and worried that they are the one at fault. They want to exit the situation as quickly as possible and move on. A pitta in stress tends to get very angry and lays the blame on everyone but themselves. They don't see their own mistakes and instead become critical, judgmental, and angry toward others. Their instinctual response is to fight the situation. Finally, the kapha in stress tends to become withdrawn and complacent, showing no reactive signs of stress. They may hide the issue or appear as if nothing is wrong but may also cling to a situation in their mind long after it is over.

I am pitta dominant with some vata, while my wife is kapha dominant with some pitta. When she makes a mistake, my pitta jumps at her. Her kapha nature stays calm, and to me she doesn't seem all that bothered. So I amp up because I don't think she is hearing me, my vata windiness starts to fan the flames of the pitta fire, and as she stays earthy and grounded, I get more agitated—until eventually her pitta fire comes in, and she yells back, "You are always mad at me about stuff, I got your point, why do you have to keep going over it again and again?" By better recognizing my own nature and also noticing when I am in a time of work overload (which aggravates pitta), I can take care to be gentler in getting my point across. I am also lucky to have three children teaching me the lessons of Ayurveda, since each of them presents a different dosha. My son is predominantly kapha: He likes to sleep in, has loyal friendships, and is very warm-hearted, loved by everyone, and great at listening. When given a task, he is methodical and maintains focus but can take a long time to finish with his measured pace. My older daughter is a vata: Creative, bubbly, and enthusiastic, she'll dance her way from one end of the room to the other. Her friendships and attitudes keep changing. She wakes up early and is restless from that moment. When given a task, she often gets distracted and strays from it. My younger daughter is a clear pitta dominant: warm and friendly most of the time, but in charge. She wants things her way. When she gets mad, there is door-slamming and name-calling. And when given a task, she is sure to complete it—and pity to the person who interrupts her.

In Ayurveda, the doshas provide insight into the roots and nature of disease and how to treat it in a tailored way. They also help when we are not sick by telling us how to maintain optimum health for our unique constitution, how to stay in balance more easily, and how to harness our maximum potential in life and work. Also, by understanding our mind-body constitution, we can understand better how we relate to people, what types of work we will naturally find ease in, and what types of relationships balance or aggravate us. We then have awareness and tools to compensate and balance our unique nature. Two people performing the same type of work may go out of balance in different ways and need different balancing techniques.

These descriptions are the quintessential archetypes, but we are all a combination of all of them, often with one or two types dominating. The doshas also often manifest differently in the body and the mind. Some may have a kapha-dominant body and a vata-dominant mind, or a pitta mind with a vata body. And depending on what is going on in your life, regardless of your constitution, any one of the doshas can go out of balance. So be sure to study them all, and notice how and when the different doshas go out of balance for you.

Anything can push our constitutions out of balance: food, exercise, relationships, work stressors, job function. Let's start by looking at food to see how too much of one dosha can send us out of balance, especially if it aggravates our dominant dosha. Popcorn, which is dry and airy, has a vata quality; ice cream—cold, heavy, and smooth—has kapha qualities; and red chilies are pitta in nature, being acidic, hot, sharp, and intense. If you are a dry and airy vata-dominant type, and you eat a lot of foods like popcorn—in conjunction with lifestyle factors such as constantly changing work responsibilities or frequent travel, especially by air (excess change and movement)—chances are your vata will fall out of balance. Like increases like, so a vata person with a lot of vata aggravators will end up with a vata imbalance. (In contrast a kapha person with a lot of vata aggravators in life would be much less affected.) It will show up subtly at first, in mental reactions and minor body ailments. But continual imbalance forms the seeds of more major health disorders, both mental and physical. Dr. Vasant Lad, a leading Ayurveda expert, uses the analogy of a leaky pipe dripping water into a bucket. If the bucket is already partially filled with a dosha, and more of that dosha "leaks" into the bucket through lifestyle factors, eventually the bucket overflows and causes damage to the surrounding floor (in our case, body tissues). If we can balance that dosha by reducing the lifestyle leakage or reducing the dosha level already in the bucket, then we keep the dosha from doing damage to our health.

Ayurveda characterizes all disease as an imbalance, and all treatment modalities seek to rebalance the imbalanced dosha. In fact, before treatment an Ayurvedic doctor will determine your unique constitution, identify the imbalanced dosha based on the disease you are suffering from, and then ask you a series of questions about your lifestyle, diet, and work to determine what is causing the imbalance. More often than not, the disease is related to a dosha that has gone out of balance through a lifestyle factor that aggravates that dosha. Treatment involves herbal medicines, diet changes, specialized treatments, and lifestyle adjustments to return to optimum doshic balance—in other words, good health. By being aware of your own subtle imbalances, you can rebalance ahead of a work disaster, regretful fight, or full-blown health problem. Use the following descriptions as a starting point to see if you are naturally inclined or currently trending toward a particular imbalance. (We'll discuss course-correcting through balancing measures in Chapter 6.) You can also use this knowledge to better understand colleagues, family, and friends and manage your relationships with them with more awareness. In my coaching practice, I even give different types of homework assignments based on a client's dosha makeup. I know I can throw a lot at a pitta, unless they are trending toward imbalance, in which case they may benefit from more relaxing assignments. A kapha might be resistant but very committed once convinced, while a vata is usually very excited to try something new—though the vata may take more of a push when it comes to follow-through.

At a mild level, vata imbalance shows up mentally as an overactive mind, anxiety, fear, inconsistency, worry, scattered thinking, and insecurity and physically as insomnia, gas, digestive issues, low stamina, constipation, arthritic pains, and bloating. Pitta imbalances show up mentally as anger, irritability, aggression, criticism, judgment, and closed-mindedness and physically as skin irritations, inflammation, high blood pressure, circulatory issues, bladder infections, headaches, indigestion, heartburn, and acidity. Kapha imbalances show up mentally as complacency, overattachment, neediness, depression, and laziness and physically as congestion (both respiratory and circulatory), excess weight gain, lethargy, lung and sinus issues, colds, and swelling. As you notice these symptoms, you can proactively balance them through lifestyle changes.

Mental Imbalance Symptoms		
Vata	**Pitta**	**Kapha**
Overactive mind	Anger	Complacency
Anxiety, restlessness	Irritability	Overattachment (not letting go of things)
Fear	Aggression	Neediness
Worry	Criticism	Depression
Scattered thinking	Judgment	Laziness
Insecurity	Closed-mindedness	Tendency to withdraw

Physical Imbalance Symptoms		
Vata	**Pitta**	**Kapha**
Insomnia	Skin irritations	Respiratory congestion
Gas, bloating	Inflammation	Circulatory congestion
Low stamina	High blood pressure	Excess weight gain
Constipation	Circulatory and heart issues	Physical lethargy
Arthritis	Bladder infections	Lung and sinus issues
Excess weight loss	Headaches	Swelling, edema
Dry skin	Indigestion	Colds
Feeling cold	Heartburn, acidity	Allergies, asthma
Poor digestion	Hot flashes, feeling hot	Achy joints

In balance however, all the doshas have strong positive qualities that lend themselves to different skills and talents. (However, when overworked, those fitting job functions can aggravate that particular dosha.) Creative vata types enjoy change, make quick decisions, think quickly on their feet, and communicate well. Full of ideas, they make great creatives, artists, industrial designers, graphics designers, and innovators. They make excellent creative leaders that can think out of the box and are flexible with change. They are also very social, build relationships quickly, and love excitement in their day. These activities do deplete them, though, and they can easily burn out. They need grounding and nourishment when in vata-type roles; they are especially sensitive to excessive travel.

Pittas are very sharp, decisive, and organized and can manage projects very well, keeping themselves and others on task. They are very persuasive and make good negotiators. They make strong engineers, project managers, and executives. They excel in marketing and sales since they can analyze data and make strong decisions and in legal professions since they can persuade and convince with sharp logic. As operational leaders, they push teams to maximum potential and achieve challenging targets and goals. Hardworking by nature, pittas often don't know when to stop and end up falling out of balance from overwork.

Kaphas are nurturing and loving, and they are very good listeners. The most grounded and stable of the types, with the most stamina, they make sound decisions considering all factors. With their nurturing and dependable natures and their ability to put people at ease, they make great counselors, psychologists, human resources professionals, and teachers. But they can suffer from listening too much and holding on to other people's issues. They need a mechanism, like journaling or talking it out, to dump that information so they don't hold on to things that don't serve them. With their excellent stamina, methodical nature, and tendency to persevere through complex situations, they also make great IT professionals, computer programmers, and accountants. Kaphas can fall out of balance from too little activity in their work, especially if their job keeps them physically stagnant. Kaphas make excellent senior leaders because of their ability to listen to their teams, process the input, and make thorough, thoughtful leadership decisions. For this reason, they are often the well-liked leader.

Outside of work, we can often spot the doshas from a mile away. The skinny artist whose mind is always flitting from place to place, the red-faced politician who is forever arguing, or the smiling counselor who listens patiently and offers sage advice. In the business world, however, with all our training, discipline, and efforts to be a team player, we cover up and compensate for our imbalances—and we're good at it. Doshas start to get hidden from view to others, and often to ourselves. We can appear very balanced and not even recognize our weaknesses before they show up as a surprise—and a real issue—in a performance review. Noticing imbalances in your approach at work and in life can be a powerful early diagnostic tool to make changes before they take root in your decision-making, family, and health. Understanding and balancing your Ayurvedic dosha is therefore a tool for you to create a foundation for peak performance, which yoga will then open up.

The following questionnaire will help you understand your own constitution with its current influences. Answer the questions at a gut level, without overthinking. Just mark the answer that comes to mind first. After reviewing your results, don't get overly attached to any dosha label on yourself. We are all a combination of all three, and they show up in different ways continuously in our life. The quiz results will simply help you understand your easiest route to imbalance at this time. With the information in the following chapters, this knowledge will help you make better diet, lifestyle, and work decisions and pursue a more optimum existence of improved self-awareness with a better understanding of others.

DOSHA QUESTIONNAIRE

The questionnaire that follows is a tool for you to under-stand your own constitution or Ayurveda type so that you can better understand your natural tendencies and propensi-ties toward imbalance. By understanding your predominant dosha or doshas, you can make better diet, lifestyle, and work decisions for your unique constitution, leading to a more optimum existence. The questionnaire results will help you understand your easiest route of imbalance. As you continue through the following chapters and beyond on your journey, you can use this knowledge as a tool for self-awareness to better manage yourself and your life.

As different events happen in your life, and as you notice your reactions to those events, you can use the awareness of your own reactions as a diagnostic tool to assess which dosha might be going out of balance for you at that time. Remem-ber, even if you are predominantly pitta, depending on the season, the circumstance, your lifestyle and diet choices, and your state of health, you might experience a vata or kapha imbalance. As you go through the questionnaire, and in the future as you refer back to it, use the dosha groupings as a framework to contextualize what is happening in your life—and to better understand the people around you—and address imbalances thoughtfully and holistically.

In this questionnaire, you'll examine each area of your physical and mental characteristics and rank attributes from most to least similar as they relate to your nature. The left-most column lists physical and behavioral categories, characteristics of which are then all grouped under the vata, pitta, and kapha doshas.

First, copy the blank table at the end onto a piece of paper; you'll use this to record your rankings. Start with the first row of physical characteristic (build), and read the vata, pitta, and kapha attributes. Find the attribute statement along that row that *best* describes you, and give it a score of five. Give the *next-best* statement a score of three and the *least fitting* statement a score of zero. Go through every row of characteristics, resulting in a single five, a single three, and a single zero in each row. Once you have ranked all the attributes along each row, add up the vata column score, the pitta column score, and the kapha column score. The highest score is your predominant dosha.

Again, answer the questions at a gut level without overthinking, and don't get overly attached to one label. We all possess qualities of all three, and we all exhibit them in different ways throughout our life.

Physical Characteristics

	Vata Attributes	Pitta Attributes	Kapha Attributes
Build	My physique is thin, and I don't gain weight easily.	I am of moderate build, and I can gain or lose weight if I put my mind to it.	My body frame is large and solid with a heavy bone structure, and it is hard to lose weight.
Joints	I have prominent joints, and they crack and pop easily.	I have medium joints.	My joints are large and well-padded (not very visible).
Eyes	My eyes are small and active.	My eyes are medium-sized, and my gaze is penetrating.	I have large, pleasant eyes.
Skin	My skin is usually dry, more so in winter.	My skin is warm, reddish, and prone to irritation.	My skin is smooth, thick, soft, and sometimes oily.
Hair	I have thin, dry, frizzy hair.	My hair is fine, straight, graying early, or balding.	I have thick, oily, dark, wavy hair.
Body Temperature	My hands and feet are usually cold.	I usually run hot and can sweat easily.	I don't like cold, damp environments.
Digestion	I can develop gas and bloating easily, and I often get constipated.	I can get heartburn or upset stomach with spicy foods. My bowel movements are regular.	My digestion is slow. I still feel full sometime after eating. My bowel movements are soft.
Eating	I eat at erratic times and sometimes forget to eat when I get busy.	I have a good appetite. I can eat a lot, and I get ravenous if I miss a meal.	I can skip meals easily without problems.

	Vata Attributes	Pitta Attributes	Kapha Attributes
Sleep	I usually have difficulty falling asleep or having a sound night's sleep.	I usually sleep well and can get by on less than eight hours of sleep.	I'm a sound sleeper and can take a while to wake up in the morning.
Energy Level	My energy fluctuates and comes in bursts.	I have good energy and am determined to complete my work.	I have a steady energy level with good endurance and strong stamina.

Behavioral Characteristics

	Vata Attributes	Pitta Attributes	Kapha Attributes
Personality	I am lively, enthusiastic, imaginative, quick, and active by nature.	I am assertive, direct, persuasive, and impatient by nature.	I am laid-back, easygoing, methodical, and relaxed by nature.
Reaction to Stress	Under stress, I get anxious, worried, and fearful, and I tend to blame myself for things.	Under stress, I get angry, critical, aggressive, and judgmental, and I tend to blame others for things.	Under stress, I usually remain calm and composed, but I can get complacent, withdrawn, or reclusive.
Learning & Memory	I am a quick learner, but I tend to forget things quickly.	My memory is moderate.	I am not a quick learner, but I am good at memorizing things and remembering them later.
Decisions	I am not good at making decisions; I can be indecisive.	I am decisive and assertive in making decision.	I carefully consider all angles before making a decision, and once it's made, I don't usually go back on it.

	Vata Attributes	Pitta Attributes	Kapha Attributes
Work Style	I typically end up multitasking and being involved in lots of projects at once.	I am organized, focused, and task-oriented, and I tend toward overwork and perfectionism. I consider myself efficient.	I work at a measured and comfortable pace. I have stamina and patience to complete long tasks.
Activities & Exercise	I like vigorous exercise and creative activities, but I can tire out easily.	I like competitive sports and activities where I feel challenged.	I like relaxing activities, but when I exercise, I can have a lot of stamina.
Idea of Fun	Being creative and imaginative and being social.	Getting things done and hitting my goals.	Relaxing, doing nothing, staying home.
Speech	I talk fast and a lot, but I can tend to wander in my conversations.	I talk moderately and with confidence and like to stay on point in a conversation. I like to convince and persuade.	I am measured in my speech, I talk at a steady pace, and I'm a good listener. Sometimes I don't really want to talk.
How Others See Me	I am considered creative and full of ideas.	I am considered warm and friendly but sometimes strong-willed and stubborn.	I am considered affectionate, forgiving, and peaceful.
Responsibility	I easily end up with too many responsibilities for me to handle.	I enjoy having responsibilities.	I am reluctant to take on new responsibilities.

Within each row, give one attribute statement a zero (worst fit), three, or five (best fit).
0 = Not really me   3 = Somewhat describes me
5 = Describes me the best

Scoring Table

	Vata Scores	Pitta Scores	Kapha Scores
Build			
Joints			
Eyes			
Skin			
Hair			
Body Temperature			
Digestion			
Eating			
Sleep			
Energy Level			
PHYSICAL SUBTOTAL			

	Vata Scores	Pitta Scores	Kapha Scores
Personality			
Reaction to Stress			
Learning & Memory			
Decisions			
Work Style			
Activities & Exercise			
Idea of Fun			
Speech			
How Others See Me			
Responsibility			
MENTAL SUBTOTAL			

————————   ————————   ————————
Vata Total   Pitta Total   Kapha Total

The highest total score is your predominant dosha if it is at least fifteen points higher than the other dosha scores. Any score within fifteen to thirty points of the top score would be your secondary dosha, which indicates the secondary slope toward which you can slip out of balance. If you have a score less than fifteen points behind your highest score, that means two doshas are in play. Some people are bi-doshic, with two prominent doshas, and some people can even be tri-doshic.

This questionnaire is not intended to replace a professional medical assessment of your doshic constitution. If you want a deeper or more accurate understanding of your dosha or a deeper breakdown of mental versus physical imbalances, we recommend consulting a qualified Ayurveda practitioner. Especially if you are suffering with a chronic disease, a medical practitioner's diagnosis and advice will be beneficial, going much deeper into your specific imbalance. But as you continue your journey, your preliminary understanding of your dosha will give you a much stronger foundation to relate to the chapters that follow.

Questionnaire adapted with permission from the works of Dr. Suhas G. Kshirsagar, BAMS, MD, of Ayurvedic Healing Inc. Santa Cruz, California.

CHAPTER SIX

Bringing Balance to Your Life

After learning your unique mind and body constitution, you may start to notice your Ayurvedic constitution influencing your daily routine. Vata types resist routine and like to change it up, sleeping at different times, eating at erratic times, and running out of energy in the middle of the afternoon and wanting a nap. Pitta types might be very routine driven, paying attention to their watch all day and getting intensely hungry right at the noon hour. Deny a pitta their mealtime and hear them roar! Meanwhile, kaphas like to hit snooze a few times, need a cup or two of coffee to get going in the morning, don't really care if they miss a meal, and tend to stay up late. These behaviors might not always present themselves quite so neatly because your body will try to correct dosha imbalances by itself. Plus, as added complexity to our underlying nature and influence from the nature of our job, the different doshas dominate at different times of day, during different seasons, and through different phases of life. By tuning in to nature, the elements, and ourselves, we can use Ayurveda to recognize imbalance when it arises and return to balance promptly— and of course, maintain balance to begin with as often as possible.

117

I was working with Shari, a senior executive at a fashion goods company with a pitta-vata constitution. At the time, vata was quite out of balance. In her high-stress position, she was constantly meeting different people and having to think quickly and be creative. She was eating a lot of cold foods at erratic times and was frequently on the run as she darted from meeting to meeting. Her main challenges were exerting confidence in senior-level meetings, standing up to bullying personalities, thinking quick on her feet, and feeling anxiety around preparation for presentations. Though she was not necessarily a vata-dominant person, the nature of her workday had sent vata out of balance, with health symptoms including bloating, poor digestion, insomnia, mental fog, confusion, anxiety, and fear. There were also some kapha-imbalance symptoms such as morning sluggishness, weight gain, exhaustion, and the desire to withdraw. Her body was trying to compensate for the airy vata imbalance by grounding itself with sleep, some extra weight, and involuntary mental rest. When an intense company fund-raising effort started, these health challenges exacerbated her stress levels, causing vata to boil over and forcing her to take time off work at a critical point.

We can tackle most imbalances proactively with simple lifestyle adjustments that don't interrupt our work. Shari started eating more nourishing and warm foods at regular times at a sit-down meal, without her phone in hand. She started meditating daily, getting regular oil massages, and walking in nature to ground her excess vata in a healthy way. She also used journaling at the end of the day as a technique to offload some of her mental anxiety and added regular blocks of focused alone time into her work schedule. As she grounded the vata imbalance with small lifestyle changes, her body sent fewer grounding signals, and she was able to find better mental clarity, confidence, sleep, and job performance. She reconnected with her sharp, analytical pitta nature, which helped her handle her senior executive role, and she prevented her symptoms from turning into a more severe health ailment. Her return to balance helped her effectively secure the financing the company needed to ensure a bright future.

In general, the excess movement and change found in periods of frequent travel, excessive meetings, job changes, moving, or transitions in relationships can aggravate vata. When you are going through these vata periods, especially if you tend toward vata, you should make regular time to ground and nurture yourself. In addition to Shari's grounding activities, try gardening, listening to soothing music, and spending time with your bare feet on soil or sand. Any type of activity in nature helps calm vata. Social interaction and activity should still be a part of regular life, and vatas thrive on this—but try to spend time with people that have a nurturing and soothing energy, rather than people that drain you. Vatas should also indulge their creative abilities through work or hobbies, but routine is very important when vata is creeping out of balance, so take caution not to overbook yourself, and schedule in regular periods of rest. Reduce or eliminate caffeine, alcohol, and loud noises; Chapter 7 covers additional diet guidelines.

Kapha (earth and water elements) becomes muddy when out of balance; it needs to be stimulated and churned up. Periods of cold, damp weather and periods of isolation, when you are not interacting with people much, can aggravate kapha. So can tasks that require long periods of unbroken, solitary concentration, or work that is so overwhelming that you don't know where to begin. Kapha imbalance can be countered with new experiences and stimulating, vigorous activities like exercise. Aerobics, running, competitive sports, dance, and more movement-oriented yoga can help. Paying attention to food intake and not overindulging is important, as is engaging in intellectually challenging activities and work. Get outdoors, move, sweat, experience new things, and whatever you do, avoid the couch; you'll only aggravate your imbalance further, becoming more sluggish and low-energy and building kapha-related health issues. Poor sleep can aggravate kapha as well, as the body will try to rest and nurture itself through the sluggishness of kapha symptoms.

Pitta out of balance needs to be cooled down. Periods of intense work, heavy task lists, too many responsibilities, and high job pressure and stress can aggravate pitta regardless of your dominant dosha. Cooling activities can include swimming, cycling or walking on a chilly evening or early morning, walking along lakes and oceans, and meditating. Any physical exercise helps release the fiery energy, but it should not be competitive, as that adds to pitta imbalance. Relaxing activities such as a soothing massage or restorative yoga can also be very helpful. Cooling drinks and foods such as raw vegetables are also soothing to pitta; refer to Chapter 7 for more diet information. Avoiding overwork during pitta imbalance is of utmost importance, as is minimizing interruptions during work hours.

TUNING IN TO NATURE

But how do we avoid getting out of step in the first place? With knowledge about our dosha preference, our lifestyles, and the world around us, we can find our own optimal lifestyle practices and adjust them as life and nature fluctuate. The first step in formulating our optimal daily lifestyle is to understand the natural rhythms of nature, which interact with all doshas differently. In our modern world of artificial lights, stimulants, meetings across time zones, and constant information flow, we tend to separate from our relationship with the cycles of nature. We have to actively reestablish that relationship.

The most obvious cycle of nature is that of the sun and Earth. Earth's rotation around the sun produces alternating cycles of day and night, corresponding to our body's circadian rhythms, or biological processes that happen every twenty-four hours. During sunlight hours, we produce more serotonin and endorphin hormones to help with activity and enthusiasm. As the sun sets, and it gets dark, we produce melatonin to help us fall asleep (and as we sleep, other hormones regulate bodily rejuvenation and repair). As the sun rises, our bodies work to detoxify, so you will often notice mucus, tears, and earwax carrying toxins out of your system in the morning. These circadian rhythms—our bodily reactions triggered by our surroundings and habits—help maintain balance and health. When we decouple from these cycles, it's like always being a little bit jet lagged—an example of circadian rhythms being thrown off. To adjust to a new time zone, we know to spend time in the light during the day, and turn out the lights completely at night. No drug has been able to match this natural reconnection to daylight and nighttime. Connecting with to these cycles regularly can help you tune your body for optimum performance.

Less obvious but also important are the cycles and effects of the moon, our closest astronomical neighbor. Of course, the moon makes its presence known on Earth by creating the tides, and given this gravitational effect on water, plenty of which is present in our bodies, it makes sense to pay attention to the moon's fluctuations.[1] The ancient yogis believed the moon had an intimate connection with the mind, and Westerners made the same connection: The word *lunatic* comes from the Latin word for *moon*. Many an ER doctor and police officer will tell you that they see the craziest cases on full moons. Vishvketu explains that in yoga the moon is also tied to our melatonin levels and the pineal gland, which regulates our focus and intuition. Dopamine levels, the so-called love hormone, often enhanced through meditative practices, is also correlated to the moon in the yoga tradition. If you're skeptical of the moon's ability to impact our lives, take only the most tangible factor to heart: Fuller moons produce more light, leaving us naturally more active and sometimes disturbing our sleep. Even such a simple awareness can help us tune in to our rhythms and make adjustments such as paying extra attention to healthy sleep routines on full moon nights. In Vedic texts, it is said that projects that start during a waxing moon tend to be more successful, while the time of the waning moon is good to analyze, debrief, and wind projects down. As you tune in to your work environment and colleagues, observe if you see any correlations with the moon cycles and the general mood and workflow at your office. Full-moon gazing is also a meditative practice that you can try to help bring emotions into balance, calming the fluctuations of your mind. Doing this simple practice for as little as five to ten minutes a few nights a month can help to temper your emotional state.

Beyond the moon cycles, notice the seasonal changes as our Earth rotates around the sun. As we go from summer to fall to winter to spring, see if you can observe the doshas at play, and adjust your routine, diet, and outlook accordingly. Western nutrition talks about eating the right foods for the season, and even culturally, particular dishes are celebrated at certain times of year, which matches up with Ayurvedic thought. The hot summer, when the fire of pitta gets easily aggravated, requires more cooling influences and cooling foods in your life to balance. Imagine biting into a cool watermelon, or taking a swim (pitta balancing activities) on a hot summer day and how it cools you to the core. Think of the cold, dry winter months when vata gets aggravated and you need more grounding and nourishment from warm drinks, root vegetables, and skin moisturizers. Then in the late winter and spring when things are damp and cold, kapha gets aggravated and you feel sluggish and congested. A lighter diet, spring cleaning, and time outside can help energize you. Being aware of the seasons and of how one dosha in excess leads to ailments gives you a powerful tool of awareness to adjust seasonally. For instance, a kapha personality with a kapha job in a kapha time of year (cold, damp weather) needs to take extra precaution to reduce kapha.

The different doshas also dominate at different stages of your life. The younger years of childhood are dominated by kapha, presenting through ailments such as colds and asthma, as well as the need for more sleep. The teenage years are dominated by pitta, with skin inflammations such as acne, hot-headedness, anger, and rebellion. As we age, we come into a vata time when our skin gets dryer, our hair thins, and our bones become frail. With awareness of our constitution and the doshas' presentation in our age, the seasons, and the times of day, we can be much more attuned to making adjustments and living from a place of balance.

With our advanced consciousness and ingenuity, we may have found ways to transcend the natural order, but optimal health over the long term requires working with the natural order. By understanding our body's connection to nature, we can better care for our bodies and maintain optimum health, happiness, and performance throughout the days, seasons, and years. A daily routine of putting your life in harmony with nature is one of those small but simple things that can have a huge impact, and it's also a cornerstone of yoga. Routines provide a nice structure for our day and help signal our body to more efficiently prepare for periods of rest and activity. Though the adjustments are minor, they add up and amplify, improving our overall harmony with far-reaching implications for our health, well-being, and performance.

OPTIMAL DAILY ROUTINE

Creating an optimal daily routine requires us to understand the influences of the Ayurvedic doshas on different times of day. We described each of the doshas as a set of qualities, founded in the five elements of nature, that can be applied to people, places, and things. The qualities of the different doshas also predominate at different times of day. There are six doshic time periods—6:00 to 10:00, 10:00 to 2:00, and 2:00 to 6:00, a.m. and p.m.—and each dosha governs two of them.

Vata, the airy dosha, governs 2:00 a.m. to 6:00 a.m. It's often the time that insomniacs—who are presenting a vata imbalance—wake up and can't fall back asleep. It's also when the most active dreaming takes place with the rapid eye movement (REM) phase. Rapidity and movement, of course, are qualities of vata. That active quality also shows up in the tossing, turning, and mental thoughts that can show up in those 2:00 a.m. to 6:00 a.m. hours. Our dreams also reflect the creative nature of vata, as we create an alternative world in our mind's eye. People who run or walk early in the morning would also notice the ethereal flow of energy at this special predawn time. Then from 6:00 a.m. to 10:00 a.m. is an earthy kapha period when you may feel more lethargic and also congested, as your body is eliminating toxins. But you can also find a lot of stamina and endurance in midmorning. While the sun is high, from 10:00 a.m. to 2:00 p.m., the fiery pitta takes over for the time of high productivity and digestive ability. Then from 2:00 p.m. to 6:00 p.m., we return to a vata time, when our minds can be very creative and full of ideas, but we can also run out of energy and crave a nap. Then from 6:00 p.m. to 10:00 p.m., we return to kapha, unwinding, relaxing, and slowing down. And from 10:00 p.m. to 2:00 a.m. we are back to a fiery pitta time: a period of transformation when most of our detoxification, rejuvenation, and deep (intense) sleep take place.

So how can we adjust our routine to better coincide with these daily dosha rhythms? Waking up a little before 6:00 a.m., in a vata time, will help us feel energized throughout the day, while sleeping deep into kapha time, past 7:00 a.m. or 8:00 a.m., may cause us to feel sluggish all day. Also, ideally we'll eat our biggest meal during pitta time in the middle of the day when we have maximum digestive capability. From 2:00 p.m. to 6:00 p.m., when vata dominates, is a great time for a short, regenerating nap (ten to twenty minutes) or energetic activity. It is best to start winding down when kapha returns from 6:00 p.m. to 10:00 p.m. Since our digestion is also slower in kapha time, we should have a lighter meal for digestive health and to avoid excessive weight gain. As we enter the second pitta time from 10:00 p.m. to 2:00 a.m., maximizing time in bed during this period maximizes the body's opportunity for detoxification, digestion, and rejuvenation. If we stay up into this pitta time, we may get a sudden burst of energy to do pitta things like organize our closet or raid the fridge. We might leverage pitta's productivity function but completely miss out on its rejuvenation function—throwing us way off balance the next day.

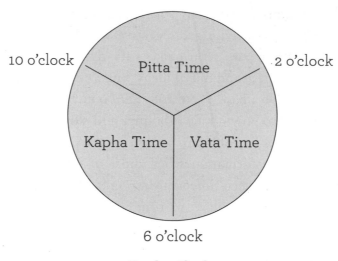

10 o'clock   2 o'clock

Pitta Time

Kapha Time   Vata Time

6 o'clock

Dosha Clock

When we can, it's helpful to also orient our workday and tasks around these daily cycles. The morning kapha time is a great time for tasks that require attention to detail, stamina, patience, and endurance. Follow your task list during these hours and you can accomplish a lot without tiring. This would also be a great time for a longer run if, for instance, you were training for a marathon. The middle of the day is a great time to tackle difficult critical-thinking tasks, challenging meetings, or negotiations. Vata time in the afternoon is a great time for creativity and innovation-oriented work, including interacting with others in meetings or creatively brainstorming ideas. This is also a good time to review task lists and come up with priorities for the next day—an excellent interplay of leveraging vata's creativity to map out the next day's endurance-oriented kapha period. Experiment with moving your schedule around and see what lines up best for you based on the nature of your work and your unique constitution.

Note how you're reacting to these structural suggestions—it might be a clue to your mental constitution. If you are a pitta, you might love the clarity and feel excited to adopt it in a disciplined way immediately, finding freedom in the structure of a logical schedule, but you'll have to be careful not to become overly attached and lose the ability to be flexible. A vata might see the doshic clock as a suggestion instead of a prescribed structure, preferring to flow through the day more freely, with awareness but not with a strict schedule—but they should be careful not to drift too far off. Vatas may also feel overwhelmed to make such a commitment of their time. If that feels like you, start with one or two adjustments at a time so you can see the benefits and develop new habits over time; don't be afraid to try just because you can't do it all right away. Kaphas may like the concept but feel deep down that they won't actually get around to trying it. Kaphas by nature do not like change of any sort, so they will have to leverage other dosha qualities in themselves to get a change going. Once in place, though, the kapha nature will maintain the structure over the long run. Regardless of how you approach experimenting with your daily routine, simply being aware of these cycles and tuning in to yourself throughout the day will help you figure out your best solution.

A template daily routine is outlined on the following pages. From this starting point, adjust to what is comfortable for you, based on your needs, your constitution, and your work and life demands. Don't worry about being too rigid, and do keep your routine straightforward. It is okay to wander from it here and there. The key is to observe balance the majority of the time, rather than being out of balance the majority of the time. Above all, keep it inspiring so that you feel happy with your life. Make sure that within your day you take time to focus, time to connect with others, time to exercise your body, time to be quiet, time to reflect, and time to breathe.

TEMPLATE FOR A BALANCED DAILY WORKDAY ROUTINE

Morning
- Wake up early (by 6:00 a.m. if possible, before sluggish kapha time).
- Drink some lukewarm water with lime to help clear the bowels and detoxify.
- Do a morning activity such as a walk, yoga, or meditation.
- Have a seated, quiet, and attentive breakfast (warm, cooked, and nourishing for vata; cooling and/or raw for pitta; light and dry for kapha).
- Head to work.
- Set your intentions and goals for the day.
- Begin your workday.
- Until 10:00 a.m. when kapha time ends, front-load tasks that require stamina, endurance, and attention to detail—heads-down work time.

Midday
- Handle any tough meetings or challenging projects just before and just after lunch (10:00 a.m. to 2:00 p.m., in pitta time).
- Take a solid, seated, and mindful break for lunch.
- Try to minimize eating at your desk while working, and stay off your phone. It is time to enjoy and recharge rather than try to squeeze in more work. Eat your heaviest meal of the day.
- Try for an after-lunch walk for ten to fifteen minutes to help with digestion and energy.

Afternoon
- Tackle creative projects, brainstorming, and meetings in the afternoon (2:00 p.m. to 6:00 p.m., in vata time).

- If you have an excess of vata, and your work environment is conducive, a ten-to-twenty-minute nap can be energizing between 2:00 and 4:00 p.m.

Evening
- Try to wind down your work between 5:00 and 7:00 p.m. and head home.
- After work is also a good time for exercise, yoga, meditation, and other self-care activities.
- Relax. Use this period of kapha time to catch up with friends, family, and social groups.
- Have a light, sit-down, mindful dinner between 6:00 and 8:00 p.m. (keep a two-to-three-hour gap before you go to bed for better digestion and sleep).

Nighttime
- Stop emails, texts, phone, TV, and other screens at least an hour before bedtime.
- Avoid alcohol within two hours of bedtime.
- Head to bed at a good hour and don't engage in stimulating conversation or intense reading material right before bed. Try to have the lights out by 10:30 or 11:00 p.m. (pitta rejuvenation and detoxification time begins at 10:00 p.m.).

If your daily routine is far off from this template, adjust gradually. Perhaps shift your sleeping and waking times by thirty minutes each week. Also notice any unhealthy cycles that have become an ingrained part of your life. Perhaps cut down or eliminate your drinks in the evening to relax (these disrupt your sleep so that you need more stimulants in the morning). How can you naturally wind down in the evening, and what might be a morning start that energizes you naturally? The goal is a healthy, balanced routine in tune with natural rhythms that better supports you in your life and work and also supports your yoga practice.

Balancing doshas is an active daily effort that should become part of your lifestyle. It requires self-awareness, awareness of your unique life and situation, and application of mindful balance considering those factors. Your mindfulness will prevent dosha imbalances from taking root as disease and, of course, interrupting your ability to do your work. Vata severally out of balance causes a range of disorders such as anxiety, insomnia, constipation, abnormal blood pressure, headaches, gas and bloating, joint pain, and food allergies. Pitta out of balance leads to inflammation, skin irritations, heartburn, circulatory issues, liver issues, ulcers, and heart issues. Kapha out of balance causes congestion, joint swelling, colds, sinus infections, edema, diabetes, and obesity. If you tend toward these dosha-related health conditions—whether mild or severe—and you see some wisdom in the common-sense approaches discussed in this book, consider visiting a reputable Ayurvedic physician to assess your unique situation and suggest a more tailored approach your daily healing. Often an Ayurvedic approach can be a powerful complement to a Western healing approach and can multiply the efficacy of a course of treatment.

SPOTLIGHT ON SLEEP

While an optimal lifestyle looks different for everyone and changes over time, the optimal sleep schedule is more uniform—and one of the most important tenets of Ayurvedic medicine and overall balance. In keeping with the solar circadian cycle, sleeping when the sun is down and waking when the sun rises supports our natural hormone production. If we stay awake many hours past sunset or surround ourselves with bright light after sunset, we inhibit melatonin production and confuse our bodies. Similarly, when we awaken with the sunrise, we produce serotonin more effectively, which naturally helps get us going for a happy day. The old "early to bed, early to rise" proverb is being proven: Sufficient and regular melatonin production is being seen as a preventive measure for cognitive decline in diseases such as Parkinson's and Alzheimer's. Inhibited serotonin production from lack of sunlight is related to depressive disorders such as seasonal affective disorder, or depression associated with winter's darker, shorter days. Chronodisruption, as it is being called—symptoms resulting from being out of sync with the natural sun's timing—has such a major effect on our physiology that it is being correlated with cancer, diabetes, migraines, and other diseases.[2] A leading Ayurveda expert and teacher of mine, Dr. Suhas Kshirsagar, believes so strongly in the correlation between chronobiology and health that he wrote a book titled *Change Your Schedule, Change Your Life,* in which he attributes major health improvements ranging from weight loss to better sleep just through adjusting one's daily lifestyle to be more in sync with nature.

In the corporate sector, however, good sleep is often deprioritized; people even seem to pride themselves on how little sleep they "need." One coworker of mine used to boast that he could get by on five hours of sleep—but he was a nervous wreck and was always falling asleep in important meetings. We have limited time and limited energy, and we must rejuvenate to get the most efficiency from our mind and body. Waking up tired should not be a regular occurrence; if it is, pay attention to your body and make adjustments.

A good night's sleep begins with a healthy and realistic attitude toward sleep: This requires us to tune in and honor the amount of sleep we truly need. The length of sleep needed does vary by person and constitution, but somewhere in the range of six to nine hours is ideal for most people. Vata imbalance requires the longer end of the range, while kapha requires the shorter, with pitta in the middle. Measuring whether you're getting enough is easy: Tune in to how energized you are during the day, and be prepared. The need for sleep can vary significantly depending on what is going on in your life. If you are able to stay awake through both meetings and meditations, you're probably getting the right amount. Observe, without sleep aids or excess coffee, how much sleep your body actually needs, and honor that. If you are constantly changing up your routine, sleeping at different times, or eating at sporadic times, it is as if you are putting your body through jet lag on a daily basis. This confuses your physiology and saps your energy. By establishing a good routine and sticking to it more often than not, you allow your body to balance and rejuvenate itself naturally and free up energy for more productive purposes.

More important than overall time asleep, though, is time spent in deep sleep cycles—when most bodily rejuvenation takes place—and our daytime choices affect this quality of sleep. From the moment you wake up, your choices—when and what you eat, when and how you exercise, and how you wind down—all determine how well you will sleep that night. You can help yourself get into a healthy, deep sleep cycle by waking up early, working productively and in a balanced way, exercising, eating healthily, winding down in the evening, eating light evening meals, not drinking alcohol within two hours of bedtime, and going to bed close to the beginning of pitta time (around 10:00 p.m.). And of course, getting off our phones and other screens early is key. Job and social demands compel us to look at screens right until the moment we try to sleep. It's often also the first thing we see when we wake up. All those electronic screens emit a blue light proven to inhibit melatonin, that hormone essential for sleep, particularly deep sleep and its corresponding rejuvenating effects.[3] Though some help can be derived from a blue light filter, there's another problem: Both the high-frequency oscillation of the screen's pixels and the information you're absorbing aggravate the active, light vata dosha, keeping us from winding down and creating a tendency toward excess vata issues such as insomnia and anxiety. Do your best to stay away from screens near bedtime, or the rest of your efforts will be diminished. Implementing these practices is easier said than done, but try experimenting with them and see if you wake up more refreshed and energized after following a healthy sleep routine for several days.

Modern business leaders are paying attention to the importance of sleep, now viewing it as a performance enhancer, not a sign of weakness. Arianna Huffington, one of the world's most successful businesspeople, had a reputation for being a workaholic. She finally drove herself to such extreme exhaustion that she collapsed at work. The event gave her a new purpose: to help Americans understand the importance of sleep. She wrote a book called *The Sleep Revolution,* explaining how sleep deprivation hurts us financially and emotionally, damages our mental and physical health, and holds back our success in business. Jeff Bezos, similarly, sees his nightly eight hours of sleep as a "responsibility to his shareholders."[4] Folks with immense responsibilities like Huffington and Bezos still find a way to manage their busy schedules to prioritize sleep since they correlate it with their ability to succeed. Whether you are relatively new in your career with a lot to prove, midcareer fighting for your next promotion, or a CEO unsure how you could possibly step back, a concerted effort at orienting your day toward a healthy sleep schedule will help you on your path to success. Challenge yourself to stop working earlier, get good rest, and come back fresh. See how much faster you can solve problems or create innovative solutions that regular busyness and tiredness hinder. This is what unlocks the "healthy, wealthy, and wise" part of the adage.

Waking up refreshed, easily eliminating toxins, feeling hungry at the right times, and finding better balance are just a few of the benefits of proper sleep as part of tuning in to the doshic times of day. Vishvketu says, "If your six to nine is inspiring, your nine to five will be good. If six to nine is rushing, fussing, and missing (buses, food, wake-up times), then your whole day will be a windstorm." To start the day well, the night has to go well, and for that to happen, the wind-down for the day has to be good, and so on. As with everything in Ayurveda, all factors work together to create balance. Tune in to your body and your mind and experiment with what works for you, and over time as you implement this knowledge, you will orient toward a routine that allows you to thrive.

CONNECTING AND DISCONNECTING

Even with our optimal lifestyle largely under control, our lives are unpredictable. We can't control the actions of others or events of the world. So how do we best set ourselves up to maintain balanced relationships and manage various sources of stress in our life?

Regular connection with friends and family, especially in relationships that fill you up, is a major factor in happiness. One can find connection in friendships, volunteerism, and community activities. If you find you are around people who are not healthy for you, find ways to minimize those interactions and counter them with positive interactions. Maintain a healthy balance in relationships with peers, family, and partners, and try to interact in as many positive ways as possible. Tune in to who recharges you and who drains you, and take active steps to surround yourself with more recharging than draining influences.

Balance can also be challenging in romantic relationships. If you're feeling unhappy in a relationship, there might be an imbalance you haven't been able to clearly identify. Using your new awareness of personality tendencies to identify the imbalance can help you nurture the relationship, ask for what you need, or leave a situation if need be. For instance, if you tend toward vata, you might need more nourishment in your relationships, while kaphas might need more activity and stimulation, and pitta tendencies might require more soothing and calming in a relationship. Sexual relations also play a role in maintaining balance. For example, excessive sexual activity can harm relationships when all the dimensions of the relationship are not being honored in a balanced way. Excessive sex also aggravates vata, while underactive sexuality in a relationship can lead to partners feeling disconnected and undernourished. Particularly in the workplace, pay extra attention to maintaining professional relationships and not mixing power, hierarchy, and status with sexual relationships; such relationships complicate your boundaries, setting up more barriers to your balance, mental health, and at times, job performance and career.

Finding balance in our need for connection becomes especially tricky in the context of social media. We've already discussed modern information overload as a sleep inhibitor, a distraction from what matters to us, and a barrier to self-awareness. The social media element is particularly fraught with barriers to holistic success. While it is a nice way to casually connect with far-flung friends and even advance your career, it cannot replace true human interaction or deep personal experience. Vishvketu always says, "Use social media, but don't let social media use you." If you are constantly checking for updates and likes and you are emotionally up and down based on what you see, or feeling envy and inadequacy, social media is starting to be in control. This is an imbalance that you'll need to address—and not just because it will cause a doshic imbalance: From a Vedic perspective, such attachment to validation and preoccupation with others' journeys will preclude you from having clarity in your own direction. Live life for your own happiness and pleasure, without need for validation of that from others. Savor your life experiences, but don't make the point of those experiences get reduced to just an input for social broadcast. Live authentically and in the present, and do things that truly make you happy, regardless of what others might think, and then post about it after the fact if it makes sense to do that. Remember, a balanced, spiritual life exists within society, so if social media is an integral part of living within society for you, then it is simply another area in which you must practice self-awareness and balance. Since this has become such a common imbalance, there are plenty of tools out there to handle this area of your life.

As you deepen your yoga practice and start regularly meditating, your ability to tune in to yourself and your needs will improve. It will open up new levels of strength and awareness in your dosha balance and lead you to healthier relationships. You will naturally sense when it is time to connect with others or disconnect from others and instead connect with yourself for rejuvenation. I enjoy social events and meeting new people, but during a party, I can sense when it is time for me to disengage and go home. Instead of extending myself too far with social interactions and then feeling energetically drained, I pay attention to what my needs are and honor them with discipline. As odd as it sounds to some of us, having a meal, watching a movie, taking a walk, or taking a trip alone opens you up to discovering you and your needs and actually improves your relationships. I start my day with a solo sunrise walk along the beach, which sets up me up for an inspired day as I interact with others. It gives me time to be with my thoughts, daydream, and rejuvenate, setting a foundation to meet my responsibilities to myself and others in balance. Experiment and determine the most effective way for you to manage your social and alone time with your unique lifestyle and constitution. The result should feel happy, intrinsically balanced, and, in a word, good.

MANAGING STRESS AND EMOTIONS

On a daily basis, tune in to the causes of stress in your life, try to understand why they are stressors, and take steps to mitigate or eliminate them. Sometimes it's unavoidable at work with the varied and complex personalities that we have to interact with, even if we're practicing our calling. Sometimes stress results from circumstances beyond our control, and we stress about trying to control it rather than letting go. Other times we set expectations for things to go a certain way and they don't, and we don't forgive ourselves for our human mistakes. The same situation can have very different reactions from person to person, and also within the same person in different frames of mind or under different doshic influences. Whatever the cause of stress, regardless of others' actions, you must take ownership of your feelings and try to understand your reactions. With an understanding of Ayurveda, you can see yourself and your reactions more clearly: Vata reactions involve more anxiety, pitta reactions present with anger, and kapha reactions show complacency (remember, we can all exhibit any dosha depending on the time and circumstance). No matter the time, the situation, the people or the mistake, you still can have influence over your own reaction. In the Vedic tradition, that power over your reaction begins with awareness.

Taking a pause and observing yourself, like a dispassionate third party looking into the movie of your life, can be a very powerful tool to start seeing things from a healthier perspective. One technique for cultivating this witnessing ability is to use every stressful situation as an opportunity to observe yourself. In a difficult situation, the moment you notice tension in yourself, stop for a brief moment, and take a deep, belly-filling breath. During this breath, be conscious of the outward and inward movement of your belly. After calming your physiology through this breath, observe the situation and your own reactions, just for a moment taking the role of observing yourself. At this moment, you are free to laugh at yourself, but if not, then just continue on as you would normally with your usual rage, anger, anxiety, sadness, or whatever it is you're feeling. Just by having recognized the very moment that you are falling out of balance, pausing, breathing, and observing, you are interrupting the cyclic pattern of stress and taking power back. The deep breath slows your reaction. Then, by observing the situation in a cool, dispassionate way, you begin to be able to interrupt your typical stress-response pattern. Even if you continue as usual, just hitting this pause button sets you up better for future stress moments. In time, your pauses will actually start to change the nature and course of your reactions and responses. Proceeding with more awareness, instead of unconsciously repeating the same cycles, serves to set deeper intentions in ourselves to shift our patterns of response to stressful events in life. To make any change, the first step is always awareness.

As you practice this technique, you may start to notice that it is actually the other person's drama and story that is pulling you in. They're upset about something, they take it out on you, and all of a sudden you are upset. Maybe their reaction, though directed toward you, had nothing to do with you, but you take it personally and so you get sucked into their drama. Recognize how their drama is becoming your drama and take stock of the situation to see what you need to be concerned with and what you can let go of. After these split moments pass (this whole technique can take a second or two), you may continue interacting as you normally would, but with more awareness each time. That awareness will give you more power and balance in future situations. You will be less reactive and more resilient, often effecting a much more positive outcome while carrying less stress around.

Sometimes our relationships can cause us a lot of pain and heartache, ranging from heated arguments with our spouse to struggles with our parents and children to challenges with colleagues and customers. In all cases, our reactions to these stressors are in our domain of control, yet we find ourselves losing control. Ayurveda looks at emotions in a very similar way to food. We can digest difficult experiences delivered in moderation and absorb nutrients from those experiences to become stronger. If there is an overload of toxic experiences coming at us, then our emotional digestive ability shuts down, and instead of being able to extract nutritive value, we end up holding on to toxic, undigested emotional matter. This toxic emotional residue can remain with us for years, lurking in our system, causing us unhappiness or emotional imbalance. Ayurveda offers deep treatments such as *panchakarma* to process deep-seated issues. However, there are simple regular tools that we can use for emotional processing and digestion—sort of like an antacid for emotions. We can talk it out with a friend we trust, or process it with a therapist or coach, or even just talk it out loud in a room by yourself. As a coach, I often see clients where a major performance blockage at work is related to some unprocessed experience from childhood, but that same experience, when appropriately processed, provides the strength to improve performance. One of the most effective low-cost techniques I have found is a "hot-pen" (or hot keyboard) method of writing things out. Revisit a difficult experience of your life, or of your day, and just write about it for several minutes, without letting the pen leave the paper. Try to also examine the nutritive and strengthening value of the experience you are writing about. When you are done, chuck the piece of paper, tear out the page of the journal, or delete the file. No further analysis necessary, just get it out of your head and physiology, offload it onto a piece of paper, and then chuck it, since it no·longer serves you! (Just like food, once you eat it, pull out the nutrients, and get rid of the rest!) A simple journaling practice, when coupled with meditation and yoga, can go a long way in keeping your emotional digestive system moving well.

Finally, look at your stress in the bigger picture of your life aims and purpose. Even when you are completely overwhelmed with responsibilities, by referring to your purpose, you should be able to clarify which responsibilities are highest priority and still deserve your stressed-out attention. Deprioritize the rest, and then experiment with other daily rebalancing techniques as you learn to tune in to your needs. One of my best anti-stress tools (second to meditation, yoga, and walking) is the conviction and power to say no. As much as I want to please everyone who depends on me, my ability to truly serve well can only be enhanced if I have the discipline and courage to say no to things that don't truly serve me.

RELAXING FOR BALANCE

We can safely say that we live in some of the busiest times ever known! Our grandparents probably thought the same thing. It seems no matter the time period, the idea of being overly busy is a theme in our Western world. In some cultures, higher value is still placed on relaxation. In Spain, an afternoon siesta is still the norm, even in business culture. North Americans, on the other hand, frown upon any kind of nap. In that type of culture, especially in fast-paced work environments, we have to pay special attention to relaxing intermittently rather than waiting until we can go no further.

I once had a stellar employee who was one of the hardest-working people in the company. Justin would often stay at work late and was always willing to go the extra mile to complete an assignment. He had one unique quirk, though: He insisted on a twenty-minute nap every afternoon. His being European and myself being a yogi in disguise, I thought nothing of this, and I was fine with him napping right at his desk. He even cut out a square of gray foam padding and emblazoned the words "nap pad" in black marker. But one day, someone from human resources wandered by and noticed my sleeping team member. The idea of relaxing seemed just preposterous! After getting over her shock, she wrote him up. Numerous meetings ensued to discuss this serious transgression, and Justin's perfect record was tarnished. Eventually, after escalating it up the chain of command and justifying Justin's exemplary performance, we finally got special dispensation for this "unusual behavior."

Research now proves Justin's theory that a midafternoon nap can be an excellent productivity boost, improving focus and efficiency, reducing stress, and cutting down on errors. Even as little as a six-minute nap has been shown to improve memory recall.[5]

It is still, however, antithetical to our culture to use relaxation as a tool for productivity. If we do indulge in something relaxing, it is only after we justify how hard we worked. And if we happen to be caught, we rush to prove our innocence! Even in Western yoga classes, the central relaxation element is often pushed aside. After all the "jumping and pumping," as Vishvketu describes the typical gymnastics-style class, the instructor often doesn't prioritize the final relaxation that is an essential part of yoga practice. A yoga teacher friend once proudly told me the style of yoga she teaches doesn't need the relaxation part. But after she took a class from me, and I took her through a true relaxation, it became her favorite part.

Building regular activities into your life that relax and rejuvenate you will help center you on your journey. Shoot for ten to twenty minutes of real relaxation per day. You might add simple techniques into your office routine such as the breathing exercises we'll discuss in Chapter 8. You might go for a stroll in a park during lunch or schedule a regular massage appointment or spa treatment. Consider scheduling time after a meeting to mentally unpack and release issues that came up—away from your computer, just with your thoughts and without agenda. I found that after an especially challenging meeting, a ten-minute walk around the building worked wonders to release a little of the pressure and allow myself to refocus and be re-inspired. For my colleague Justin, his built-in relaxation was a regular afternoon nap. Simple, regular rest sometimes has to be engineered into our lifestyle. If you feel self-indulgent, you're doing it *right*. And you'll be on the path to improved self-awareness, balance, and fulfillment. After all, all of these tools for balance come back to one thing: your ability to better tune in to yourself.

NOTES

1. "World's Highest Tides," bayoffundytourism.com, http://
    bayoffundytourism.com/worlds-highest-tides/; "The Water in You,"
    United States Geological Survey, https://water.usgs.gov/edu/propertyyou.
    html.
2. Maria Angeles Bonmati-Carrion, et al., "Protecting the Melatonin Rhythm
    Through Circadian Healthy Light Exposure," *International Journal of
    Molecular Sciences*, Dec. 2014, 15(12), 23448–23500, https://www.ncbi
    .nlm.nih.gov/pmc/articles/PMC4284776/.
3. "Blue Light Has a Dark Side," *Harvard Health Letter*, May 2012, updated
    Aug. 13, 2018, https://www.health.harvard.edu/staying-healthy/blue-light
    -has-a-dark-side.
4. Arianna Huffington, "10 Years Ago I Collapsed from Burnout and
    Exhaustion, and It's the Best Thing That Could Have Happened to Me,"
    Thrive Global, Apr. 6, 2017, https://medium.com/thrive-global/10-years-
    ago-i-collapsed-from-burnout-and-exhaustion-and-its-the-best-thing-that
    -could-have-b1409f16585d.
5. Kenny Kline, "Why Power Napping Can Improve Your Productivity—
    and 4 Ways to Do It Right," *Inc.*, https://www.inc.com/kenny-kline/why
    -power-napping-can-improve-your-productivity-and-4-ways-to-do
    -it-right.html; George Dvorsky, "The Science Behind Power Naps, and
    Why They're So Damn Good for You," *io9*, Sept. 26, 2013, https://io9.
    gizmodo.com/the-science-behind-power-naps-and-why-theyre-so
    -damne-1401366016.

SELF-REFLECTION QUESTIONS

1. Based on your dosha, what regular habits and lifestyle choices of yours aggravate your dosha?

2. What are the major causes of stress in your life, why do they cause you stress, and how can you better handle it?

3. How could you improve your sleep quality?

4. What changes will you make to your daily routine? What will be your regular relaxation activity?

5. What will be your regular emotional processing practice?

6. What will you start saying no to in life?

CHAPTER SEVEN

Eating for Balance

"You are what you eat." This often-used but rarely digested phrase sums up the Vedic view on food. As you have seen from the preceding chapters, we are developing an overall foundation for fulfillment and success through an understanding of Vedic philosophy, healthy lifestyle guidelines, an understanding of ourselves, and sound perspective on our journey through life. All of these life lessons, from knowing your purpose to understanding your unique constitution to living in harmony with natural rhythms, are all integrated to help extract the most benefit from the yoga and meditation practice that will hopefully become a part of your regular life. One of the most important factors in developing this solid foundation for living is expressed in that opening proverb: All the food you put in your body, several times a day and hundreds of times a year, contributes to your overall health and well-being—including sustained career success. Athletes know well the intrinsic connection between their food and their performance, but in business, often we don't realize that our performance can also be influenced by our food choices. By eating in context of Ayurvedic dosha constitutions, you can

145

better feed yourself toward higher performance. Changes in my diet influence my work performance, my efficiency, my moods, and the quality of interactions with my colleagues.

In Western society, we're quite attached to body image and weight loss, and everyone has a different approach that they swear by. Various diet approaches have worked for our peers, others are endorsed by celebrities, while others are medically necessary for certain individuals. Ayurveda offers quite a different view on diet. Perhaps most importantly, diet must be understood as an integral complement to all the other areas of the Vedic tradition presented in this book—another tool to help improve our work and life performance. We'll practice using food as a healthy and measured balancing mechanism rather than a coping mechanism or a side thought. As with everything in the Vedic knowledge system, tune in to yourself and do what works for you based on your health, constitution, and lifestyle needs. We are working to build awareness around your eating habits and identify diet approaches that don't serve *you* well. Bearing in mind your unique dosha along with your work and lifestyle, you'll assess how your food choices might be supporting or aggravating your nature and how you can adjust your diet to support better balance.

The Vedic tradition teaches that the food that you put into your body becomes a part of your consciousness, and at a cellular level that food becomes awake in your body. When you eat something, it goes into your gastric system, and during the digestion and assimilation process, the nutrients are absorbed into your physiology. As the nutrients combine with the enzymes and produce chemical reactions in your body, life is sustained and energy is created. The food is the building block of who you are, and some part of it becomes a part of your machinery. Vishvketu explains that if you give a machine high-quality parts, it will run well and require less maintenance. If you give a machine low-quality parts, things will break down, making the machinery expensive to maintain. Except, with our bodies, you can't replace a gear with a higher-quality one when the first one fails. If you continually ingest low-quality food, over time, the buildup becomes harder and harder to fix. The fix is not a simple gear replacement but rather a complicated system-level issue. Conversely, when you put quality food into your body, though it may cost more up front, you avert expensive, system-level breakdowns in the future. Modern science agrees: Research has proven that poor diet and disease are correlated, and dietary changes can slow or even reverse the progression of major disease.[1]

Similar to Western nutritional thinking, Ayurveda eschews highly processed foods and recommends fresh, whole foods for all types of people. Where Ayurveda breaks from Western nutrition, however, is in its argument that the same foods will have different effects on different constitutions and in different situations. Each of us must observe our own body, mind, and current life situation and make appropriate food choices based on that insight. Ayurveda also recognizes that the same food will have a different effect at different times of day, different times of year, and different times in your life. A heavy meal in the middle of the day (when pitta dominates) is digested very differently than the same food late in the evening at kapha time, when digestion can be more sluggish. A slice of watermelon in the height of summer affects our physiology differently than it would in winter. And foods that agreed or disagreed with you when you were young may affect you differently as you move from a kapha-dominant life stage to a vata-dominant life stage.

The Western approach also tends to seek definitive answers on the "best" foods; articles and advertisements often say cut food A out completely and replace it with food B. Ayurveda takes a gentler approach, suggesting you balance and adjust without shocking your system by increasing foods that are balancing for your dosha and situation while reducing foods that aggravate it. Drastic methods may be needed to counter full-blown disease, but in normal health, we are just aiming for balance. And of course, depending on what is going on in your life, what time of day it is, or what season it is, the foods that promote balance will vary. If that sounds complicated and overwhelming, just remember, you're not trying to orchestrate all the parts; you're using knowledge and practice to better tune in to the needs of your body and mind and making small adjustments. For example, a heavy travel period in your work schedule, with lots of movement and time in airplanes, will increase vata; with practice, you will feel innately that you need grounding foods, massages, and gentler exercise activity in such a period.

In my studies of yoga and Ayurveda, I have realized that these traditions are absolutely obsessed with food and digestion. It even spills into Indian culture. For instance, in my family, the first question out my dad's mouth in the morning was often about how your bowel movement was. He would even talk about various dishes served at dinner and estimate their bowel-movement smoothing potential. To Western society, this might sound like "inappropriate" dinner-table conversation. But this awareness of digestion has powerful implications for health.

HAPPY, GRUMPY, AND JUNKY

As Vishvketu explains, "Yoga begins in the kitchen," where we prepare our fuel. He divides food into three general categories: happy food, grumpy food, and junk food. Happy food helps support your being in harmony with your environment, and we should primarily eat food from this category. It is typically plant based, locally grown, and in season, including foods that are easy to buy, easy to prepare, easy to eat, easy to digest, and, of course, as my dad prioritized, easy to eliminate. It includes a healthy amount of vegetables, fruits, nuts, and seeds. These shouldn't be cooked so long that most of the nutrients are gone, and it's better if the produce is in season. Pay attention to where your food comes from and how it is produced. The farther the food is from its source, in terms of distance, processing, and time from being extracted from the earth, the less harmonized it is with nature. Happy foods are also processed quickly and efficiently by our digestive system without sapping our energy. Meat tends to take a very long time for the body to digest and process, and much of it today is heavily altered with chemicals and growth enhancers and hence is typically not a happy food. Also, meat is often produced in an unhappy way. From a pure yogic point of view, any creature that is killed is automatically an unhappy food, but for practicality, if a plant-based diet isn't viable for you, you can temper this approach by favoring meats that led happier lives. Also be aware of the portion of meat you consume as it uses more energy to digest than typical happy foods. Assess in your own mind whether it fits into the happy category or not, and try to ensure that the majority of your diet comes from the happy group.

Grumpy food makes our body grumpy (even if we feel happy when we ingest it). These are foods that take a long time to digest or require the body to create a lot of acid. Meat typically falls in this category, as do foods eaten at suboptimal times of day such as raw cabbage eaten at night during slow-digestion kapha time, creating a lot of bloating and gas (grumpiness). Also, if the method of food production is careless and heartless—for instance, factory farming of fruits, nuts, vegetables, and animals—and the production involves suffering and harm, it is grumpy food. Typically, food in this category increases pitta and fuels angry tempers, skin diseases, inflammation, and liver disorders. As I learned the hard way, grumpy food contributes to stress, irritation with colleagues, and impatience.

Junk food is generally overprocessed or unnaturally preserved. Most processed foods are laden with chemicals and severely altered from their natural state. This type of food is prevalent in our modern convenience-oriented society. In pursuit of longer shelf lives and easy preparation, scientists and engineers have found ingenious ways to defy nature with food products that last months and years beyond their natural versions. Lab-developed foods, processed "cheese products" or "meat products," or foods with an uncannily long shelf life fall into this category. Look for additives on labels; you should recognize every word as a natural ingredient. Radiation-based heating devices (that means our beloved microwaves) turn even previously happy food into junk. Because it is so heavily altered, junk food is hard for our digestive system to read and understand. Our metabolic systems get confused and are unable to extract nutrients or properly eliminate the excessive toxins. Because the body does not recognize how to process this food and doesn't feel satiated, we end up consuming excess amounts. And usually because we are eating junk food quickly, out of convenience, we are less mindful in our consumption, further confusing our body. Junk food leaves behind toxins that our body takes a long time to eliminate, and over time, complicated health problems and obesity tend to develop.

When I studied Ayurveda at the Chopra Center in Carlsbad, California, I learned Deepak Chopra's acronym for food to avoid: FLUNC. (I thought this was brilliant since you're *flunking* your diet.) It stands for frozen, leftover, unnatural, nuked, and canned food. In the Vedic tradition, food is said to carry *prana*, or "life force," within it, and the closer the food is to its source form, the more prana it contains. Therefore, when food is frozen, eaten a day or two after it's prepared, heavily processed, microwaved, or canned, the food contains less of its vitality and nutritional value. The more whole the food, the more natural the food, the more vital energy it contains. Try to reduce FLUNC types of foods, and never let them become a majority of your diet—and Western science agrees, correlating such a diet with higher incidences of diabetes, obesity, cancer, and damage to our gut bacteria and the corresponding suppression of our immune sytem.[2]

We all deviate from time to time, even when we know the basics of what's healthy and what's not. Given that kama—pleasure— is part of life's purpose, the enjoyment of food and sharing it with others is an integral part of happiness. Attachment to perfection in diet is not helpful on our journey. Severe restriction creates its own sense of stress and dissatisfaction; that is not the goal of proper diet in the Vedic tradition. Some people eliminate carbs, others cut fat, and then there are the pescatarians, the Paleos, the vegans, and the vegetarians. Those can all work in the context of the Vedic tradition, as long as you are eating mostly happy foods and eating in context of your dosha and life situation. For example, if vata is out of balance, dairy products can be an easy source of nourishment. If you are vegan, however, you might have to balance it with nourishing, non-dairy foods such as heavier grains and cooked foods and supplement it with non-diet-related changes such as more frequent oil massages. Pittas who go Paleo will either have to temper their red meat intake due to its fire-aggravating nature or find cooling activities to balance it. I like the concept of a "flexitarian" diet, where you eat what is right for you for the most part but moderately indulge every now and then as part of life's enjoyment. Ayurveda, when used for maintaining good health (as opposed to targeted disease treatment), is about balance and adjustment rather than rigid rules that create unnecessary worry.

DIGESTION

The next step is to maintain our digestive system so that we can efficiently process our food. Digestion in Ayurveda centers around the concept of fire, or *agni* in Sanskrit. Agni is the digestive fire, and as you know, pitta constitutions and time periods possess this powerful digestive property. When this digestive fire is burning brightly, it has the capacity to properly digest and metabolize food in the most complete way. The positive nutrients are extracted, increasing our vitality and health, while the negative waste matter is expelled. But when the agni fire is burning poorly and our digestion is weak, or when we eat too much grumpy or junk food (like throwing wet logs on a campfire), we are unable to fully extract the nutrients or fully eliminate the waste. This waste accumulates over time and these toxins in our system end up leaving us feeling lethargic by dampening our agni, leading to poor nutrient absorption from our food. At this point a fast or cleanse is a useful tool to flush out the toxins and reinstate that agni. We'll cover this in more detail later in the chapter. Ayurveda places primary importance on keeping that agni burning bright, and to maintain it, we should avoid Vishvketu's grumpy and junk foods and the Chopra FLUNC foods.

Even within "happy" foods, there are different foods that help balance different constitutions and avoid straining your unique digestive system. Observe dietary balance in the context of your dosha makeup, and you'll avoid the accumulation of toxicity in your system that dampens your energy and eventually produces a health disorder. The common-sense wisdom around foods for different constitutions is quite simple. When vata is high, reduce dry, airy foods, and increase grounding, nourishing foods. When pitta is high, reduce hot, spicy foods, and increase cooling foods. When kapha is high, reduce rich, heavy foods, and increase lighter or spicy foods. Observe which dosha is predominant in you, both from your natural constitution and from what aggravators are taking place in your life, and adjust your food intake accordingly to pacify that dosha.

Let's explore each dosha's counteracting foods in more depth. When vata is out of balance or threatening to be, avoid dry foods such as dry cereals, popcorn, or crackers. Also, since vata is already quite a stimulated dosha, caffeine, alcohol, and spicy foods are aggravating. Counter the wind element with grounding, heavy, nourishing foods that are warm in temperature. Creamy foods, oily foods, and heavier whole grains such as rice, wheat, and oats are all good (though leavened bread can be a bit aggravating because of the air in it). Also very grounding are heavier, moist vegetables, such as squash, zucchini, root vegetables (such as potatoes, beets, and turnips), and cooked leafy greens. If you do eat a cold salad, counter it with oily or creamy dressings. I love popcorn, but when I find myself on track to vata imbalance (with public speaking, travel, and an overloaded schedule), I put olive oil or butter on it to make it more of a grounding food. Nuts, seeds, and legumes are good vata-balancing foods, though they can produce gas and bloating unless soaked prior to cooking. Heavier fruits such as bananas, oranges, and mangoes are grounding, as are warming spices such as cumin, cardamom, ginger, and cinnamon. Ginger specifically helps detoxify the body and solve digestive issues and can also be consumed as a tea. Vatas can usually eat meat with fewer adverse effects than the other doshas. Sesame oil is warming and good for vata cooking. It can also be used for massage, as can almond oil, as a way to nourish vata. To pacify vata, it is important to stick to routine, eating on a regular schedule rather than erratically. Alcohol tends to be hard on vata dosha, with its drying and evaporative qualities. Beer and other carbonated drinks also contribute to this airy element. Red wine in moderation is probably the best choice for vata with its warming quality.

Pitta out of balance is pacified with foods and drinks that are cooling by nature—not just cold from being in the fridge but cooling in properties and quality. Lettuce, spinach, kale, collard greens, artichokes, and asparagus, as well as raw foods such as salads, are very good for pitta. Grains in general, such as rice and pasta, are cooling to pitta. Milk and dairy are also cooling; yogurt can have a nice cooling effect, though its sourness needs to be cut with some sweetener, since sour tastes tend to aggravate pitta. Acidic tomatoes can be aggravating, which is a tough one for me: I enjoy a bowl of pasta and tomato sauce accompanied by a glass of red wine, and though the pasta is cooling, the tomato sauce and red wine are heating. Adding cooling cheese helps; softer and less salted cheeses are best for pitta. Salt in general should be reduced for pitta since it aggravates the fire element (the Western-medicine correlation is that salt increases blood pressure). Cooling fruits and vegetables such as cucumbers, dill, mint, watermelon, potatoes, zucchini, broccoli, and sweet potato are great. Coconut water is especially refreshing. Oils and fats should be taken in moderation, as pitta nature has enough oiliness to it. Spicy foods should be avoided since they fan the fire, as do red meats. Beer is fine in moderation, as is white wine, but hard alcohol (especially darker alcohols) and red wine generally fuel the fire of pitta. Spices that are considered anti-inflammatory include coriander, fennel, cinnamon, cilantro, and turmeric. Peppermint or fennel tea, even consumed warm, is a nice cooling drink for pitta physiology. For cooking and massage, cooling oils such as coconut, olive, or sunflower oil work well. Eating cooling foods in the pitta-dominated lunchtime is especially beneficial for balancing the pitta dosha.

Light and stimulating foods help balance kapha. Spicy food works very well, as do dried fruits and lots of vegetables, especially leafy greens. Heavier or oily foods are not beneficial to kapha, so avoid heavy grains, fried foods, nuts, milk, and dairy during kapha imbalance. Quinoa is an excellent light grain for kapha, as is couscous. Pungent, stimulating vegetables such as onions and peppers are great for kapha (but not fried). Dry foods such as cereals and crackers are good for kaphas, and kaphas can enjoy dry popcorn all they want. Stimulants like coffee and tea can be positives for kaphas, and kaphas can also handle alcohol in balance better than the other constitutions. For meats, white meat and seafood are preferable. Fiery spices such as cayenne, black pepper, and chili peppers are good, as are cardamom, cloves, and ginger. Lighter oils such as olive oil or sunflower oil work well for cooking, but for massage, kapha types or others experiencing kapha imbalance are better off with a dry, oil-free massage of a more vigorous nature.

Foods to Balance Doshas

Vata (Airy)	Pitta (Fiery)	Kapha (Earthy)
Nourishing foods	Cooling foods	Stimulating foods
Cooked vegetables	Raw vegetables, salads	Raw fruits, vegetables, and salads
Root vegetables such as potatoes, turnips, beets, sweet potatoes	Lettuce, spinach, kale, collards, potatoes, zucchini, broccoli	Any vegetables and leafy greens
Leafy greens	Artichokes, asparagus	Onions and peppers
Moist vegetables such as squash, zucchini	Cooling fruits such as cucumbers and watermelon	Dried fruits
Heavier fruits such as bananas, oranges	Sweet noncitrus fruits such as apples, pears, plums	Reduce sweet, sugary foods
Milk and dairy	Milk and dairy (add sweetener to yogurt), soft cheeses	Reduce dairy products

Foods to Balance Doshas, continued

Vata (Airy)	Pitta (Fiery)	Kapha (Earthy)
Heavier whole grains	White rice and pasta	Light grains such as quinoa, buckwheat
Rice, cooked oats, wheat	Barley, oats, wheat	Dry foods such as cereals, crackers, popcorn
Oily and buttery foods	Reduce red meats	Spicy foods
Cumin, cardamom, ginger, cinnamon	Coriander, fennel, cinnamon, cilantro, turmeric, mint	Cayenne pepper, black pepper, cardamom, cloves, ginger
Reduce dry foods, caffeine, and spicy foods	Reduce salty, spicy, oily, and acidic foods	Reduce rich, oily, heavy, and fried foods

Everyone's digestion system is different and varies over time depending on the dosha or doshas at play. Adjust and balance your diet according to your natural constitution, your current lifestyle, the time of year, the season, and your age. Practice tuning in to your body and mind and learn to assess your needs and feed yourself accordingly. You can refer back to the questionnaire in Chapter 5 to see which dosha-affecting factors are presenting in your life. If you notice several factors within a particular dosha, you can address that imbalance by adjusting your diet. If diet change is challenging, you can counter with lifestyle changes or other means from Chapter 6. Remember the bucket analogy: When the bucket is overfilling with one dosha, you can drain the excess through diet, lifestyle, work style, daily routine, or other habits. With Ayurveda, you are working gently toward balance, so don't beat yourself up if you end up eating the wrong foods once in a while. Make good choices at each meal that are right for your body, but if you indulge now and then, don't fret. Be flexible to your circumstances and adjust as you need depending on all the variables going on in your physiology, psychology, and environment.

Diet and daily routine combined in a thoughtful way can lead to major changes in your health and work performance. No single fix will change your life. But diet, exercise, and overall lifestyle can harmonize to create a powerful transformation that is greater than the sum of the parts. In conjunction with yoga, meditation, and the ensuing self-awareness, Ayurveda helps us better tune in to our body so we can innately know what is good and what is bad for it and start to make the right choices on a daily basis on an overall trend toward healthy living. Though each change may seem minor, it creates a domino effect in which pressure is relieved in one area of life, making room for the mental clarity to better handle other challenges. Each way you care for yourself frees up bandwidth and makes room for a significant restructuring and improvement of your career and life.

My client Jody, a financial advisor, had just taken over a new leadership role as a partner in her firm. She tended toward vata, being very bubbly, cheery, talkative, and creative. The job change had aggravated vata, on top of her long commute. After an erratic night's sleep and consistent insomnia, she would wake up around 3:30 a.m. (vata time) to go for a brisk run (vata-increasing). In addition, each morning she regularly drank about five cups of black coffee, a stimulant to a naturally stimulated constitution. Her diet was also vata aggravating—her mealtimes were erratic, and she tended to mostly eat raw vegetables and salads, knowing that they are nutritious. She was experiencing heightened anxiety and showing up to business meetings with that anxiety, preventing her from consistently closing deals and meeting her aggressive growth targets.

We worked on a vata-pacifying lifestyle for a few weeks. Jody began eating more cooked vegetables at regular mealtimes, with minimal snacking of dry foods in between. She reduced her raw food intake and added nourishing grains and pastas to her diet to help ground her system. When she did eat a salad, she would include a little extra oil and avocado to help it better pacify vata. She also delayed her morning wake-up time to be closer to the kapha 6:00 a.m. time and reduced her coffee intake to two to three cups a day, but with a healthy dollop of milk and natural sweetener to add a nourishing, soothing quality. She slowed the pace of the run to a jog and began meditating for fifteen minutes a day. Within two weeks, the change was unmistakable. In coaching sessions, I saw a much more measured pace of speaking and thinking. She was sleeping better, and the insomnia was gone. With clients, she was presenting more confidence and much less anxiety. She started consistently winning business and also not dwelling on business she lost. And as a wonderful health benefit, her doctor was able to take her off her blood pressure medication.

The foundational lifestyle changes set Jody up for success in business—and in health, improving her ability to have a long, fruitful career. To this day, she has maintained increased sensitivity to her constitution and awareness of her lifestyle choices, giving her the health and performance foundation to continue to succeed in her role as a partner at her firm.

Food is a source of pleasure as well as nutrition (remember kama from Chapter 3), but using food (or alcohol or drugs, of course) as a comforting mechanism can easily throw us out of balance. It is important to build awareness of what is out of balance and tackle those things directly rather than relying on food or substances to temporarily mask things. When we embark on the journey toward a healthy and balanced existence, incorporating the tools of yoga and meditation into our lives, many of our socio-emotional needs feel more fulfilled, and the addictive needs wane as the Vedic practices nourish us on a deeper level.

Finally, when it comes to eating, it is important to slow down and be mindful of this activity. Eat at regular mealtimes and in quantities to coincide with the natural dosha cycles of the day. When you do eat, try to not distract your attention with other activities such as reading, working, smartphone snacking, or TV watching. As our parents taught us, take small bites and chew your food thoroughly. This helps signal your digestive system to activate so it can better process the food coming at it. A moment of silence or a prayer prior to eating is also beneficial to signal your physiology ahead of receiving your sacred fuel. Savor the textures, flavors, and experience of a nourishing, rejuvenating mealtime. After your meal, see if you can sit quietly for a few minutes or take a leisurely stroll to help with the digestion and assimilation process. Observing this simple awareness at mealtime will automatically improve your body fueling process.

FASTING

In yoga, periodic fasting is used to occasionally cleanse the system, giving the digestive system a rest and boosting the agni digestive fire. Over time, especially when we eat heavy doses of grumpy and junky food without doshic awareness, our systems end up overloaded with residual toxins. If you feel achy when you wake up, tired during the day, or mentally foggy, and you find yourself eating emotionally rather than out of hunger, a fast can be a wonderful reboot. It is also starting to show up in modern medical research studies as a way to reduce inflammation, encourage cellular regeneration, and slow the aging process. Though the research is still early, yogis have long used intermittent fasting as a way to let the body and digestive system rest, rejuvenate, and detoxify.[3]

There are many trendy cleanses and fasts these days, but they rarely consider doshic constitutions. For instance, kaphas are fine to fast since their constitutions can handle going without food for long periods, but fasting can adversely affect vata types. A healthy fast also must care for our intestinal microbiome—the good bacteria essential for digestive health. Many juice fasts disturb sugar levels and also flush out healthy bacteria that we need. As always, use common sense and pay attention to your body and its needs. If you start to feel dizzy or light-headed, you may consider breaking your fast. The following are a few ideas for quarterly fasting that work for all constitutions. For anything beyond Level IV, or if you have any hesitations, questions, or other health issues at play, it is important to seek the guidance of a qualified professional. Also be aware that if you are at a time of extreme stress or work overload, a Level III or IV fast may not be appropriate.

OCCASIONAL FASTING SUGGESTIONS

Level I: Fasting Between Meals and Plant-Slant

Fast between meals for three to five days—eat breakfast, lunch, and dinner, and nothing in between meals except water and tea. This kind of simple fast can help with your willpower and have a good cleansing effect (and some weight loss, if this is very different from your normal routine). Stick to happy foods, especially fresh foods that are easy to digest and heavily plant-based. You can even try a vegetarian or vegan diet during this type of fast and observe the effects on your body.

Level II: One or Two Meals for the Day

For one day, skip lunch: Have breakfast and absolutely no snacks until dinner. Make both meals happy and plant based. Alternately, have a late brunch as the only meal, with no dinner. This fast can help prepare you for the more intense fasts that follow. Skipping meals on a regular basis is not healthy, but once in a while it is helpful for digestive rest.

Level III: Fruit Fast

Only consume fruits and water for twenty-four hours. You can do this with multiple fruits or just stick to one single fruit. The fruit allows your body to feel somewhat satiated, while still cleansing and healing itself. You can time your fruit intake with your regular mealtimes or try fasting by only eating a single serving of fruit when you feel extreme hunger. All doshas should be able to manage a fruit fast. If you are pitta, do not only rely on citrus fruits for this fast, as the acidity may be too high for you.

Level IV: Total Fast

Consume only water for twenty-four hours. (Vata constitutions should take caution with a total fast and have some fruit if they feel light-headed during this type of fasting.) This can promote mental clarity; you will find that you have very deep meditations during a total fast. Avoid strenuous physical activity. This type of total fast has the most powerful detoxifying effect and is a marvelous reboot for the digestive system. If you are able to handle twenty-four hours, then the next stage is to fast for thirty-six hours. For a fast of this length, you would have your dinner, fast the full next day, go to bed, and then break the fast on the morning of the second day.

Level V: Advanced Cleanses

More serious fasts or cleanses, such as a yogic water cleanse or a castor oil purge, are beyond the scope of this book. They are very effective and can cure major dosha imbalances. You should gather more information and consult experts before introducing these techniques into your life.

With food as with life in general, try to put on your plate only what you can digest. In the Western world, we make food very complicated, but it is very simple. It just requires common sense and tuning in to your body's needs. Eat consciously, be flexible, and follow the diet that works for you. You have enough understanding of your body and what it needs without having to look outside for much more information. Rather than consuming volumes of contradicting information on what and how to eat, just tune in to your innate understanding of what is right for you. Indulge a little here and there, but for the most part look at food as the foundation for you to live happily and work well. And know that your awareness and choices will only improve with your yoga practice and overall balanced living

NOTES

1. "Diet, Nutrition and the Prevention of Chronic Diseases," Report of the Joint WHO/FAO Expert Consultation, WHO Technical Report Series, No. 916, https://www.who.int/dietphysicalactivity/publications/trs916 /summary/en/.
2. Thibault Fiolet, et al., "Consumption of Ultra-Processed Foods and Cancer Risk: Results from NutriNet-Santé Prospective Cohort," *thebmj*, Feb. 14, 2018, doi: https://doi.org/10.1136/bmj.k322; Lindo Thrasybule, "Why the Western Diet Keeps Making Us Sick," *Everyday Health*, Jan. 17, 2018, https://www.everydayhealth.com/crohns-disease/diet/why -western-diet-making-us-sick/.
3. Kris Gunnars, "10 Evidence-Based Health Benefits of Intermittent Fasting," *healthline*, Aug. 16, 2016, https://www.healthline.com/nutrition/10-health -benefits-of-intermittent-fasting#section4.

SELF-REFLECTION QUESTIONS

1. What are some grumpy and junk foods that you regularly indulge in that you could reduce to a more moderate level?

2. Think through the nature of your work and lifestyle. Based on this reflection, which dosha do you think is most affected on a continual basis in your life, and how can you rebalance it using your diet?

3. What is the timing and atmosphere of your mealtimes, and how could you improve your timing and awareness during meals?

CHAPTER EIGHT

Take a Breath

Breath is the primary source of our energy and life. It is our constant companion, silently and constantly taking in oxygen and expelling carbon dioxide, without a conscious thought needed. In addition to keeping us alive, our breath also links to our emotions and mental state. For example, in tense moments, our breath automatically quickens. Conversely, by managing our breath, we can manage our emotions and feelings. We can use it to energize, rejuvenate, or calm ourselves. As Vishvketu often says, you can take as much breath as you want, and it is tax free. Central as breath is to our existence, it is also central to yoga—for balance and awareness, and also as the first challenge in letting go.

Breathing techniques in yoga are called *pranayama*, *prana* meaning "life-force energy" and *ayama* meaning "extension of." Pranayama, in essence, is therefore the extension of life-force energy, or a way of efficiently extracting more life-force energy. Yoga sees life-force energy, or prana, as the central vitality of our existence—the thing that animates our very existence and without which we would cease to exist. It is recharged through four distinct sources, the core source being breath. The others are food, connection with our higher self, and the environment around us, including people and places that rejuvenate us. Conversely, poor-quality food, lack of connection to our higher self (including failing to honor our gifts and talents regularly), dangerous situations, and negative environments and people can drain us of this life-force energy. Pranayama's specific breathing exercises and techniques are yoga's method of helping us harness more life-force energy and helping it flow through us more freely.

Prana is what keeps us healthy, vibrant, and creative. When it is depleted, we feel tired, lethargic, uncreative, and sometimes ill. Our modern world wears heavily on prana with factors like multitasking, lack of rest, overexertion, chronic stress, forced interaction with people who drain us, imbalanced work environments, and toxicity through diet, air, or water. Pranayama is meant to quickly and efficiently counter that daily depletion of prana, accelerating cleansing, nourishment, and rejuvenation.

Yoga's breath work techniques are designed to help our body better access, absorb, and process prana so that we can cultivate and reap more of our built-in energy. Through pranayama, we can better use oxygen to restore our energy and help us think clearly and positively. Depending on the exercise, we can fully oxygenate our entire physiology quickly, calm our emotional state, or recharge our spirit. Our body is the instrument that carries out our work, so by improving the body's prana-processing abilities, we make the instrument healthier and more efficient, and we are able to carry out our work better.

In addition to oxygenating the system, pranayama opens up circulation channels, eliminates toxins, accesses the full extent of our lung capacity (often not used), and helps make our rib cage more flexible. Even when we run, we don't always fully expand the lungs, but through pranayama techniques we can exercise the lungs more fully and improve their capacity. Vishvketu tasked a group of trainees with teaching someone in their family the most fundamental pranayama technique: full yogic breathing. A trainee named Margaret came back sullen, saying her husband, Chris—an Olympic-level skier—had rejected the approach. He said he's been an athlete his whole life, he knows the best breathing techniques, and he doesn't see the point of this one (remember, pranayama is a first step in letting go). Margaret asked Vishvketu to use his expertise to appeal to Chris. Vishvketu then trained a slightly better-behaved Chris on the technique and asked him to try it for a week. When Chris checked back in, he reported that his performance times on the hills had improved by *20 percent*. As Vishvketu explains, once you learn how to make proper space in your body for breath by taking advantage of your full lung capacity, you are able to expel a larger amount of carbon dioxide, freeing up your muscular system to perform at a better level.

Our lungs are also connected to our brain activity. We regularly experience our breath affecting our emotions and thinking; think about the instinct to take a deep breath when you need to calm down. Our breath and emotions are intrinsically linked: Our breath reflects our emotions, and conversely, we can use our breath for emotional modulation and detoxification. By improving our ability to subconsciously connect to our breath in times of difficulty, deep breathing work can have a transcendental effect in counteracting stress, clearing unnecessary emotions, and clearing the mind to perform more creatively and without resistance. With sensitivity to our breathing—by tuning in to subtle changes in our breath as we encounter different situations—we can better read business situations, deduce when challenges arise, and alter our patterned behavioral reactions to change the outcomes of tense situations. Researchers have been proving this, correlating emotion to breath changes and showing that breath techniques can measurably change our emotional state. Breath exercises are now being prescribed by psychologists to manage a host of emotional disorders, from anxiety to PTSD.[1]

Within every yoga technique, there is a deliberate approach to breath that supercharges the pose's efficacy. Like the other teachings so far in this book, understanding and exercising breath is another way of getting the most out of our yoga practice. But before you add yoga poses to pranayama, practice the breathing itself first. In the remainder of this chapter, we will share some powerful introductory breathing techniques that you can use to cultivate a stronger connection to your breathing, better manage stress, improve lung capacity, and boost overall well-being. You should practice these techniques in any comfortable sitting posture (unless instructions say to lie down): crossing your legs in front of you with your feet under your lower legs, kneeling with your glutes resting on your heels, or sitting on a chair. Feel free to use cushions and find your most comfortable position, ensuring that your spine is straight, shoulders are relaxed, chin is level, and face muscles are relaxed. You can perform these techniques at home or the office, and they are especially beneficial when performed outside in fresh air, for instance at a park or nature preserve. It is not safe to perform these techniques while driving, since your attention can falter, and also avoid doing these exercises in poor air quality (such as an airplane), so you don't pull the toxins in the air deep into your physiology.

Full yogic breathing (*dirgha pranayama*)

Benefits: The first pranayama technique that students of yoga should master is full yogic breathing, sometimes called a three-part yogic breath. This fundamental technique forms the basis of many pranayama techniques, so it must be mastered over a few days before you attempt other techniques. In Sanskrit, it is sometimes called *dirgha pranayama*, *dirgha* meaning "long" or "full." Though simple, it has powerful effects if done on a regular basis. It tunes you in to the functioning of your lungs, calms your physiology, and helps release stress and anger. It stabilizes your emotions and balances your hormones. It also improves your sleep quality and helps trigger the relaxation response in your physiology. And with the deep inhalation and exhalation, you are in effect "pranating" your system—oxygenating, circulating, rejuvenating, and detoxifying in an efficient way.

I had a client, Sanjay, who was a vice president of product development working in a tense operating environment. His stress kept him up late, and he was experiencing random anxiety attacks in the middle of the day. Just by regularly practicing this breathing technique, he noticed a remarkable reduction in his stress levels and better sleep through the night. He was more skillfully able to handle tough situations at work, his anxiety was gone, and he had more energy throughout the day. His performance did not go unnoticed, and in a matter of six months, he was promoted. At first he found that the technique felt very difficult and abnormal; his abdominal muscles had never been stretched or activated in such a full and complete way. I've seen similar transformations with many clients, showing how leveraging our entire lung capacity is a tool for performance in business as well as in sports.

Additional benefits include voice projection and rib cage flexibility. An executive coach of mine once watched me practice a speech. She put her hand on my belly and asked, "Vish, are you even breathing? You *are* a yogi, aren't you?" I wasn't integrating my practice into this situation given my nerves around public speaking. I was breathing from a shallow place in my upper lungs, not reaching the full tone and projection of my voice. I did a few rounds of full yogic breathing, and soon I was projecting with a deep voice all the way to the back of the room.

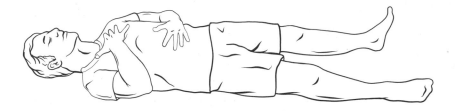

Technique: The best way to begin this technique is to lie flat on your back with your right hand on your belly and your left hand on your chest, over your heart. Then with your left hand, reach your index finger and thumb to rest on your collarbone. Use your hands to monitor the filling and emptying of your lungs. Your belly rising and falling indicates the lower part of the lungs being activated, your chest rising and falling indicates the middle part of your lungs being activated, and the finger on your collarbone indicates the shallow upper part of your lungs being filled. While your chest is rising, you should also feel your rib cage expanding; you may feel this under your left forearm.

While lying in this manner, inhale deeply through your nose, feeling first the belly rise, followed by the chest, followed by the collarbone. If all three rise sequentially, then you are doing the technique correctly and are filling the entire chamber of your lungs with air. Inhale as much as you can, hold the breath with the lungs fully expanded for a second or two, then exhale all the way out through the nose, feeling the collarbone lower, the chest lower, the ribs contract, and finally the belly lower all the way, fully expelling air from all parts of the lungs. Keep breathing for a few minutes, conscious of all three parts of your lungs activating, and you'll have a good sense of how it feels to completely fill and empty the lungs. Once you have mastered this technique lying down (i.e., all three parts of the lung mobilize during a breath), you can perform the technique sitting up. If you are a highly stressed person, as I often meet in my coaching practice, you may tend to have a very tight abdominal region (to hold it all in!), and you may notice very little belly movement. It will take practice and patience to start to stretch and move this area of your body.

Try to practice this technique for three to five minutes per day if you are under heavy stress. Or, once you begin your yoga practice on the mat, practice full yogic breathing regularly as part of your routine for seven to ten rounds. You can also do a few rounds of this technique any time you are feeling anxiety, stress, frustration, or anger. It is especially beneficial for pitta types or those with pitta-aggravating work.

Purification breath (*kapalabhati kriya*)

Benefits: The next breathing technique is known in Sanskrit as *kapalabhati kriya*, which translates as "shining skull purification exercise." It is targeted at the frontal lobe of the brain, activating and energizing this area to help bring shining clarity to one's thoughts. It is an invigorating technique that uses forced exhalations to oxygenate the system, expelling toxins and unnecessary emotions that accumulate in the frontal lobe. It also helps move mucus out of the sinus passages, so it is good to have some tissue nearby. Only attempt once you are comfortable with the full yogic breathing technique, as kapalabhati kriya requires a sensitive understanding of the lungs and relative looseness and flexibility in the abdominal muscles. This technique has great benefits for immunity, blood purification, and allergies and sinus problems. It is also a good for toning the abdominal muscles and improves digestion. You should not practice this technique if you have high blood pressure, a headache, constipation, or severe sinus blockage. It is not advisable for women who are pregnant or are on their menstrual cycle.

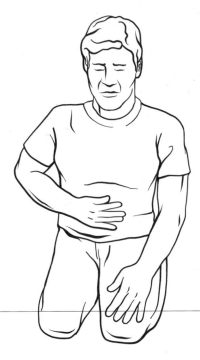

Technique: Kapalabhati is performed in a seated position with the spine upright and the eyes closed. Start by deeply inhaling and exhaling through the nose, filling and emptying the lungs completely using full yogic breathing. Then inhale through the nose, and keeping the mouth closed, exhale actively through the nose, drawing your belly sharply in and slightly up. It is an active exhale followed by an automatic, passive inhale, so you focus your attention only on the exhale, while the inhale comes naturally. You repeat this exhale through the nose while drawing the belly in at a rate of about one to two breaths per second. As you perform this, it is important to keep your spine straight, your shoulders relaxed (not hunched over), your chest open, and your head upright, not nodding down. The exhale should be active but not forceful or such that your body contorts or shakes. There should be no sound or intention on the inhale; the intentionality and sound should be on the exhale only. Rest a hand on your belly at first to get familiar with the belly's movement inward. You can use your hand to gently guide the belly inward during the exhale as you familiarize yourself with the technique. Make sure both your inhale and your exhale are through your nose and that your mouth is closed. You should not make a wheezing or rasping sound in your throat or chest and there should be no constriction in your nose.

Perform the breathing exercise for twenty repetitions (for beginners), then completely exhale, and hold the breath out for five seconds. Then fully inhale, filling the lungs completely, and hold the breath in for five seconds. Exhale and relax for a few breaths, and observe the sensations in your physiology before performing another round. Beginners should start with two to three rounds of twenty repetitions, eventually building up in a few weeks to three to four rounds of thirty to forty repetitions. After you complete this technique, you should sit quietly for a few moments experiencing the clarity and energy that it provides.

Alternate-nostril breathing (*anuloma viloma pranayama*)

Benefits: The third technique is called alternate-nostril breathing, or *anuloma viloma pranayama*. This gentle technique has powerful healing capabilities. It balances the active and passive energies of our body (solar and lunar), which are said to flow through our right and left nostrils, respectively. Solar energy is the energy we send brightly into the world, standing for our beliefs, having a strong sense of self, getting things done, and growing. Lunar energy is our compassion, our receptivity to learning from and connecting with others, and our ability to perceive the reality around us. It also helps us rest. When we are overly solar influenced, we become forceful, aggressive, and hot (relating to excess pitta). When we are overly lunar influenced, we become too passive, dispassionate, and unproductive. By balancing both energies, we can better leverage each of them. Alternate-nostril breathing cools the system, creating a sense of calm and peace, while simultaneously energizing us, boosting our immune system, and purifying the blood. It quickly tackles the usual culprits of stress in business life, dissolving anxiety from the mind. It also improves concentration and focus. Research has shown that alternate-nostril breathing has an immediate effect on toning the parasympathetic nervous system and calming the entire physiology.[2]

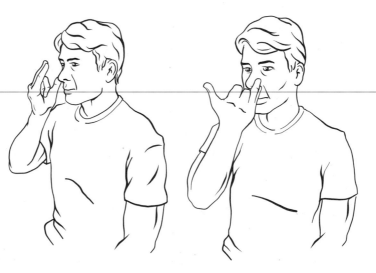

Technique: Anuloma viloma can be practiced on the floor or in a chair. Sit upright with the spine straight and the shoulders down and relaxed (not drooping or rising). Hold your head upright, taking care not to nod your head down or back. Holding your right hand up with fingers extended, curl your index and middle fingers down to rest at the base of your thumb. Your thumb and your ring and little fingers remain outstretched. Close your eyes and take one full inhale and exhale as you would in full yogic breathing. After the exhale, close your right nostril using the pad of your thumb, and inhale gently through the left nostril all the way down to the belly (the bottom of the lungs). Hold your breath in for a moment, close the left nostril with your ring and little fingers, then release your thumb from the right nostril and exhale completely through your right nostril, from the bottom of your lungs. Hold the emptiness for a moment, then inhale through the right nostril all the way down to the belly. Holding your breath for a moment, open the left nostril, close the right nostril, and exhale completely, from the belly up, out of the left nostril. This completes one round. Throughout, take care that your breathing is silent and your body is still. Time your inhales and exhales to six to eight seconds and your holds to one to two seconds. If you find it helpful, you can silently repeat "om one, om two" to keep track of the seconds, counting one "om" for every second.

Always begin this practice with one full yogic breath, then inhale through the left nostril, exhale right, inhale right, and end with an exhale through the left nostril. About seven to ten rounds of this sequence will offer great benefits to working professionals, especially those who want to calm an overly reactive nature. You can increase the rounds to up to twenty over a few weeks if you are seeking deeper benefits.

Variations: Once you have mastered the basic technique of anuloma viloma, you can try a couple of variations: Try using a faster alternating nostril breath of two seconds in and two seconds out (which will produce some nostril noise), and also try a four-second inhale with an eight-second exhale. The former is a more energizing technique, while the latter is a more calming technique. This latter is also an excellent technique to practice prior to meditation.

Ocean breath (*ujaii pranayama*)

Benefits: This fundamental breathing technique is used often during yoga practice on the mat. It creates tremendous focus, power, and internal stability during yoga poses. It involves breathing through a constricted glottis. In Sanskrit, it is known as the *ujjai pranayama*, which translates to "breath of victory." This technique stimulates heat and digestive fire, draws awareness inward, creates strength and steadiness, and increases concentration and willpower. During yoga practice, it allows one to remain calm, poised, and aware, enabling deeper internal activation of the postures. It also stabilizes the pelvis, helping to prevent injuries. Ocean breath is especially good for vata and kapha types and helpful during winter when the body could use some heating.

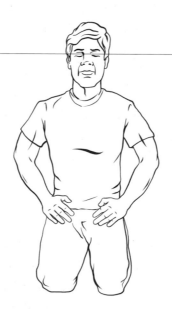

Technique: To understand this technique, imagine breathing out of your mouth to fog up a mirror. It is a soft *ha* sound, with a raspy noise in the throat area through constriction of the glottis.

(It is a bit like pretending to be Darth Vader.) To perform ujaii breathing, maintain this glottis constriction and mirror-fogging breath setup, but close your mouth and breathe out your nose instead. Inhale and exhale this way, with the mouth closed and throat constricted, creating a hoarse rasping sound in the back of the throat. This technique can be performed while seated or while doing yoga poses. In both cases, it is important to inhale fully to the belly and exhale fully from the belly as in the full yogic breathing technique, but with the constriction in the throat.

Precautions: This technique should not be practiced by individuals with excessive pitta, as it creates a lot of heat. It should be avoided by those with high blood pressure, heart disease, or severe constipation, and by pregnant women.

Honeybee breath (*brahmari pranayama*)

Benefits: *Brahmari* breathing is a simple yet powerful yoga technique that is especially beneficial for people in high-stress roles. It calms the mind and releases negative emotions and built-up stress. It balances serotonin and melatonin levels by stimulating the pineal and pituitary glands and also helps with adrenal fatigue by balancing the adrenal glands. It helps with health problems such as high blood pressure and insomnia through its stress-relieving properties—use it during the day to prepare for better sleep, or during a sleepless night, provided you are not disturbing your partner. I also find this technique very helpful if I have a sore throat, head cold, or headache (for some, it addresses migraines). You may notice that people who are suffering extreme pain spontaneously start performing this technique as the body's natural way of trying to relieve itself of pain. It is also a very powerful preparation for meditation and can be used throughout yoga practice. It works particularly well during child pose.

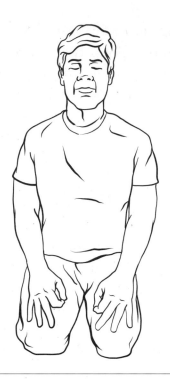

Technique: The technique can be performed in a sitting posture, while lying down, or during yoga poses. After inhaling deeply, exhale, making a loud humming noise (similar to the buzzing of a honeybee) while resting your tongue against the palate in the roof of your mouth. Continue to hum loudly until all of your breath is released, then inhale deeply again and repeat. This technique can be performed for several minutes at a time.

Cooling breath (*shitali pranayama*)

Benefits: *Shitali* cools down the physiology. Western society values pitta traits and solar energy, especially in the corporate sector, so we can run very hot. (Perhaps this is why North American restaurants serve ice water immediately, to cool you down—but unfortunately this dampens the digestive agni right before the meal!) Shitali pranayama can help with balancing pitta and managing excess solar energy, improving conditions such as inflammation, skin irritation, heat flashes, fever, and blood pressure.

Technique: First, slightly stick your tongue out of your mouth and roll your tongue lengthwise, forming a tube. Then gently inhale through the tube for as long as you can, and exhale slowly through the nostrils. About eight to ten rounds of *shitali* breathing will help cool down your system.

Variations: If you are unable to roll your tongue, a variation is to rest the tongue gently under the front two teeth and breathe in this manner.

NASAL IRRIGATION (JAL NETI)

Benefits: Related to pranayama is a powerful nasal cleansing technique called *jal neti*, which translates to *water cleaning*. In the yoga tradition, it is used to maximize the depth and effectiveness of pranayama by opening the breathing pathways. It has been adopted in the West for relief from allergies and sinus issues, and many drugstores now carry neti pots. It can be filled with a saline solution and has a long spout that can be inserted into a nostril. Performing this technique can relieve sinus issues, congestion, headaches, and allergies. It also helps improve eyesight, is a great way to cleanse the nasal passage of pollutants and irritants, and helps prevent and relieve the common cold.

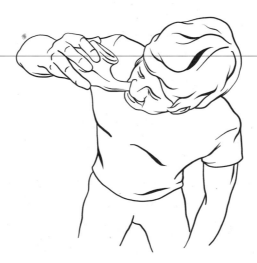

Technique: Your neti pot may come with specific instructions, but in general the technique is as follows. Fill the neti pot with lukewarm water and about half a teaspoon of salt (preferably rock salt). Mix the solution, then raise the neti pot and insert the spout gently into one nostril. Standing with your legs slightly apart and leaning your body forward to almost a 45-degree angle, tilt your head sideways (away from the neti pot). Breathe calmly through your mouth as the water drains through the top nostril and out the bottom nostril. After you've used half the pot, remove the spout, bend forward, and do several gentle but active exhales through the nose. Then, to remove excess water, move your head to each side, repeating the gentle but active exhales on each side five to seven times. Do not hold your nose or blow too hard, as you can hurt your ears or force water into them. Repeat the neti pot in your other nostril, and once again blow out the excess water.

If the neti pot solution is too salty or not salty enough, it may be painful as the water passes through your nostrils, so adjust the saltiness according to your comfort level. If you have a cold, a little extra salt is helpful. After the cleansing, put a drop of sesame, almond, or coconut oil in each nostril with the little finger or a cotton bud to keep the nostrils from drying out and trap dirt before it travels into your clean nasal passages. (I also use the nostril oiling technique before a long flight to avoid dryness and help trap germs.)

This practice is very good to do daily and before pranayama practice as it increases the efficiency of the absorption of prana. You can also just use it on an as-needed basis whenever you feel allergies or congestion coming on, or if you have been in an environment with poor air quality. This is a technique I have relied on for years to get me through allergy season, dusty manufacturing environments, and international travel.

Precautions: Do not practice this just before bedtime or if you have an ear infection. Also be careful not to exhale too strongly when you are clearing out the water, especially if you have some blockage in your nostrils. Consult your doctor before using this technique if you have severe congestion or more serious sinus issues.

PRANA AND YOGA

Pranayama is an integral part of yoga, even getting its own recognition as the fourth limb. You can increase your life-force energy by using conscious breathing techniques and doing other prana-enhancing activities such as surrounding yourself with positive people and environments and indulging in your higher calling regularly. The next chapter on yoga asanas (postures) will help you take this prana energy and amplify it to create a life full of energy, health, and effectiveness.

NOTES

1. Anjali A. Sarkar, "Functional Correlation Between Breathing and Emotional States," *MedCrave*, May 18, 2017, 3(5), 157–158, https://medcraveonline.com/MOJAP/MOJAP-03-00108.pdf.
2. Anant Narayan Sinha, Desh Deepak, and Vimal Singh Gusain, "Assessment of the Effects of Pranayama/Alternate Nostril Breathing on the Parasympathetic Nervous System in Young Adults," *Journal of Clinical and Diagnostic Research*, May 1, 2013, 7(5), 821–823, doi: 10.7860/JCDR/2013/4750.2948.

SELF-REFLECTION QUESTIONS

1. Which pranayama techniques would be beneficial to your life? How would they change things?

CHAPTER NINE
Move Your Body

*A*tha yoga anushasanam: "And now begins yoga." This is the famous first sutra from Sage Patanjali's two-thousand-year-old Yoga Sutras text, and it can open up a lifetime of learning. At this auspicious moment, after all your preparation, now begins the yoga (union) with the higher self. You have adjusted your moral behavior, diet, work performance, life direction, daily disciplines, and breathing techniques, building the foundation for a physical practice that integrates these teachings into a transformational set of body movements and poses. Without the foundational work, yoga practice on the mat would just be exercise; with the foundation, the practice assimilates the entire philosophy into the physical cellular structure of your body. It is your foundational work that enables a thirty-to-sixty-minute practice to have such a profound transformative effect that few other activities can match. As Vishvketu explains, "Now is the time that you can begin to reprogram your body-mind connection to let go of negative patterns, habits, and limiting beliefs and open yourself up to better alignment with your higher self."

Yoga asanas (poses) are a healing practice. It is said that the ancient seers observed animals in nature and noted how they moved their bodies in order to heal themselves. From these profound observations, along with heightened intuition, self-awareness, and inner experimentation, emerged the yoga asanas. The physical postures are used to heal the body and in turn heal the mind, releasing mental tension that has manifested in the body and opening up channels for a deeper connection to our true nature. Yoga connects and harmonizes our physical, mental, and spiritual layers so that we can perform better in life.

Physically, yoga asanas are designed to realign the body and keep it healthy in order for it to better perform its duties in carrying out our life work. Especially after the daily contortion of our body and our mind at the office, we need regular realignment on all levels. Slouched at our desks focused on emails and tasks, huddled around conference tables, hunched in cramped airplanes, we abuse and neglect our bodies. Yoga asanas move the joints and muscles through opposing forces of compression and expansion, massaging all of our muscles, joints, and organs to realign our bodies. Asana practice keeps the muscles supple and flexible and lubricates and flexes the joints to keep them performing well. The weight-bearing nature of some of the postures strengthens the bones and keeps them from becoming brittle as we age. Yoga postures also activate the glandular system, rebalance hormones, promote circulation, and help detoxify the body.

Though yoga treats the whole body and mind, it concentrates heavily on spine health; among the physical components of yoga, taking care of the spine is second only to breathing properly. The spine is the frame that supports your entire body and carries communication between your brain and vital organs. Keeping the spine healthy ensures proper motion throughout the body and helps tone the nerve fibers and neurological pathways. Vishvketu often says that aging begins in the spine, so if you keep the spine healthy, you slow the aging process. Our working lives aggravate and neglect the spine and neck; between sitting, lugging around heavy bags, and squinting into our phones, we can end up aging quite quickly! Asana practice involves bending and twisting the spine to counter these effects, keeping it healthy and young to better support you and keep your systems running smoothly.

Yoga poses are designed to exercise several layers of our system, promoting energy, balance, and healing. The Vedic literature explains that alongside our physical anatomy, a subtle anatomy of energy channels carry our *prana* or life-force energy. When we feel depleted mentally and physically, it is because our life-force energy is drained. Yoga helps to recharge this system, and this active energization is why many people feel rejuvenated after practicing yoga. Asana practice also helps balance the body, eliminating excess fire (pitta) or air (vata) elements that can be easily accumulated during a twenty-four-hour period. Vishvketu likes to say that asana practice is how you reorganize the five elements of nature within you on a daily basis. Your body is always striving for balance, but its attempts to rebalance without your assistance can take a long time at best and cause new problems at worst. We know that balancing our doshas prevents disease and promotes healing; a regular yoga practice continually accelerates this balancing process, healing your body so that you can perform at your best. In the yoga tradition, illness results from a combination of physical, mental, and energetic factors, and by working on all these systems in the integrated way yoga provides, we can heal ourselves faster. Taking medication can help us on a physical level, but it can work more effectively or become unnecessary alongside a yoga practice. Research is indeed starting to detect improvements in immunity and reduction in inflammation (the root of many diseases) through yoga.[1]

Stiffness in the body is often connected to inflexibility in the mind, and as we improve our body movement, our mind opens up to new perspectives. Asana practice releases tension, stiffness, and toxicity, creating space for positive energy and healing positivity to flow in. As the mind rests, we start to cultivate a spiritual lightness and calm that heals our emotions and gives us deeper strength to conquer our challenges. We become creative problem solvers in life and expand our consciousness to understand things in life more profoundly. As the body stretches and twists, we massage our organs and muscles and expel toxins from the tissue while drawing in nourishment in its place. We exercise the respiratory system and the digestive system so that they operate more efficiently and improve our overall health. In massaging various glands, we also help regulate hormonal secretions and bring them back to balance from the stressors of modern life. Then, the emotional excesses of anger, jealousy, anxiety, depression, and indecisiveness start to dissipate. Through a regular yoga practice, our decision-making improves, and we gain poise and grace in difficult situations. Confidence and determination strengthen as we make a habit of unloading physical and emotional toxins. We start to feel more rooted and emotionally stable through the ups and downs of our careers, relationships, and lives.

The whole system of yoga is intricately designed to move the body, mind, and spirit toward wholeness and deeper connection. For many, the path of yoga is a purification methodology to rid the body and energy channels of toxins and blockages on a path of meditation and higher spiritual experience. The benefits of the practice, however, are applicable and available to all of us, whether we are on a spiritual path or not. We can use these methods to improve our well-being and decision-making to live more effectively and more consciously. We can create the holy grail of success without guilt. We can perform well in our work and be rewarded for it financially but without sacrificing morals and decency. This is what yoga can make available to us in the business world.

Balance within our exercise habits is important for our pursuit of optimal mental and physical health and, ultimately, our optimal earthly and spiritual existence. In the Vedic tradition, exercise should be performed most days of the week, comprising a blend of strength, flexibility, and cardiovascular activities. Strength exercise can be weights at the gym, body-weight exercise at home, or anything else that subjects the joints and muscles to a comfortable strain. Flexibility exercise keeps your joints limber and your muscles supple. Yoga tackles both strength and flexibility, as you balance your body weight on various bones, joints, and muscles while performing deep stretches. Cardiovascular, of course, can be anything that gets the blood flow moving and the respiratory and heart rates up. Regular yoga practice and cardio exercise most days of the week make for a complete and balanced exercise regimen.

PREPARATION FOR YOGA PRACTICE

Your mind-body preparations have set you up to make the most of your practice on the mat, and your practice on the mat further deepens your pursuit of self-knowledge and balance off the mat. But your on-the-mat practice can be weakened if you approach your practice without clarity of body and mind. The more you clear your body and mind of clutter like digestion issues, illness, and stress prior to asanas, the more space the asanas have to do their work unencumbered.

Yoga is ideally performed on an empty stomach, with the bladder and bowels evacuated. Try to wait at least three hours after eating before performing yoga asanas, and empty your bladder before the practice. The asanas involve deep organ-level stretching that promotes intense circulation; we must empty the bowels to avoid circulating those toxins. It is also best to bathe before yoga to remove dirt, sweat, and other toxin buildup from the skin. The original practice of yoga is gentle and does not create much sweat, so after practice you can continue on with your day. I find the ideal time to practice is in the morning, after I wake up and bathe and before breakfast.

It is also best to practice yoga when you are generally healthy and clear of emotional stress. If you are suffering moderate to severe ailments such as headaches, serious colds, severe constipation, or other serious diseases, it is better to address the underlying issues and perform yoga when the ailments clear, or take the guidance of a yoga therapist for a more targeted, healing practice. If any serious illnesses are at play, consult your doctor before doing asana practice. Though they may not be aware of the holistic approach of yoga we are taking here, they will be able to address any physical stretching concerns related to the illness. Also wait to practice yoga if you are experiencing overly strong emotions such as anger or sadness, as you don't want that to be the underlying experience of your practice. If you perform yoga while having significant negative emotions, you won't gain the benefits of the practice, nor will your other issues resolve through yoga asanas alone. You can also hurt yourself by pushing too hard or not paying attention to the stability of your poses. Try to resolve any such issues prior to practicing, and if today is not a day to practice, accept that, seek rebalance today, and try again tomorrow. (The sound work in Chapter 11 can help you resolve these issues before engaging in the physical postures.) Finally, if you are menstruating, you want to encourage downward flow, rest, and reflection, so avoid inversion poses and intense stretches. This might also be a time when you increase the meditation component or the relaxation part of your practice.

Before you begin your practice, set a positive intention that will carry you through the practice and help set a tone for your day. It might be an affirmation or a quotation that speaks to you. As you sit with your eyes closed, center yourself and bring this intention to mind, dedicating the practice to that intention. Throughout the practice, bring the intention back to mind so that it permeates your body, mind, and spirit. The following are some intention examples that you might use. They begin "I am" rather than "I will be" or "I can" to assert ownership of the affirmation without hesitancy. You can structure the intention in whatever way suits you; the important thing is that you step into it and become it, rather than only aspiring to it.

I am happy.	*I will heal.*
I am confident.	*I will win.*
I am a good speaker.	*I am free.*
I am content.	*I am loved.*
I am whole.	*I am competent.*
I am secure.	*I will succeed.*
I am organized.	*I am supported.*
I am intelligent.	*I am disciplined.*
I am relaxed.	*I am present.*
I am fun.	*I am calm.*
I am healthy.	*I am energized.*

Before you begin your practice, let's bring another aphorism of Sage Patanjali into mind: *Sthira sukham asanam,* or "steady, comfortable pose," explains that during a pose the body must be steady, firm, alert, and comfortable while the mind remains quiet. The word *sukhum* connotes comfort, pleasure, and joy, so in contrast to popular Western exercise practices, yoga should be comfortable not painful, pleasurable not competitive, focused on inner joy rather than comparison to others or to some ideal we set for ourselves. At different times of day, on different days, and at different times of life, our body will have different capabilities, so we must be compassionate to ourselves during yoga practice. It is not a practice of pushing past physical limits and pain but rather a physically comfortable practice that helps us indirectly push through mental limits and strengthen our spirit. So do only what is comfortable for your body, even if it is just a slight movement toward the full pose; you should only feel a healthy strain in your body, not any outright pain in a pose. (If you are ever in a yoga class where a teacher pushes you to a point of pain, take charge of the situation and protect yourself from ending up with an injury.) With daily practice, your body will gradually gain flexibility. When I first met Vishvketu and started doing yoga, I couldn't reach my hands past my knees in a forward bend. He would say, "Bend forward," and then repeat himself, thinking I had not heard him. Then he would walk over and try to gently assist me to move farther down, but I couldn't budge! He couldn't believe a twenty-year-old had so little flexibility! Today, he still tells this story, partly to tease but mainly to teach the lesson that we all have to start somewhere. Twenty-some years later, I can bend forward and put my hands under my feet. It was a gradual, patient process of opening up flexibility of body and mind.

Your yoga asanas are integrally connected with your pranayama techniques. During yoga poses, you will perform deep three-part full yogic breathing, filling your lungs completely (expanding belly, chest, and collarbone simultaneously), holding for a second or two, and exhaling completely. As you advance in your practice, you can incorporate the ocean breath (*ujaii pranayama*) along with your poses for deeper effect. The yoga teacher Mark Whitwell once told me to think of a yoga pose as a vehicle for the breath: As we put our body into a different position, we move the breath through our lungs in a different way. Your breathing is also a signpost for whether you are comfortable or straining too much. Just as observing your breath in life tunes you in to your emotions, observing your breath in yoga tells you if you are correctly positioned in a pose. In Vishvketu's words, "If you can smile and breathe deeper during asana, then it is a joyful strain. But *pain* is not good."

As you schedule your practice, you should plan enough time to end with a calm conclusion: a relaxation pose, a period of meditation, and some sound work. The relaxation pose is where you reap the benefits of the physical practice, and the post-practice meditation is especially powerful because your practice has prepared the entire being for meditation. Whether or not you perform the meditation, conclude your practice with a deep chant of the mantra *om*, which links three sounds: *ah* (as in *ahhh*), *oo* (as in *loop*), and *mm*. Om, considered the primordial sound of creation per the Vedic knowledge system, activates a calming, grounded, and connected inner feeling. For this chant, take a deep full-yogic breath, and then chant the mantra across the length of a full exhale. (See Chapter 11 for more detail on the benefits of a sound practice.)

After you complete your practice, you'll want to avoid eating heavily, drinking anything stimulating, or engaging in any vigorous activity since you are usually in a calm state after the final relaxation and meditation. Try to leave a gap of fifteen to twenty minutes to remain in this state and enjoy the results of your practice.

The following three sequences include the preparation, posing, and conclusion elements essential to your complete on-the-mat yoga practice. They are sequentially more complex, building off of one another. Each begins with centering through an intention, breathing and warm-up exercises, and poses (standing, crouching, seated, lying on belly, lying on back, and inversion) before closing with relaxation, meditation, and sound work. Each sequence moves the spine in six ways: bending left and right, bending forward and backward, and twisting or rotating left to the right. The individual poses are explained after the sequence lists. After you have practiced the sequences for a few months and you start to feel intuitively familiar with your body's needs, you can adjust and add in extra poses or hold poses longer, as you feel you need. If you need to skip a pose because it doesn't feel right or one of the precautions listed applies to you, you can continue on to the next pose in the sequence. The breathing techniques are described in Chapter 8, the meditation techniques in Chapter 10, and the sound techniques in Chapter 11.

ASANAS AND AYURVEDA

As you go through your yoga sequences, be aware of your Ayurvedic constitution and adjust your practice accordingly. As practitioners of yoga and Ayurveda, Vishvketu and I are always amused at how different constitutional types are drawn to different types of yoga. Vata types, who are always on the move, gravitate toward vinyasa yoga, a movement-heavy style that aggravates vata. Kaphas, who prefer to relax, take restorative yoga, which aggravates kapha. Pitta types, who are already fiery, are attracted to hot yoga or the athletic ashtanga yoga, which both aggravate pitta. Remember the bucket analogy: If your bucket is already filling up with one dosha, adding more of that dosha through your yoga practice can make the bucket overflow. As a pitta, I also struggle to let go and just feel what my body needs. If I set aside thirty minutes for yoga, I want to do thirty minutes—not twenty-nine, not thirty-one—and I want to hold every pose for an exact number of breaths, all aggravating my pitta dosha. So if your tendency is vata imbalance, restorative is best for you—aim for a nourishing and grounding practice. If your tendency is kapha, hot yoga is perfect; you will benefit from a stimulating and energetic practice. And if you have a pitta imbalance, you should practice gentle flows in a cool environment and seek to let go of stringent expectations and competitive tendencies.

I—FOUNDATIONAL SEQUENCE (20–25 MINUTES)

Start with this sequence if you are beginning a new yoga practice or restarting a dormant practice. The foundational sequence is also useful to maintain your well-being when you have very little time in your schedule. The poses in this sequence will prepare the body and mind for the intermediate and advanced sequences to follow. You can start by practicing this sequence without the meditation at the end, and layer in the meditation after you have read Chapter 10.

- Set opening intention
- Full yogic breathing (7–10 rounds)
- Cat-cow breathing (7–10 rounds)
- Mountain pose (5–7 breaths)
- Horse lunge, hands down (5–7 breaths each side)
- Standing forward bend (5–7 breaths)
- Palm tree pose (5–7 breaths)
- Half-moon pose (5–7 breaths each side)
- Squatting pose (5–7 breaths)
- Knee-supported plank pose (5–7 breaths each side)
- Sitting spinal twist (7–10 breaths each side)
- Cobra pose (5–7 breaths)
- Child pose (7–10 breaths)
- Legs-raised pose (5–7 breaths)
- Final relaxation (3–4 minutes)
- Breath awareness meditation (3–4 minutes)
- Final *om* chant (1–3 times over a full exhale each time)

II—INTERMEDIATE SEQUENCE (30–35 MINUTES)

Use the intermediate sequence when you are willing to invest some extra time and want to deepen your practice. Beginners should complete 4–6 weeks of daily practice of the foundational sequence before moving on to the intermediate sequence.

- Set opening intention
- Kapalabhati breathing (2 rounds of 30)
- Cat-cow breathing (7–10 rounds)
- Mountain pose (5–7 breaths)
- Horse lunge, raised arms (5–7 breaths each side)
- Standing forward bend (7–10 breaths)
- Palm tree pose (5–7 breaths)
- Chair pose (5–7 breaths)
- Warrior pose I (5–7 breaths each side)
- Squatting pose (5–7 breaths)
- Plank pose (3–5 breaths)
- Knee-supported side plank pose (5–7 breaths each side)
- Cobra pose (5–7 breaths)
- Child pose (7–10 breaths)
- Sitting spinal twist (7–10 breaths each side)
- Head-to-knee pose (5–7 breaths each side)
- Legs-raised pose (7–10 breaths)
- Fish pose (5–7 breaths)
- Wind-relief pose (5–7 breaths)
- Final relaxation (4–6 minutes)
- Humming meditation (4–6 minutes) (described in Chapter 10)
- *Ah, oo, ee* vocal toning (described in Chapter 11) followed by final *om* chant

III—ADVANCED SEQUENCE (40–45 MINUTES)

When you feel comfortable with the intermediate sequence, and you are holding the poses for longer breaths—which may take a couple of months—you can move on to the advanced sequence, which will offer deeper benefits of flexibility, calm, and rejuvenation. The advanced sequence also includes some more esoteric practices around chakras that will be explained in Chapter 11.

- Set opening intention
- Kapalabhati breathing (3 rounds of 30)
- Cat-cow breathing (7–10 rounds)
- Mountain pose (5–7 breaths)
- Palm tree pose (5–7 breaths)
- Balancing tree pose (5–7 breaths each side)
- Triangle pose (7–10 breaths each side)
- Warrior pose II (5–7 breaths each side)
- Dynamic chair breathing (10–15 rounds, then hold 5–7 breaths)
- Standing forward bend (7–10 breaths)
- Mountain pose (1–2 breaths as a transition)
- Plank pose (3–5 breaths)
- Full side plank (5–7 breaths each side)
- Sitting spinal twist (7–10 breaths each side)
- Inverted table pose (5–7 breaths)
- Sitting forward bend (5–7 breaths)
- Cobra pose (7–10 breaths)
- Child pose (7–10 breaths)
- Shoulder stand (7–10 breaths)
- Fish pose (5–7 breaths)
- Wind-relief pose (5–7 breaths)
- Final relaxation (5–7 minutes)
- Alternate-nostril breathing (7–10 rounds)
- SoHum meditation (6–10 minutes) (described in Chapter 10)
- Chakra tuning (*lum, vum, rum, yum, hum, om*) (described in Chapter 11 followed by long closing *om* chant)

YOGA ASANA TECHNIQUES

The poses are titled with a Western name along with a transliteration of the Sanskrit name. As yoga has permeated the West, many popular pose names have been modified, changed, or mistakenly used across different schools of yoga. Vishvketu undertook research of original texts, and with his expertise as a PhD in yoga, he published the authoritative *Yogasana: The Encyclopedia of Yoga Poses*, listing over eight hundred yoga poses with their accurate names and translations. In this book we have followed his nomenclature of poses but used some unique translations and transliterations for simplicity in teaching. You may find in some cases that our convention may be different to what you find in a Western yoga class.

Cat-cow breathing (*marjariasana*)

Benefits: Helps create a supple spine and improves mobility in the thoracic spine. Helps regulate the thyroid and thymus glands and releases emotional tension. Stimulates lymph flow and improves health of the digestive system. Helps prevent back issues and constipation. This pose is an excellent preparation to warm up the spine for yoga practice.

Precautions: If you have wrist issues or carpal tunnel syndrome, use your fingertips or knuckles instead of laying your hands flat. Use a folded blanket under your knees if they are sore.

Technique: Support yourself on your hands and knees, with knees hip-width apart and directly under your hips and hands shoulder-width apart and directly below your shoulders. The tops of your feet and palms of your hands are flat on the ground while you look down to the floor, head and neck parallel with the ground. Spread your fingers slightly and engage your wrists so that they are stable and not collapsing. (This is called a tabletop position.) Start with the cow: Inhale, moving your head up to look at the ceiling while dropping your navel downward, curving the back, opening the chest, and lifting your tailbone upward. Keep the shoulders relaxed. Then exhale into the cat, moving the chin down toward the chest, rounding the spine, tucking your tailbone in, and bringing your navel upward toward your spine. Moving from cow (head up inhale) to cat (head down exhale) completes one round. Repeat this sequence seven to ten times slowly and in sync with your breathing.

Mountain pose (*parvatasana*)

Benefits: Strengthens the wrists, arms, shoulders, and back. (Very good after desk work!) Improves bone density of legs and arms. Strengthens the nervous system and sends blood and oxygen to the brain. Lengthens and stretches the spine, glutes, hamstrings, and calves.

Precautions: If you have carpal tunnel or wrist issues, perform this with your forearms flat on the ground. If you have shoulder problems, do not hold this for too long or for more than one repetition in a sequence.

Technique: *Parvat* means "mountain" in Sanskrit, and so this pose is grounded and stable. (Western yoga classes sometimes apply mountain pose to *tadasana*, or palm tree pose, in which one stands still, or to a downward-facing dog pose, which is similar to parvatasana but involves a different head position and outcome.) Start in a tabletop position: on your hands and knees, with your hands and knees hip-width apart and fingers spread. Tuck your toes, coming to the balls of your feet. Inhale, raising your hips up, straightening your arms and knees, and pressing into your hands, particularly at the bases of the thumb and the index and little fingers. Exhale and drop your head down so it's even with the arms, and intend the tailbone upward toward the ceiling while creating space in the small of your back—try to open the space between the vertebrae in the lower back. Maintain a flat back as much as you can while keeping your ears between your arms. (If you move your head down past your arms, you are entering a different pose, downward-facing dog.) If you need to bend your knees slightly to maintain a flat back, then do so. If your knees are comfortably straight, then work on bringing your heels down. As you breathe, make sure to keep space between your shoulders and ears, and keep your belly in. Hold this for five to seven breaths before slowly lowering your knees to the ground.

Horse lunge pose (*chetakasana*)

Benefits: Stretches the hip flexors, the lower back, the groin, and the psoas muscle (one that doesn't get stretched much). Builds confidence and determination and releases blocked emotions. Improves stamina and lung function.
Precautions: Take caution if you have knee or lower back issues. You can add a folded blanket under your knee for cushion.

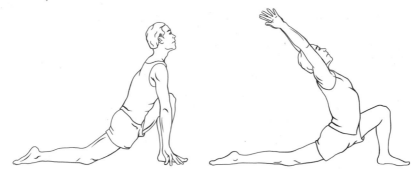

Technique: Starting on your hands and knees (tabletop), ground your hands, and inhale while stepping your right foot forward between your hands. Then extend your left leg farther backward, left toes pointing back and left knee still touching the ground. (You can also enter this pose directly from mountain pose.) Your right knee should be near the right side of your chest, directly above your right ankle and not swinging out to the side. As you exhale, open your chest and shoulders and intend the crown of your head up toward the ceiling while looking straightforward. Keep your hips square and your belly in. Your hands or fingertips can rest on the ground or on your right knee, and you should feel a deep stretch at the top of your left thigh. Work on lengthening the spine and the neck, and press into the right foot. Ensure again that your forward knee is aligned vertically and not collapsing outward. Hold for five to seven breaths, and then slowly bring your right leg back and enter a quick mountain pose before bringing the left knee forward to perform the pose on the other side.

Advanced: Once in horse lunge pose, inhale, raising the hands overhead, raising the torso, and opening at the chest as you maintain your solid and aligned base. Holding this position, inhale and exhale deeply, keeping your torso engaged and your pelvis even.

Standing forward bend (*prsthauttanasana*)

Benefits: Stretches all the muscles of the back as well as the hamstrings and glutes. Increases flexibility of the hip joints and spine. Massages the digestive organs. Increases blood and oxygen flow to the brain while stimulating the pineal, pituitary, thyroid, and parathyroid glands. Improves concentration and calms the mind.

Precautions: If you have lower back pain or sciatica, bend the knees and keep your forearms on your thighs. If you have low or fluctuating blood pressure, avoid this pose. Also avoid this pose if you are severely constipated. If you experience dizziness during this pose, come out of it very slowly.

Technique: Stand with your feet slightly apart, and inhale while you raise your arms up above your head. As you exhale, hinge forward at the hips, keeping the back flat as long as possible as you lower your upper body down toward your knees. Keep your knees soft (not locked) and thigh muscles engaged. As you reach your comfortable bend limit, round your back and rest your hands on your knees, shins, ankles, or feet or the floor, depending on what makes sense for you. Tuck your head downward, intending the crown of your head toward the floor while intending your tailbone upward. With each inhale, relax the hamstrings, and with each exhale, fold deeper into the pose while engaging your core muscles. Keep your shoulders relaxed and away from your ears. Maintain good alignment of your knees, feet, and hips. Hold this pose for seven to ten deep breaths. To transition out of the pose, keep your knees soft, further activate your thighs, inhale, and slowly begin to raise the torso, flattening the back and then coming up slowly. Raise the arms overhead when you come to upright, and lower them to your sides to finish exiting the pose.

Palm tree pose (*tadasana*)

Benefits: Lengthens the spine, increases concentration and self-confidence, improves posture, and increases lymphatic system flow. It is also the foundational pose for all standing yoga poses.

Precautions: Do not hold your breath during this pose if you have high blood pressure or dizziness or if you are pregnant.

Technique: This pose is sometimes called mountain pose in Western yoga classes. Stand with your feet hip-width apart, grounding the feet while slightly lifting at the arches. Lift your thigh muscles upward, keep some ease in your knees, level your pelvis, keep your belly in, open your chest, and lift slightly at the collarbone. Roll your shoulders back and then to neutral, keeping them level and open. Have your hands by your sides, palms turned inward, and head and chin level, looking straight ahead. Lift at the center of your crown. Make sure your spine is straight and you are not leaning in any direction. Center your weight. Hold this pose for three to five breaths while staring at a point in front of you. Observe the muscles involved in just standing still, and notice any areas of your body that may need some extra attention during your practice. Though this part of the pose appears simple, its subtleties can take a lifetime to master, and its practice brings grace to all standing yoga poses. Then, inhale, raising the arms overhead with your palms facing inward, fingers spread wide, ears in line with your arms, and shoulders relaxed, and on that inhale also lift your heels so that you are balancing on the balls of your feet and your toes. Pick a point in front of you to stare at, and remain still with your heels lifted for five to seven deep, full breaths. You should feel the base of your toes grounding into the floor and your body lengthening upward. On the final exhale, slowly lower down.

Half-moon pose (*ardhachandrasana*)

Benefits: Stretches and alternately compresses the ribs, lungs, and side muscles of the back and abdomen. Activates the nervous system and stimulates lymphatic flow in the armpits. Balances left and right hemispheres of the brain. Improves and prevents scoliosis of the spine and improves posture.

Precautions: Be gentle if you are suffering from scoliosis, and avoid if you have had recent surgery. Also be gentle if you feel strain in your lumbar area.

Technique: Stand with your feet hip-width apart and raise your left arm overhead with the palm facing inward. Stretch your left hand upward while resting your right hand on your right hip bone. Inhale as you lengthen, then exhale, bending to your right side while keeping your body in an aligned plane and knees straight. Keep your shoulders relaxed and do not allow the head to tilt too far to the right or nod forward or backward. Also make sure your belly does not jut out. Keep your body aligned front to back and both your feet firmly grounded, with equal weight on each. Continue to breathe while lengthening the left side and bending toward the right. Keep your shoulders down and your left ear near your left arm. Hold for five to seven breaths, then repeat on the other side.

Advanced: Put both palms together overhead as you bend sideways. Remember to keep your body aligned in a plane from front to back. This is the full version of moon pose, called *chandrasana*.

Balancing tree pose (*dhruvasana*)

Benefits: Strengthens the nerves and muscles of the whole body. Improves balance, concentration, willpower, and confidence. Stimulates lymphatic system flow and strengthens the bones to help prevent osteoporosis.

Precautions: Not advisable if you have knee problems or a condition that prevents you from balancing on one foot.

Technique: Stand with your feet hip-width apart, spread the toes, and begin to shift your weight onto your left foot. Pick a point in front of you to focus your concentration on, then lift your right foot and place it on your left shin or thigh, with toes pointing downward and knee pointing out to the side. You can use your hands to help place your right foot on your left leg. To protect your knee, make sure you place your foot below or above the knee, not directly on it. Bring your hands together in front of your chest or raise them above your head with palms touching. Hold this for five to seven deep, long breaths, then slowly come out of the pose and repeat on the other side.

Variation: If you find this pose challenging, just raise your knee in front of you at a 90-degree angle as if you are about to march, balancing on the other foot. Stretch your arms out forward or raise them above your head, with palms touching.

Triangle pose (*trikonasana*)

Benefits: Strengthens the side and core muscles and lengthens the hamstrings. Increases spine flexibility, improves posture, opens the hips and groin, and flushes the kidneys. Helps ground emotional energy, alleviating nervousness and depression. Relieves bloating and gas.

Precautions: Do not perform this pose if you have a slipped disc, sciatica, or inflammation of the vertebrae.

Technique: Stand with your feet spread wide, approximately one leg-width apart, with toes pointing forward. Turn the right foot so that it is pointing outward. The arch of the left foot should be in line with the heel of the right foot. Engage your leg muscles, inhale, and raise your arms to shoulder level, expanding the chest. Turn your head to the right side, shift your upper body slightly toward the right, and soften at the right knee (to protect it). Exhale, lowering your shoulder to the right and lowering your right hand to rest on your shin or ankle. Take care not to collapse the hip or the shoulders, and keep your abdominal muscles engaged. Look upward if your neck allows. Keep your left arm straight up. Hold for five to seven breaths. On your last inhale, slowly come up, adjust your feet so that the right toes point forward and the left point outward, and then exhale, lowering down to repeat on the other side.

Warrior pose I and II (*veerabhadrasana* and *mahaveerabhadrasana*)

Benefits: Increases self-confidence, stamina, vital energy, and willpower. Strengthens the thigh muscles and the ankle, knee, and hip joints. Alleviates depression and anxiety. This is an excellent pose if you want to set an intention to overcome a difficult challenge. When I was preparing to climb Mount Whitney, Vishvketu told me to practice this daily to strengthen my legs and willpower.

Precautions: Not advisable if you have knee problems.

Warrior I technique: From a standing position, step your right foot forward so that your feet are about one leg-length apart, with the toes of both feet pointing forward. Face toward your right foot, and square and level your hips. Inhale, raising your arms overhead, palms facing inward, and then exhale, lowering your hips down while bending at the right knee. As you come down, your left heel will lift off the ground so that you are supported at the toes and ball of the left foot. Keep your left knee straight, and keep your right knee bent at a 90-degree angle, positioned directly over your right ankle. Keep your hips square while you lengthen your spine, and lift your chest upward. Look up to the ceiling, continuing to lengthen the arms overhead. Hold this for five to seven breaths before switching sides.

Advanced Warrior II technique: Stand with your legs about one leg-width apart, with both feet pointing forward. Turn the right foot out so that it is pointing sideways, and ensure that the heel of the left foot is in line with the heel of the right foot. Square your hips forward so that they are in a plane with your legs. Inhale and extend your arms out to the sides at shoulder level. Turn your head to the right, and then, exhaling, bend the right knee to a 90-degree angle so that the right thigh is parallel to the ground. Widen your stance so you can feel some comfortable strain in your thighs but stay balanced. Make sure the right knee is aligned over the right ankle, not beyond the ankle (to protect the knee), and keep your hips pointing forward, your belly in, your left knee in, and your chest lifted and pointing forward. Keep your fingers steady, and stare with intensity at the tips of your right fingers. Keep the shoulders relaxed, feet firmly planted, and chin level with the ground. Breathe deeply for five to seven breaths. Come up slowly before beginning on the other side. The full translation of mahaveerabhadrasana is "great, beautiful warrior pose," a great intention for this practice.

Chair pose (*utkatasana*)

Benefits: Strengthens feet, knees, glutes, and thighs. Improves endurance, willpower, and inner strength. Opens the chest and improves lung capacity and vital energy.

Precautions: If you have knee pain, ankle issues, or Achilles tendon issues, don't squat too deeply.

Technique: Stand with your feet hip-width apart and inhale as you raise the arms overhead, palms facing inward. As you exhale, bend at the knees and ankles as if you are sitting into a chair. Open the chest, lengthen the torso, engage the abdominals, and look straight forward, keeping the shoulders relaxed and down. Breathe into the thighs and hold for five to seven breaths. To transition out, inhale, straightening the knees and reaching the hands upward. When the knees are straight, exhale and release your arms to rest beside you.

Dynamic chair breathing variation: Chair breathing is an active form of this asana. While standing upright, inhale and move the elbows out and back, bringing clenched fists near your armpits with fingers curled downward around your thumbs. Then, as you exhale actively through the nose, punch forward with both arms, opening the hands and bending the knees into chair pose. Then, as you inhale, come up to straight legs, fists back near the armpits, with elbows out and back. Perform ten to fifteen rounds, and then hold in the lowered chair pose with arms straight out for five to seven breaths before coming up and releasing the hands to your sides.

Squatting pose (*malasana*)

Benefits: Opens the hips and groin and helps relieve tension in the hips and lower back from excessive desk work. Strengthens the leg muscles and helps relieve constipation and gas.

Precautions: Not advised if you have stiff knees.

Technique: Squat into a baseball catcher's position, with your feet flat on the ground and toes pointing outward at 45 degrees. If it is difficult to squat with your feet flat, you can come up on your toes and rest your sit bones on your heels. Intend your hips downward and maintain your balance. Bring your hands together to meet at your heart center, and lengthen your spine. Then place your elbows inside your knees and use them to spread the knees outward, opening up at the lower back. Look straight ahead, keeping your shoulder's relaxed, and hold this pose for five to seven breaths.

Plank pose, knee-supported side plank, and side plank (*dandasana*)

Benefits: Strengthens the core muscles and helps with wrist flexibility and carpal tunnel prevention. Builds concentration and willpower.

Precautions: Be cautious if you have issues in your wrist, shoulders, or lower back.

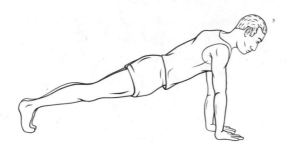

Plank pose technique: Starting from mountain pose (or horse lunge pose), shift your shoulders forward to be over your wrists, coming up on your toes, flattening your back, and tightening your abdominal muscles. Lengthen the body from the crown of your head to your heels while pressing your palms and toes into the ground. Ensure your belly is not collapsing downward and your hips are not raised; intend your body to be straight like a plank. Also do not hyperextend your elbow. Breathe deeply and hold for five to seven breaths.

Beginner variation: This is a challenging pose, and if you find you need strength to build up to it, place one knee down for support and alternate the supporting knee halfway through.

Intermediate knee-supported side plank pose technique: From plank pose, lift your left hand off the ground, reaching upward and rotating your body to the left while dropping your right knee to the ground for support. Rotate your left leg outward so that the arch of your foot is resting on the ground. Your left leg is straight, and your right leg is bent with the knee and top of foot resting on the ground. Your arms should be in a straight line with each other, with your left hand reaching straight up and your right hand planted on the ground directly below your shoulder. Your head should be in a neutral position, in line with your torso, looking to the wall on your left or upwards. Hold for five to seven deep breaths. This is also known as half side plank.

Advanced full side plank pose technique: From supported side plank, raise the right knee off the ground so that both legs are parallel and your weight is resting on the outside of your right foot. Raise the hips to keep the body in a straight line. Look upward instead of straight ahead, grounding through the right hand and lengthening through the left hand. Apart from the right hand, the only other contact with the ground is the outside of the right foot. Full side plank pose is an excellent pose to build strength in the core muscles, the arms, and the wrists, and to improve one's willpower and determination. Hold for five to seven breaths.

Sitting spinal twist (*vkrasana*)

Benefits: Deeply stretches the back muscles and helps to release tension in all parts of the back. Helps stretch the abdominal organs, specifically the colon, improving elimination. Massages the pancreas and helps regulate the kidney and adrenal glands. Helps to balance one's mental and emotional state and increases equanimity.

Precautions: Do not perform this pose if you have ulcers, abdominal hernias, or severe constipation. This is best performed when your bowels are empty.

Technique: Sit with your legs straight out in front of you, back straight, and hands beside your hips. Bend your right knee and place your right foot outside of your left knee. If you have limited flexibility, you can place your right foot inside your left knee. Make sure both your sitting bones are firmly planted into the ground, and your back remains straight and vertical. Wrap your left elbow around your right knee, then inhale, raising your right arm above your head while lengthening your spine. As you exhale, twist your torso to the right and place your right palm behind you on the ground, a few inches from your back. Squeeze your right thigh into your lower abdomen, compressing the colon while continuing to breathe. With every inhale, lengthen the spine, and with every exhale, twist a little farther. Your head should be turned as much as possible to the right as you keep your gaze at eye level and look over your right shoulder. Make sure your core muscles are engaged and you are not collapsing your lower back. The twisting of your torso should take place at the naval, and your sitting bones should remain grounded throughout the pose. To come out of the pose, take a final inhale while raising the right arm up, and then exhale, bringing the body back to center.

Head-to-knee pose (*janusirsasana*)

Benefits: Stretches the hips, knees, ankles, and spine while also lengthening the hamstrings and the calf and back muscles. Massages the kidneys, liver, and pancreas, and tones the reproductive organs. Reduces gas, tones the digestive system, and helps bring blood flow to the thyroid and parathyroid glands.

Precautions: If you have lower back pain or sciatica, only bend down halfway.

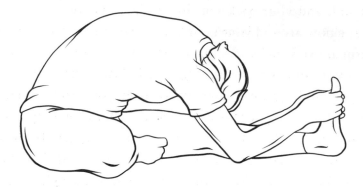

Technique: Sit with your legs together and straight out in front of you, with ankles touching and back straight and upright. Flex your toes upward, then bring the bottom of your right foot to rest on your left thigh, as far up as you can, while the right knee moves outward and down to rest on the ground. Ensure both sit bones are grounded, and turn your torso to the left slightly so that your chest is facing your left foot. Then inhale, stretching upward, and exhale, bending at the waist and folding forward over the left leg. Maintain a flat back to start, hinging at the hip joint, then as you travel downward, begin to round the back, intending your forehead to the knee. (As a beginner, even if you feel like you haven't bent far, stop and breathe as soon as you feel the stretch in your back. Pushing beyond that point will only create a sore back without much additional benefit.) You can hold your shins, ankles, or toes depending on your flexibility. If you are a male with overly active sexual energy, you can try to have the heel of the right foot contact and press into the perineum, which is a Vedic energy center related to nourishment and connection. As you perform this pose, ensure the right knee does not rise up and that you keep your left toes flexed upward. Breathe into the pose for five to seven breaths before slowly coming out, resting for a moment and then switching sides. This is a key pose in learning to be content with your capabilities. You may feel you are not bending far enough, but do not strain or push yourself into injury. This is a moment to be content with where you are and feel the stillness and subtle energies of the pose.

Sitting forward bend (*paschimottasana*)

Benefits: This is an excellent pose for calming mental stress and energizing the prana of the body. It also is a deep hamstring, spinal column, and overall back stretch. It activates the kidneys, liver, pancreas, and digestive system, helping detoxify the organs and improving excretory elimination. For women, it also helps regulate the menstrual cycle.

Precautions: Not recommended if you have back pain, a herniated disc, or sciatica. Also avoid this pose if you are severely constipated.

Technique: Sit with your legs together, straight out in front of you, with knees touching, back straight and upright, and toes flexing upward. Place your hands on the ground beside your hips, and lengthen from the waist up to the crown of your head, elongating your spine. Inhale, raising your arms up above your head, then as you exhale, fold forward at the hips, keeping your back flat and chest open (don't hunch your shoulders inward or downward). When you feel the stretch, stay in that position and rest your hands wherever comfortable, on your thighs, shins, ankles, or feet. Let go of any self-judgment and find contentment wherever you are in the pose. Ensure your back remains flat and your chest open, intend the crown of your head toward your toes, and keep your belly in. Try to keep making space in the small of your back, and keep flexing your toes upward. Hold this pose for five to seven deep breaths. If your hamstrings are tight, you can slightly bend your knees. Slowly come out of this pose on your last inhale, raising your arms overhead and returning to the upright position.

Inverted table pose (*purvottanasana*)

Benefits: Strengthens the wrists, ankles, arms, and legs while releasing tension in the shoulder and neck areas. Helps relieve fatigue and build stamina and can be very emotionally grounding.

Precautions: If you have weak wrists or high blood pressure or you have recently had surgery in the chest area, perform this pose very gently and with caution. If you have carpal tunnel, use your knuckles instead of your hands on the ground.

Technique: Sit on the ground with your knees partially bent to allow your feet to be flat on the floor. Place your hands on the ground slightly behind your hips, with the fingers pointing toward the toes. As you inhale, lift your hips upward, pressing your feet and hands to the floor and intending your navel to the ceiling. Gently engage your glutes and keep your feet and knees hip-width apart. Your knees should be directly above your ankles and your shoulders directly above your wrists. Keep the chest open and lifting upward while letting your head drop backward if your neck allows. If you have neck issues, you can instead tuck your chin toward your chest. Hold for five to seven breaths.

Cobra pose (*bhujangasana*)

Benefits: Strengthens the back muscles, arms, and wrists and massages the abdominal organs, helping with digestion. Helps balance the thyroid and parathyroid glands while enhancing immunity through its effect on the thymus gland. Helps stretch the lungs and improve heart function.

Precautions: Avoid if you suffer from high blood pressure or carpal tunnel syndrome. Be gentle if you suffer from lower back pain.

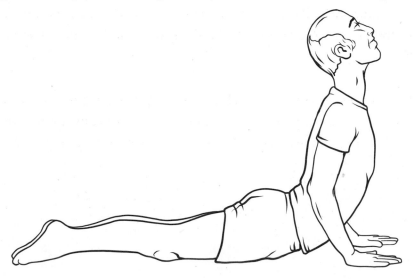

Technique: Lay flat on your stomach with your legs slightly apart. Engage your glutes and inner thighs while pressing your pubic bones down into the floor. Place your palms on the floor just below chest level, near your rib cage. Inhale, raising the head up, followed by the chest, then exhale. To rise up, avoid relying only on your hands; instead, use your back muscles to lengthen and lift the upper body, then place the hands on the floor, pushing down slightly for some additional lengthening and lifting. Keep your elbows slightly bent and tucked into the sides of the body. Make sure to keep the shoulders relaxed and down while pressing the roots of the fingers into the floor. The spine should have an even curve upward, while the tops of the feet should be resting on the ground. Hold for five to seven breaths while gazing in front of you. After a final inhale, exhale to come out of the pose.

Child pose (*balakasana*)

Benefits: Releases lower back tension, relieves headaches, prevents migraines and hypertension, and helps you feel grounded and nourished. Balances the pineal gland and calms the mind. Helps to open the groin and shoulder joints and improves spine flexibility.

Precautions: If you have neck issues, keep the neck in a neutral position. Avoid if you have a bad head cold, bad constipation, or knee issues, and avoid when you are in the midst of a migraine.

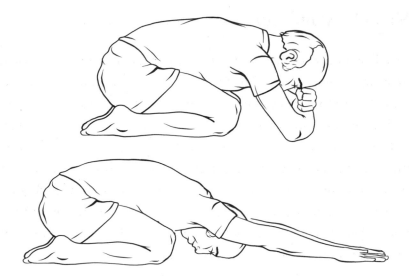

Technique: Sit on your heels in a kneeling position, with your feet and knees together, knees bent. If this is uncomfortable, move your knees out slightly or place a rolled-up towel on your ankles to raise your seat. From this position, inhale, raising your arms overhead and lengthening your spine, before exhaling and folding forward, bringing your stomach down to your thighs and your head toward the ground. You can reach your arms out forward and rest your forehead on the ground, or if your shoulders are tight, you can stack your fists and rest your forehead on them. This pose can be performed with the knees together or with the knees apart giving space for your abdomen to sink farther. Keep the shoulders relaxed and breathe deeply into the lungs. Hold for seven to ten breaths before inhaling and slowly coming up and out of the pose. This is an excellent resting pose that can be performed after any challenging posture.

Shoulder stand (*sarvangasana*)

Benefits: Improves spinal flexibility, particularly in the cervical area and upper spine. Improves blood circulation and detoxifies the abdominal organs by inverting them. Relieves stress and insomnia and is particularly effective at countering jet lag. Balances the thyroid gland and metabolic rate and helps with melatonin and serotonin secretions, which in turn help prevent depression and anxiety. Improves the immune system and energetically balances the system for enhanced meditation. Often referred to in yogic texts as the mother of all asanas because of its powerful physiological effects.

Precautions: If you have back issues or tight hamstrings, you can bend your knees during shoulder stand. If you have a headache or are menstruating, stay with the legs-raised pose.

Legs-raised pose technique: Lying on your back with your legs together and palms facing downward beside your body, take a deep inhale and slowly raise your legs up to a 90-degree position so that your toes are pointing up toward the ceiling. Hold the legs at this 90-degree angle for seven to ten breaths before taking a deep inhale, followed by a long exhale as you slowly lower your legs back to the ground. After completing the pose, rest for two to three breaths while lying flat on the ground. This pose is also known as half shoulder stand.

Full shoulder stand technique: Starting with legs-raised pose, inhale, lifting your back and hips off the ground, reaching your legs upward, and making your torso vertical. Then exhale, keeping your knees straight, lowering your legs down over your head, and moving your toes toward the floor behind your head. Bring your palms to your back for support, and then inhale, lifting your legs up toward the ceiling. Draw the shoulder blades together, and bring the palms closer together, walking them up your back to lengthen and lift the spine to a more vertical position. Also walk your elbows closer together, keeping the legs and toes pointed straight up. You may start with the torso at an angle and over time intend to make the torso vertical for the full shoulder stand pose. Focus on your toes, and take seven to ten deep, full breaths. To come out of the pose, take a deep inhale, bring your toes back behind your head, and with your hands on the ground (or on your back if you need the support), slowly unroll your back down to the ground while holding your breath. When your pelvis is on the ground, exhale and slowly lower your legs to the ground, keeping your head on the ground.

Fish pose (*matsyasana*)

Benefits: Expands the chest, helps improve lung capacity, and stimulates the thymus gland. Stretches the chest muscles, the shoulders, and the thoracic spine. Stretches the muscles around the heart, helping to relieve tension and stress, and also stimulates the thyroid, parathyroid, pineal, and pituitary glands. Helps keep arteries flowing well. It is a very good counter pose for the shoulder stand. Sometimes this pose can trigger emotional releases.

Precautions: If you have high blood pressure or upper back or neck issues, perform this pose with caution.

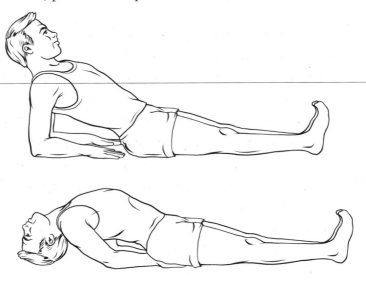

Technique: Lie on your back with your legs together, and place your hands underneath your glutes, palms facing downward. Inhale, lifting the head and chest up, bending at the elbows, and grounding through the forearms. With the chest up, exhale, arching backward and lowering the head back down so that the crown of your head touches the floor and your sternum is lifted up toward the ceiling. Keep your mouth closed and continue to lift and open at the heart area while squeezing your shoulder blades together. Keep your toes flexed and pointing upward. Hold for five to seven breaths before a final inhale, followed by an exhale to come out of the pose.

Wind-relief pose (*pawanamuktasana*)

Benefits: As the name implies, this is an excellent pose to relieve bloating and gas in the digestive system. It helps with elimination and creates a nice massage for the colon. It strengthens the abdomen and improves overall colon and uterine health. It is also a good lower back stretch, creating space in the sacrum.

Precautions: Practice this pose carefully if you have been constipated for a few days or if you have deep lower back or sciatica issues.

Technique: Lying on your back, inhale and raise your knees to your chest, rounding your back. Exhale, compressing your abdomen with your knees, and wrap your hands or arms around your knees and pull them in toward your chest. Inhale and raise your head, intending the forehead to the knees. Make sure your shoulders are relaxed and not hunching toward the ears. Keep the sacrum grounded into the floor. Hold this pose for five to seven breaths before a final inhale followed by an exhale out of the pose.

Variation: You can perform this pose with one leg at a time for a deeper colon massage and a deep release of sciatic issues.

SAVASANA: LEARNING TO RELAX

The relaxation at the end of a yoga practice, corpse pose (*savasana*), is a critical part of a complete practice. Vishvketu explains that performing your asanas is like climbing a fruit tree, and skipping savasana is like failing to actually pluck the fruit you worked so hard to reach. It is the final relaxation that gives the body time to energetically integrate and absorb all the benefits of the practice. It also helps us complete the detoxification process that the asanas set into motion and offload any stressors, imbalances, and negative emotions that we are carrying from the previous day and night. The effects of this cellular-level rejuvenation will continue on through the day and actually improve your deep sleep cycles that night. But savasana also gives our brain space and calm in a way that even sleep cannot match, complementing as well as supporting sleep: In sleep we are often not fully relaxed, the stress of the day lingering in our minds and manifesting in our dreams, shortening deep sleep cycles. We're left lethargic and alarm-clock dependent even after a full eight hours. Vacation might offer that elusive good night's rest—but the rest of the time, savasana can provide the relief we're missing at night—while at the same time improving the night's sleep. At a purely physiological level, savasana is a type of conscious sleep that elicits a deep relaxation response in our body and in our mind. So if you are particularly busy or stressed, make more time for this practice, not less. Vishvketu is famous for taking savasana every afternoon, and I think this twenty-minute "Indian siesta" is his secret to immense productivity running an ashram, a charitable school, a yoga teacher training program, and a global speaking-engagement schedule.

Connoting a lifeless state, savasana teaches us to let go and just be. Through it, we learn to let go of our bodies, our thoughts, our worries, and even our sense of self. Vishvketu explains that as we practice savasana regularly, we cultivate the ability to let go on a daily basis and, ultimately, prepare for the end of our life. As you build your natural ability to let go of things, you will move toward a life of more flow, ease, and contentment. The yogis see this practice as training for the final letting go, when we leave this earth, letting our soul move on, unattached to the ego, body, and life it once occupied.

By using "autosuggestion"—directing attention to relax different parts of our body one by one—yogis are able to relax their bodies deeply, down to their organs and subtle energies, and enable detoxification, rejuvenation, and healing at those deepest levels. Autosuggestion is a psychological technique related to the placebo effect; we almost hypnotize ourselves to effect an outcome. It is called autosuggestion because we both suggest and receive the suggestion. Even when we are sick, we can avail of this technique to help accelerate our healing process. We can direct our healing intention and positive energy to a particular area of trouble in our body within a savasana practice. This intentional focus can send healing energy to help support the area of concern and accelerate recovery.

Corpse pose (savasana)

Benefits: Savasana completes your yoga practice and allows the body to absorb the benefits of the yoga postures and breathing techniques and completes the balancing effect that yoga has on the glandular system and body chemistry. It is also very grounding for the body and mind and is excellent preparation for meditation after yoga practice.

Precautions: If you have back pain, a herniated disc, or sciatica, you can use a bolster under your knees to relieve any tension on the back.

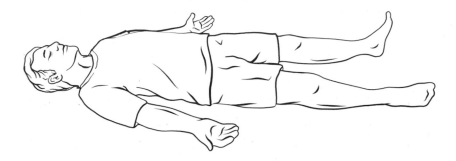

Technique: Savasana may appear simple, but as with any yoga pose, its subtleties are what make it a challenge. Lie flat on your back on a firm surface with your feet about one to two feet apart and your palms facing upward and resting about eight to twelve inches from your sides. Ensure your head and neck are straight and your body is symmetrical. It is best to be in a silent environment for savasana. Take two deep breaths, inhaling fully and exhaling fully through the mouth, sighing out loud if you are feeling especially tense. Then, letting your breath return to normal, begin to visualize your body relaxing into the ground, body part by body part.

Start by relaxing the toes one by one. Feel them getting heavier and sinking downward. Then take this visualization down the soles of your feet, to your heels, then up to the tops of your feet and into your ankles. Relax the shins, then the knees, and then the thighs and hamstrings. Relax your glutes and pelvis. When you get to this point, briefly scan your waist all the way back down to your toes, visualizing relaxation and sinking. Then continue relaxing the waist, the stomach, the hips, the lower back, the ribs, the chest, the upper back, and the shoulders. Then relax the arms, elbows, forearms, hands, and fingers. Now, scan from the collarbone all the way down to the toes, again visualizing relaxation and sinking. Then relax the neck, chin, tongue, cheeks, lips, nose, ears, eyeballs, eyelids, forehead, and whole head. Feel your entire head sinking into the ground. Now visualize all of your skin relaxing, and feel a pause here. Then imagine relaxing all the muscles in your body. Feel a pause again, and then imagine the relaxation of all the organs of your body, getting heavier and sinking down into the ground. Imagine all of your bones relaxing, getting heavy, and sinking downward. Then, just rest like this for as long as you feel is needed. Feel free to add in more specific body parts and autosuggestions that help you reach full relaxation. For example, you can imagine you are on a beach sinking down into warm sand as part of your visualization. A three-to-seven-minute savasana is suggested for the sequences in this book, but you can extend it as you need. For instance, if you are particularly tired or stressed, your body may need a longer rest.

To come out of the pose, start to return to your body, deepen your breath, wiggle your fingers and toes slightly, and move your head gently from side to side. Then gently raise your right arm above your head. Turn your body to rest on the right side in a loose fetal position, with the right arm now outstretched and resting along the ground. Keep your eyes closed, and rest in this position for a moment, feeling the benefits of the pose. Then, using your hands to help you up, come to a seated position. At this point, you would be very receptive to a meditation practice.

Variations: If you are in times of extreme stress or illness, or if, like Vishvketu, you find immense benefit from savasana, you can extend this pose up to thirty minutes. You can also use this technique as an aid if you are having trouble falling asleep, by just letting sleep naturally ensue from the savasana practice. While reduced sleep is never ideal, during periods of difficult deadlines or intense travel, a daily thirty-minute savasana can help supplement sleep (and replace excessive caffeine). During periods of insomnia, I use this technique while lying in bed, so even if I don't sleep, I am still getting some rejuvenation. If you have illness in a particular part of your body, you can also use the autosuggestion relaxation technique to visualize and set your intention on particular organs, muscles, or other body parts to relax and release them in order to aid in their accelerated healing.

For a special treat, you can also have a friend or partner read through this technique, doing the suggestion for you by calling out each body part one-by-one, so that you can have a deeper relaxation experience. This is the foundation of a technique called *yoga nidra*, in which a qualified practitioner can help you experience deep healing. Yoga nidra is now being used in the West to treat a variety of disorders, including high blood pressure, hormonal imbalances, depression, and PTSD.[2]

YOGA FOR DAILY RENEWAL AND BALANCE

As you incorporate a daily yoga practice on the mat, along with all the foundational work in the preceding chapters, you will be setting up your lifestyle for daily renewal, rejuvenation, and balance. Make your best effort to practice daily, even if just for fifteen or twenty minutes. Consistency and regularity are much more powerful for transformation than doing longer practices every several days. Just as you regularly brush your teeth to remove plaque, your yoga practice is a daily cleanse for your internal physiology and psychology, preventing calcified buildup. As with any routine, give it at least thirty days of disciplined regularity in order for it to stick, but don't beat yourself up if you miss a day or two here and there. Along with your daily practice, for some social interaction and connection, you can supplement with classes at a local studio. Practicing with others makes you feel part of a community and a qualified teacher can help correct any misalignments in your practice. Just be aware to do what is right for *your* body, and don't let any teacher overrule your innate wisdom. As Vishvketu says, "Listen to your body first, and to me second." The role of any teacher in the Vedic tradition is to be a facilitator of your own intuition and inner guidance rather than a hijacker of it. With your tuned-in approach to yoga, you will find more clarity in life, improved resiliency through challenges, and better decision-making at work. Your career, life, and relationships will take on a different trajectory with this better mental, physical, and spiritual health.

NOTES

1. Marlynn Wei, "New Research on How Yoga Boosts Your Immune System," *Psychology Today*, Feb. 22, 2018, https://www.psychologytoday .com/us/blog/urban-survival/201802/new-research-how-yoga-boosts-your -immune-system.
2. Emily Hill, "How 'Yoga Nidra' Works," *Huffington Post*, Apr. 14, 2017, https://www.huffingtonpost.com/entry/how-yoga-nidra-works _us_58efcea5e4b048372700d692.

SELF-REFLECTION QUESTION

1. How will you incorporate a daily yoga asana practice into your life? What time of day, how long a session, and how often will you practice?

CHAPTER TEN

Meditation:

Transcend Your Limitations

Just close your eyes, and stop thinking—that's it, right? This is what many of my clients initially think meditation is: the cessation of all thoughts. And therefore, they say, there is no way they can meditate. They think too much! In fact, meditation is the opposite: If you can think, you can meditate. Thinking is a natural product of being human, of being alive, and is therefore also a natural occurrence in meditation. Think of Descartes's *cogito ergo sum*—"I think, therefore I am." The average human being has over sixty thousand thoughts a day, and they are impossible to stop. So rather than seeing meditation as a means to stop thinking, see it as a means to let go of attachment to our thoughts and the world around us—so that we can connect to the level of our being that is behind those thoughts.

Meditation is the ultimate purpose of yoga. The practices we've covered so far are the foundation from which a powerful meditation practice can ensue. The practices and life guidelines of yoga—developing a clear sense of meaning in life, living in harmony with your surroundings and your own nature, eating the right foods, practicing breathing, yoga, and sound work—are designed to prepare our body, mind, and energetic system to go deeper into meditation. And synergistically, meditation enhances all those choices and directions, enabling us to transcend our limitations. Meditation is where we come to a deeper understanding of our true nature and where we tap into our potential. When we want to manifest more of who we are in our bodies, our minds, and our careers, meditation is what integrates all the various practices to send us on that path.

But what exactly is meditation, and what does it do? From Sage Patanjali, we learn the sutra *yogas chitta vritti nirodha*, which means that yoga is the progressive settling of the fluctuations of the mind. Meditation, as the culmination of all yoga practices, is the pinnacle of that sutra: Little by little, it settles the constant chatter of the mind. It is our mental chatter that precludes us from seeing the true reality around us and manifesting our deeper potential. As we question ourselves, sell ourselves short, or overthink things, we cloud our minds with false perceptions instead of confidently going forth. All of our dramas, self-perceptions, and self-limiting beliefs impede our greatness. Meditation trains us to calmly detach from this chatter and settle into the calm and clear mind beneath all those waves. *Mizu no kokuto*, a Zen saying, explains how meditation helps create "a mind still like water," where there are no ripples of our own perception, just calm, serene stillness with a true reflection of reality. Meditation is therefore a progressive practice that unfolds over time, not a here-and-there relaxation exercise. Its purpose is to help us develop a certain power of observation, without attachment or judgment, and a way to see the world more clearly.

Meditation is not about stopping thoughts but about listening—exploring the quiet that is already within us. I think of it as ducking down below the waves of life and experiencing the quiet that already exists below the surface. It is taking a break from the constant cyclic tumult of the everyday. It is a journey deep into the essence of your being, and it helps you live a life of more clarity. It is the ultimate practice toward an evolution of ourselves.

Before we go through a detailed meditation training, first it is important to understand what will result from a dedicated meditation practice. Meditation may be trendy to talk about, read about, and post about, but you must choose to practice it regularly in order to gain any of the benefits. Understanding the benefits intellectually also helps us sustain a practice when the going gets tough. The yoga texts describe a series of obstacles in meditation known as the *kleshas*. As meditation releases us from the grip of our thoughts, our thoughts mount a counterattack by coming up with ideas like "This isn't working," "I'm not making any progress," or "I liked things the way they were before all this meditating." I find the perfect response to the kleshas is to use that same intellectual mind to rationalize the health benefits of meditation. So when you feel meditation isn't working for you, just remember it is probably those pesky kleshas at play, and remember the ways the practice will benefit your life.

HEALTH, HAPPINESS, AND PEACE

Meditation has been shown to reduce stress and improve health, immunity, focus, and overall life satisfaction and happiness.[1] Our stress builds up from the fight-or-flight responses we experience daily—often without realizing it. Getting cut off in traffic, having an argument at work, or handling a family dispute triggers a physiological response in us that, through our evolutionary biology, is on par with a life-threatening danger.[2] During these daily, seemingly benign fight-or-flight events, hormones release to increase our heart rate, trigger our stress response, suppress our immune and digestive systems, and thicken our blood in preparation to handle injury—typical responses to emergency situations in the wild. Repeated occurrence of this stress response leaves our system depleted, leading to mild to extreme fatigue. I have had clients who, after years of chronic stress, suffer from adrenal fatigue—their overtaxed adrenal glands can no longer release life-saving hormones in actual dangerous situations.

The body's physiological response during meditation has been measured to have the diametrically opposite reaction as it does during the fight-or-flight response.[3] During meditation, our heart rate slows down, blood pressure normalizes, breathing slows, and digestive and immune functions reengage. Time spent in that mode gives us memory of that restful but aware state, and with regular practice, that peaceful awareness shows up in day-to-day life and actually lessens the duration and severity of the fight-or-flight response. Scientifically proven as a powerful antidote to stress, meditation is thus showing up in corporate offices around the world, helping employees have better mental health, relationships, and performance.

Meditation also gives us more sustained relief than we get from other vehicles for relaxation. We resort to alcohol, drugs, TV shows, spa days, vacations—all of which offer a temporary fix with varying degrees of negative fallout. Meditation offers us balance that sticks, integrating into our lives rather than only providing relief during the activity itself. To study this, the Mount Sinai School of Medicine (now the Icahn School of Medicine at Mount Sinai) partnered with the Chopra Center, a wellness center at the Omni La Costa Resort. They measured stress levels through blood samples and wellness surveys in people attending a weeklong meditation training at the Chopra Center versus a normal vacationer staying at the resort. Both groups exhibited an initial reduction in stress levels (vacations do help!). But a few months later, the vacationers presented higher stress levels than pre-vacation, and the meditators maintained the low stress levels measured during the retreat with their continuing meditation practices.[4]

The improved focus that results from meditation is a powerful benefit for those of us in the corporate world. Meditation itself is a practice in attention and concentration, so it builds those skills in our daily life. Major companies such as Target, Google, Aetna, and General Mills have recognized these benefits and have been instituting meditation and yoga programs for years as a tool for better performance and wellness in the workplace.[5] Meditation is also being used to improve counseling and coaching abilities, helping counselors stay focused on what a client or employee is saying rather than getting distracted and thinking about other things. By improving our ability to listen to our colleagues and focus in meetings, meditation offers us a daily practice in returning to the topic at hand.

Meditation is also scientifically shown to slow the aging process. Anecdotally, I have always noticed that the longtime mediators in my life appear so youthful. And research has proven it: Scientists know that the telomeres that cap each DNA strand start to fray as we age, somewhat like the plastic end of a shoelace, and that triggers the aging process of our cells. But meditators' telomeres have actually been shown to repair themselves, slowing the aging process.[6] Furthermore, neuroplasticity research has shown an increase in cortical thickness of meditators. This simple practice can have far-reaching effects on improving our lives as well as our actual cellular makeup.

IMPROVING AWARENESS AND INTUITION

The term *mindfulness* is deeply connected to meditation. It seems that the word *meditation* at one time connoted a religious practice of Buddhists or Hindus that might have offended those of other belief systems. So the term *mindfulness meditation* was a way of bringing a once esoteric practice to the mainstream. Though the term connotes awareness, don't make the mistake of thinking *mind*fulness indicates only mental awareness. Meditation is about transcending the mind to the level of spirit so that our mind can get out of the way. We are decluttering our minds—creating space in our minds, as Vishvketu says. From this space comes fuller awareness, allowing us to be more present in our experiences, more productive in daily life, and wiser in aligning our choices with our direction.

This improved awareness is why meditation is a powerful tool to cultivate better intuition. With less chatter in our minds, and a more heightened awareness, our observation skills improve. The mind becomes less cluttered, and our absorption and processing of information improves. We start to become more sensitive to our surroundings, to the people around us and their energies, and we start to hone an almost predictive ability. A friend of mind was the meditation teacher to a professional soccer team, and he explains how meditation gives athletes the edge over the competition through a more predictive sense for where the ball will go next. Vishvketu talks about meditation improving our ability to connect with our subconscious mind and use it to make more positive things happen in our life—hence why meditation is being used in psychology to heal the subconscious from past trauma.

This is also why Vishvketu is always able to tell if I have been doing my yoga and meditation practice diligently. I tried many times over the years to fake it, but he always saw through me. He can sense immediately from the outside if one of his students is happy on the inside. The way someone walks, their choice of words, their energy, and how they look are all subtle clues for whether a student has been practicing regularly. Indeed, research has shown that meditators are better able to read the microexpressions that more deeply reveal another. What a boon for business if you can better read your colleagues and business partner. A study performed by the preeminent facial expression researcher, Dr. Paul Ekman, found that meditators were able to detect microexpressions better than trained policemen, lawyers, psychiatrists, customs officials, judges, and even Secret Service agents, who are all typically trained and skilled at this.[7]

Not only do you read people better as a meditator, but you also have a better ability to disconnect from other people's drama and not see it as your own. By connecting to your inner calm, you can separate yourself from challenging or complicated situations. The clarity this provides makes it easier to find compassion for others and their disconnection from their own calm. You start to see someone's drama as separate from their higher potential. In a way, you start to separate the good person from the bad problem they might be having. By separating the problem from the person, you also realize, it is not your problem either; it is nothing that should knock you off-kilter. They are just struggling on their own journey, and you happened to get some flak from their issue. How often in life do we get pulled into someone else's negative story and start to lose sight of our own positivity? Through the awareness cultivated in meditation, we can better recognize someone else's drama as separate from ourselves, assert our own positivity, and naturally pull more positivity around us.

DIGESTING EMOTIONS AND REBOOTING THE SYSTEM

We've mostly discussed meditation in relation to yoga, but it is also a powerful tool in the mind-body tradition of Ayurveda. It is seen as a "digestive" tool for the emotional stressors of life. With food, if our digestive system is weak and we overeat or consume poor-quality food, our system cannot properly absorb the nutrients or fully eliminate the waste. A type of toxic residue known as *ama* in Sanskrit remains behind in our system, and as it accumulates, it becomes the seed of health issues—hence the fasting, cleansing, and diet techniques that flush the body of these excess toxins. Our mind and emotions also need to digest what we put into them. If we are hit with too many emotional traumas and dramas, or if we are at a susceptible time in our lives, we cannot properly absorb the nutrients from the experiences and gain the power and strength that could come from them. Instead, the traumas are imperfectly metabolized, and a toxic mental residue of emotional ama remains behind that becomes the seed of psychological health issues. Therefore, we need cleanses for the mind. Various techniques, including journaling, talk therapy, yoga, and massage, can be effective for this residual processing. But meditation may be the simplest and most powerful technique for regular and rapid ama processing (and the cheapest). During the states of consciousness involved in meditation, deep-seated memories and traumas are digested at a subconscious level, though the meditator may not be aware of what memories are being accessed and processed. This is why people in meditation sometimes experience odd sensations or emotional reactions, see colors, recall forgotten memories, or even experience bodily pain. A person's breath may speed up, or they may feel a sense of extreme restlessness. These are all signs of deep emotional processing taking place. Vishvketu likens a daily meditation practice to taking a bath for the mind, clearing off all the negativity and residual emotions from the mind's encounters with daily situations. It is no surprise, then, that clinical psychologists are prescribing meditation to people experiencing mental health challenges ranging from depression to anxiety to childhood trauma.[8]

Because of its mental cleansing and processing effect, meditation also improves sleep. We typically rely on active dreaming as the mechanism to subconsciously process emotions and experiences. The continual clearing of emotional residue reduces that reliance, decreasing our mind's chatter during sleeping hours and enabling us to achieve deeper and more restful sleep. The *Journal of the American Medical Association* (*JAMA*) published a study in 2015 outlining the sleep benefits of meditation, including improvement in sleep quality (reduced frequency of sleep disturbance incidents) and reduction in daytime impairment (measured through cognitive assessments).[9] Vishvketu describes meditation as a reboot for the brain—he likens our busy minds to having lots of applications open on your phone; eventually the phone will start acting up. If you just put the phone to sleep, it will wake up with the same issues. But if you reboot it, which shuts down all the applications, it will regain its quickness and efficiency. Rest only goes so far when we're never closing all our "applications" completely.

INTERPERSONAL PERFORMANCE

As we process our emotions, reboot our system, and develop a more lucid awareness of the world around us, we become calmer, more grounded in who we are and less reactive to other people's effects on us. As we gain these qualities, we naturally start to become better at interpersonal interactions, and our relationships improve. Compounding this effect, researchers have identified brain waves being released during meditation that mimic those of love and compassion. As we regularly experience these deep brain waves during meditation, we become more familiar with our mental capacity for compassion and love in our nonmeditating hours. We also start to find a sense of nonattachment to the drama that others might have triggered in us in the past. All of these outcomes help improve our human relations. Specifically in business relationships, we can maintain calm through stormy projects and discussions and also understand and empathize with our colleagues better, reducing tension and contributing to progress.

Improved awareness creates more productive conversations by tuning you in to the flow of the conversation and improving your understanding of the particular person in front of you. The book *Crucial Conversations*, a classic treatise on business communication, describes a successful conversation as one in which both parties equally contribute to a "shared pool of meaning."[10] We can imagine a faucet of information flowing from both parties. If only one faucet is filling up the shared pool, then the imbalance will result in the conversation going sideways. If both parties equally fill up the pool, then there is a healthy exchange of viewpoints and a more productive outcome. A regular practice of meditation improves our overall awareness so that in the midst of conversation, we are better able to sense those two faucets and their relative fill rates and adjust to ensure a more constructive and equal-sided conversation. The improvement in recognizing microexpression signals gives us another clue to read emotions better, which can help us adjust an interaction or even avert a full-blown disaster. By cultivating our intuition, our compassion, and our ability to focus and detach as needed, we start to see more clarity in all our human interactions and are able to better experience happiness for ourselves and the people around us.

STAYING ON PURPOSE

Meditation is also a powerful tool to help manifest our life purpose. After we discover our inner calling, it is the meditation practice that allows us to commune with our inner potential to help manifest that calling. As discussed previously, in yoga, the concept is called sankalpa shakti: the power of intention. It begins by setting a clear vision and goal for what we want to manifest in life. It then relies on actually letting go and not obsessing over the steps along the way to achieve the goal. If we get too obsessed mentally and try to over-engineer an outcome, our mind gets in the way of our success. A set-and-forget approach is much more powerful; we set our vision and then let go of sweating all the small stuff. The clarity we get from meditation helps us tune ourselves to naturally and gracefully orient every microdecision toward manifesting our goals and desires, making it easier to stay focused on the important parts of life. Vishvketu explains that meditation helps you stay on your right path and helps to inspire your life purpose and goals. It is during meditation that we integrate our physical, mental, and spiritual layers toward the manifestation of those goals. Just pointing your body in the right direction won't send you to your full potential. By adding the mental intention and integrating it at the spiritual level, you can achieve powerful results.

My transition from being a corporate executive to a Vedic teacher required innumerable coincidences and serendipitous events. I could not have forcefully engineered the significant events and people in my life to orient things this way. But, toward the end of my executive days, I did set my intention toward a life of more fulfillment and toward a career in which I could better leverage my deeper talents. My meditation practice heightened my sensitivity to what served me and what didn't and also increased my awareness of what a fulfilled life might look like for me. I set an intention and vision for what I wanted my life to be, and through diligent meditation practice, I cultivated the ability to tune in and orient myself toward that direction. I believe that setting my intention helped orient conversations and meetings with the right supporters to take place. It also tuned me into when to say no and when to say yes.

Your meditation practice can also help lead you toward smaller components of your broader life purpose and the fulfillment of your potential. Years ago, during my work at DaimlerChrysler, I was on one of my semimonthly trips to Mercedes Benz headquarters in Stuttgart, Germany, and ran into an old colleague I hadn't seen in many months. Being both German and an engineer, and quite direct in his mannerisms, Thomas pinched my belly and said, "Vish, you have come with something extra!" Wow, was it that noticeable? After months of regular transatlantic travel, meals out, long hours, and limited exercise, I had indeed gained about ten pounds. I resolved to lose the weight. I started calorie counting and exercising, but after two months, my weight had not changed. So I gave up—in a sense. I resolved to deal with my stress first. I replaced my weight-loss regimen with diligent meditation, every day for twenty minutes, no matter where on the planet I was, to try to get my mind in order. In just five weeks from honoring this resolution, I lost the ten pounds! To this day, I struggle to explain how it worked. It might have been my intention manifesting better with meditation, or reduced stress leading to less stress-related eating and drinking, or wiser dietary choices from an intuitive understanding of what suited my constitution. Whatever combination it was, I ascribe my most successful weight-loss program to meditation, and it can have the same effect on whatever factor of life is currently challenging you.

SLEEPING, MEDITATING, AND PRAYING

Sleep, meditation, and prayer are separate but complementary processes, with meditation serving to deepen and expand the benefits of the other two. The brain waves emitted during deep sleep are primarily delta waves, which are characteristic of a restful state without alertness. During meditation, theta waves are emitted, which are characteristic of wakeful, alert relaxation. Both have their benefits, but the aware relaxation of meditation has a specific function in processing our emotional residue and connecting to our higher self.

Prayer is also part of the yoga tradition, within the second limb of personal guidelines, known as ishvar pranidhan, the surrender to a higher power. It does not specify a particular faith but rather suggests prayer as a healthy practice of devotion, no matter the religious path. While prayer is a faith-based, devotional practice where we hold a dialogue with a higher power that we have faith in, meditation is more of a silent form of connection that detaches us from our concrete dialogue with ourselves or any higher power. Within prayer, we may ask for something we want, seek forgiveness, or express gratitude. In meditation, we move to a place where we are no longer asking for anything or even expressing anything. Both practices are a powerful way to feel connected and set powerful intentions. Both can provide healing energy and help us surmount difficult obstacles. But one is through a conscious effort and the other through a subtler connection. If you have a devotional practice in your life, it is excellent to maintain and connect with it on a regular basis. A regular meditation practice opens up a deeper connection and faith in prayer. Dr. Deepak Chopra, a world-renowned meditation and alternative medicine expert, explains that he thinks of prayer as talking to God and meditation as listening to God: In prayer, we ask for what we need and for divine grace; in meditation, we stop talking, stop asking, and listen to what God has to say back to us—whatever God means to you.

MEDITATION TECHNIQUES

The types of meditation techniques taught today probably number in the thousands. There are Buddhist meditations, Zen meditations, walking meditations, mindfulness meditations, guided meditations, and a host of other variants, some with more popularity than others. The first descriptions of meditation and its techniques, however, show up in the ancient Vedic texts from five thousand years ago. The Vedic knowledge system manifested through the insights gained during the deep meditations of the ancient sages. They described their techniques as a means to access the deeper layers of human insight. Yoga, at its core, is a meditation tradition, with all the frameworks, philosophies, and body movement techniques as support mechanisms for meditation itself. In the yoga framework, meditation does not stand alone as a solo practice; it is the crowning halo of the full system of well-being described in this book.

Vishvketu explains that the myriad approaches to meditation fall into two distinct categories. The first, *sakaar dhyan*, is meditation where the attention is focused on some concrete object or form, *sakaar* connotating form, and *dhyan* connotating attention. The other category is witnessing meditation, where the meditator is in a state of subtle observation of the self, without focus on any form; this is known as *nirakaar dhyan*, where *nirakaar* connotes formless. For instance, a mantra meditation is sakaar dhyan, since there is focus on a mantra. Any meditation that focuses on an image, sound, object, breath, or other object of attention is part of this category. Techniques that involve observing oneself as an external witness, observing thoughts with non-attachment, or just being fully aware of the experience of the present moment all fall into the formless nirakaar dhyan category. With any meditation practice, the object of attention (focus) or observation (witnessing) helps facilitate the mind's inward journey.

Lucy, a meditation teacher of mine, once explained that the mind is like a monkey, always jumping around from one thought to another. To calm the monkey, we give it a banana—a distraction. In meditation, the banana is the mantra, image, sound, breath, or witnessing task. That banana occupies the monkey for a little bit until it gets bored, drops the banana, and jumps to another thought. If you examine any meditation technique, you can always find the banana that is drawing the monkey mind away from the thoughts to a higher realm.

Every time you lose the banana is an opportunity for you to return to the object of your meditation. Lucy calls it exercising the "comeback muscle": every time your mind wanders in meditation, it is an opportunity to strengthen your comeback muscle. The practice of strengthening this muscle every time your mind drifts is the reason that meditation helps cultivate presence and focus. If you are like many of my clients who think they think too much for meditation, then meditation is a great opportunity to work out that muscle. Be patient with yourself; as with any training program, it takes a while to build your muscles to handle more and more repetitions. If you had a meditation session with lots of thoughts, think of it as high-intensity day at the gym.

Though there are many popular meditation techniques, formal and casual, the most powerful and basic technique is a quiet, close-eyed sitting practice. In this sitting practice, we look to the last four limbs of yoga (from Chapter 2), which specifically describe meditation. The fifth limb, pratyahara, is the withdrawing of the senses—not engaging with the senses of sight, sound, touch, taste, or smell. As we withdraw completely from the senses, we start to be able to focus on the object of meditation; this focused concentration is the sixth limb of yoga, dharana. Dharana precipitates the next limb, dhyana, which is the absorption of our body, mind, and spirit in meditation. Without any external stimulus—without the brain processing input signals from the eyes, ears, or other sense organs—we quiet down to the true state of meditation, where we can experience complete disconnection from our current space-time reality. When we are absorbed in deep meditation and unaware of time or sensation, we enter the state of transcendence, described by yogis as samadhi, the eighth limb of yoga. (Samadhi has multiple stages within it, but in a state of meditation, everyday people like us who aren't enlightened saints can experience the early stages of samadhi.) It is connection with this eighth limb that enables all the benefits of meditation to manifest in our lives. This is why it is recommended to perform meditation in a quiet place, sitting still, with our eyes closed to enable that sensory withdrawal. Guided meditations can help new meditators gain momentum, and they can also serve as powerful relaxation techniques. But the sound stimuli and consequent brain activity from that input prevent the full withdrawal of the senses described by pratyahara, so we don't get as much return on investment from our meditation time, so make sure that more active and guided meditations are supplemental and not your full practice.

HOW TO MEDITATE

Like your yoga asanas, your meditation practice is best conducted in an environment that is supportive to your practice. Ideally, you will create a dedicated place and time for your practice. The place might be a corner of a room or a small altar with a cushion or chair and objects that are meaningful to you. It should be quiet and free of noises, smells, TVs, pets, and other distractions. The routine and props signal to you that it is meditation time when you are in that space—much like when you feel relaxed when you see your bed nicely made.

Sit in an upright position so that your energy channels are able to flow freely. An upright spine enables the chakra system of your subtle anatomy (which will be discussed in Chapter 11) to properly activate during meditation. Lying down confuses your physiology between meditation and sleep. You can sit in a chair, on a cushion, or on the floor, ensuring your spine is straight, your chin level, and your shoulders relaxed. If you are on a cushion or on the floor, it is best to sit cross-legged. If it makes you more comfortable, use cushions to raise your hips to knee level or higher and to support your knees. You can rest your hands with palms turned upward on your lap or on your knees. To facilitate the withdrawal of the senses, close your eyes and turn off any music or background noise. The most important thing is to ensure that you are comfortable, as any discomfort will disturb your meditation.

It is best to meditate on an empty stomach and not immediately after vigorous exercise. Yoga asanas are a great way to prepare the body for a deeper meditation experience, so ideally meditation is performed at the end of a yoga practice after the savasana relaxation pose. If your schedule does not allow this, you can modify; perhaps meditate in the morning after waking up, and do your yoga practice later in the day. If you enjoy other types of meditation, such as walking meditation or guided meditation, you can continue those. But attempt a formal, quiet, seated practice on a daily basis for a few weeks and see if you notice any different results. It is wonderful to meditate twice in a day; as a saying in the Zen tradition goes, "Meditate every day for twenty minutes, unless you are very busy—then meditate twice a day for twenty minutes." You can always make one of your meditations one of quiet sensory withdrawal and the other the guided or moving meditation that you might be used to. The formal practice has a specific purpose beyond relaxation and stress-relief: to help connect to your deeper potential within. It is important to honor that for yourself. With full sensory withdrawal, you can experience the subtler realms of consciousness described in the yoga tradition.

In this book, we will explain three separate meditation techniques that you can use, from a beginner level to a more advanced level. (These are found in each of the yoga sequences presented in Chapter 9.) No one technique is better than the other, and after trying them you are free to choose the technique you like most and use that one. As you practice the meditation of your choice, you can start to lengthen the time up to twenty minutes. If you are ready to increase your meditation time and study more advanced techniques, be sure to seek the guidance of a qualified teacher.

BEGINNER PRACTICE—BREATH AWARENESS MEDITATION

Sit comfortably with your spine upright and your hands resting in your lap or on your knees with palms turned upward. Close your eyes, and begin to settle into your seat. Let go of any lingering thoughts or concerns for this bit of time you have put aside. Begin to pay attention to your breath. Don't force your breath or inhale or exhale in any particular manner. Just breathe in a natural, nonconscious way, in and out of your nose, keeping your mouth closed, and begin to observe the pattern of your breath.

Pay attention to your inhalation; notice where you feel the inhale. You may feel a heaving in your chest, a coolness in the back of your throat, a dryness as the air flows through your nostrils, or movement in your rib cage or abdomen. Wherever you primarily notice the inhale, gently rest your attention on that location during every inhale.

Now pay attention to your exhalation, and notice where you feel the exhale. Again, you may notice it in your rib cage or your chest, or you may feel a coolness or dryness at the back of your throat or in your nostrils. Gently rest your attention during each exhale on this natural spot of your exhale.

As you continue to inhale and exhale naturally and without deliberation, gently rest your attention on the inhale and exhale points. Continue to meditate with this awareness on your natural inhale and exhale. Note the companionship of your breath. It has been with you since the moment you were born, and it will be with you every moment of your life. If you notice your mind starting to drift to thoughts, this is that comeback muscle opportunity for you to notice the drift and gently return to the object of your meditation, your natural inhale and exhale. Similarly, if you hear sounds in the environment around you, feel sensations in your body, or visualize images and patterns in your mind's eye, just gently return to the spots of your inhale and exhale.

Continue to meditate on your breath, each time returning from a drift in attention to the spots of your inhale and exhale. Notice that you are not criticizing yourself for having thoughts or analyzing those thoughts, but simply observing that you are having a thought and returning your attention to your breath. If you have a breakthrough idea during meditation, it will come back to you after meditation if it is important enough, so let go of that idea and return back to your banana. Practice this for about three to ten minutes depending on the time you have available; you can set a timer with a pleasant sound so that you don't have to worry about keeping track of time. When the time is up, keeping your eyes closed, gently let go of the breath attention, and sit quietly for a minute or so, observing how your body and mind feel. Rest in this state of pure being before gently opening your eyes.

INTERMEDIATE PRACTICE—SOUND AND WITNESSING AWARENESS MEDITATION

Sit comfortably with your spine upright, your hands resting in your lap or on your knees with palms turned upward. Close your eyes, and begin to settle into your seat. Let go of any lingering thoughts or concerns for this bit of time you have put aside. Take a deep inhale, filling the lungs completely, then exhale using the brahmari honeybee breathing technique, making a humming noise with your mouth closed. Continue to hum until you have expelled all your breath, then take another inhale followed by the honeybee exhale. Repeat this for about five to seven rounds, and while doing so, gently examine in your mind where this sound is coming from, how it is being produced, and where it travels to. Observe the texture and tone of the sound and how it permeates your being and surroundings.

After the final round of brahmari, start to breathe normally without any conscious effort. Begin to observe yourself in meditation. Be a silent witness to yourself and your thoughts. As thoughts come to your mind, be a silent witness to them, observing them from afar but not engaging or indulging them. If a thought takes root and pulls you further from your witnessing perch, imagine the brahmari humming sound washing away the thought, and return to your witnessing observation. If the thought is too powerful, and you can't let it go by silently imagining the humming sound, you can take a brahmari breath out loud to wash away the thoughts and return to your witnessing awareness.

Continue to meditate in this manner for three to ten minutes (set a timer with a pleasant sound to tell you when your time is complete) before gently letting go of the meditation and returning to your being. Rest for a minute in a state of pure being, observing how your body and mind feel before gently opening your eyes and ending the practice.

ADVANCED PRACTICE—SOHUM MANTRA MEDITATION

Sohum is a very powerful mantra that acknowledges ourselves as existence personified. Its meaning could fill a book, but a direct translation is "I am that," or, "I am the soul," or, "I am beyond me."

In a seated position, with your spine upright, gently close your eyes, resting your hands on your lap or on your knees with palms turned upward. Settling into your seat and letting go of any thoughts or emotions that don't serve you right at this moment, begin to notice your breath, observing the points of inhale and exhale. Without forcing or controlling the breath, just observe and listen for any faint sound that correlates with your inhale and exhale.

As you inhale, imagine the sound *so*, and as you exhale, imagine the sound *hum*. On each inhale and exhale, feel the faintest sensation of these sounds. You are not forcing the sounds in your mind, rather faintly imagining and listening to them.

If you mind drifts away to a sound in the environment, a sensation in your body, or an image in your mind's eye, or you drift away to a thought or series of thoughts, without any judgment on yourself or analysis, notice that you have drifted, and gently return to the silent repetition of *so* and *hum* in sync with your inhale and exhale.

Continue to meditate on the mantra for about ten to fifteen minutes. When your timer goes off, keeping your eyes closed, gently let go of the mantra and rest for a minute. Rest in this state of just being and observe any feelings in your body or mind. Then gently open your eyes to end the meditation.

CHANGES OVER TIME

As you continue to meditate regularly, you will start to have an innate awareness of time. You will automatically come out of meditation when time is up, no timer required. This sense will carry over to sleep, where you set a wake-up time in your head when going to bed, and the next morning, you wake up at the time you intended.

As you begin to deepen your meditation practice, you may have different experiences each time. In some cases, you may have a lot of turbulent thoughts, whereas on other days, you may find a deep calm and rest. It is important not to ever judge your meditation sessions. It is a practice and a process. Whatever happens is right for where you are on your journey. Some days, you might be processing deep emotional residue that causes a more agitated meditation; other days you may be accessing deeper layers of your subconscious and not even be aware of what is taking place during your meditation. The important thing is to practice regularly to cleanse the mind and benefit from the cumulative effect that meditation offers. The expectation you may set based on one session may disrupt the experience of another session. Instead of analyzing each meditation, over a period of time, you will start to notice subtle changes in your behavior, and that is the sign that the meditation is working for you. You may be calmer, less prone to emotional trigger, more aware and present, or happier and more joyful overall.

As you incorporate the different techniques and frameworks in this book, your meditation practice is what will bind all the pieces together and propel you forward to a life of much more grace and flow. You will find that your meditations become much smoother, often not even being aware that a span of time has passed, as you enter states of transcendental consciousness. You will also find your intuition improving and things working out more easily in your work and life. As you become aware of the more subtle aspects of your personality and abilities, you will start finding value in some of the more esoteric aspects of yoga, which we will begin to explore in the final chapter.

NOTES

1. Emma M. Seppälä, "20 Scientific Reasons to Start Meditating Today," *Psychology Today*, Sept. 11, 2013, https://www.psychologytoday.com/us /blog/feeling-it/201309/20-scientific-reasons-start-meditating-today.
2. "Understanding the Stress Response," Harvard Health Publishing, May 1, 2018, https://www.health.harvard.edu/staying-healthy/understanding-the -stress-response.
3. Jeffery A. Dusek, et al., "Genomic Counter-Stress Changes Induced by the Relaxation Response," *PLoS ONE*, July 2, 2008, https://journals.plos.org /plosone/article?id=10.1371/journal.pone.0002576.
4. Monique Tello, "Regular Meditation More Beneficial Than Vacation," *Harvard Health Blog*, Oct. 27, 2016, https://www.health.harvard.edu /blog/relaxation-benefits-meditation-stronger-relaxation-benefits-taking -vacation-2016102710532.

5. Kimberly Schaufenbuel, "Why Google, Target, and General Mills Are Investing in Mindfulness," *Harvard Business Review*, Dec. 28, 2015, https://hbr.org/2015/12/why-google-target-and-general-mills-are-investing -in-mindfulness.

6. Marta Alda, et al., "Zen Meditation, Length of Telomeres, and the Role of Experiential Avoidance and Compassion," *Mindfulness*, Feb. 22, 2016, doi: 10.1007/s12671-016-0500-5; Richard J. Davidson and Antoine Lutz, "Buddha's Brain: Neuroplasticity and Meditation," *IEEE Signal Process Magazine*, Jan. 1, 2008, 25(1), 176–184, https://www.ncbi.nlm.nih.gov/ pmc/articles/PMC2944261/.

7. Daniel Goleman, "The Lama in the Lab: Neuroscience and Meditation," *Lion's Roar*, Mar. 1, 2003, https://www.lionsroar.com/the-lama-in-the-lab/.

8. J. Mark Williams, Ian Russell, and Daphne Russell, "Mindfulness-Based Cognitive Therapy: Further Issues in Current Evidence and Future Research," *Journal of Consulting and Clinical Psychology*, June 2008, 76(3), 524–529, doi: 10.1037/0022-006X.76.3.524; Roger Walsh and Shauna L. Shapiro, "The Meeting of Meditative Disciplines and Western Psychology: A Mutually Enriching Dialogue," *American Psychologist*, Apr. 2006, https://escholarship.org/uc/item/7885t0n6.

9. David S. Black, et al., "Mindfulness Meditation and Improvement in Sleep Quality and Daytime Impairment Among Older Adults with Sleep Disturbances: A Randomized Clinical Trial," *JAMA Internal Medicine*, Apr. 2015, 175(4), 494–501, doi: 10.1001/jamainternmed.2014.8081.

10. Kerry Patterson, et al., *Crucial Conversations: Tools for Talking When Stakes Are High* (New York: McGraw-Hill, 2011).

SELF-REFLECTION QUESTIONS

1. What benefits of meditation appeal to you the most, and how will those benefits improve your life?

2. What will your meditation practice look like? How often, for what length of time, and where will you practice?

CHAPTER ELEVEN

Tuning Your System
Through Sound

Yoga is a system of healing and connection with your true potential that relies on your body as an instrument for transformation, thereby preparing the body to be our instrument for life's journey. Since the philosophies of the tradition are cultivated through the physical and mental medium of our bodies, the practice of yoga must also seek to purify that bodily instrument. In that way, the body can better perform our journey across all aspects of life, including career, relationships, and spiritual growth.

One of the ways yoga helps purify its bodily instrument is by leveraging sound as a tuning mechanism. Just as we tune a guitar using the sound of a piano key, we can use specific sounds to harmonize our entire being. I have been to many a modern yoga studio where no sound is used in the practice, not even an *om* at the end, suggesting a salient missing piece in yoga's modern embodiment. In the trend toward exercise-oriented yoga, and in fear of offending customers, many studios and gyms refuse to incorporate chanting without realizing the powerful comple- mentary effect they are missing. To keep the bodily instrument of yoga's work balanced, tuned, and running smoothly, a complete yoga practice must involve sound and vibrational work, as well as specific chakra-tuning techniques and devotional work. All of these practices relate to tuning your system through energy and vibrations. This work can balance and heal your system by input- ting positive vibrations, and also tune your system like a radio, improving your awareness and energy flow.

TUNING INTO VIBRATIONS AROUND US

Sound is a fundamental theme in our human existence, affect- ing our bodies and minds more than we realize. Before we could write (or text!), we could only communicate with one another through sound. In the early days of human existence, we were highly attuned to sound and vibrations, since careful listening was central to our very survival and security. Hearing approaching predators, sensing weather changes, and hunting for dinner all relied on keen sound perception. As our technologies improved, we became less reliant on these acute faculties. Today, we are so desensitized to sound that a walk in the forest may seem silent to us, though there is so much taking place around us. If we really tuned in, we could become newly aware of the world around us. Animals can hear a sound alerting them to danger from miles away, sense changes in atmospheric pressure, or even sense the subtle thoughts or intentions of beings around them. Even domes- tic pets tend to gravitate toward visitors with a positive attitude and sense negative people much more quickly than we do. And during natural disasters like tsunamis, it is the animals that first sense the energetic and sound change in the atmosphere and begin to run to safety—hours before humans have any sense of danger. This skill was highly developed in our ancient ancestors, but as we moved away from living in nature, we started to disconnect from these senses as we no longer relied on them.[1]

We have access to the same vibrations around us that animals do, if we tune our senses and improve our attention. Sound waves travel through the atmosphere at varying frequencies and amplitudes. When those waves reach our ears, they elicit a vibration in our eardrum that our brain then processes and interprets as sound. Everything in nature has a vibration, from the subatomic level to the gross level. Everything is in motion, in vibration, even our bodies, down to our cells. The vibrations of sound around us therefore have a physical effect on the natural vibratory systems in our physiology. Just imagine a subwoofer booming; people say you can feel the bass in your liver. Sound vibrations are felt at every level of our body, mental, physical, and spiritual.

The concept of music can help new yoga students understand that vibration has a profound effect on healing our mind and body. Turn on some music that you love and observe your mental, emotional, and physical reactions to it. You might feel happy, sad, or reflective. Your body might relax, or it may want to get up and dance. Music affects our mood, manages stress, energizes us, and even improves our health. And it's not just anecdotal: Research on neonatal units playing classical music in the background has shown improved health metrics on preterm infants, including improved oxygen saturation levels, improved heart and respiratory rates, and reduced heart and breathing disruptions.[2] Music is also being used as therapy for acute pain, Parkinson's, and fibromyalgia because of its ability to trigger the relaxation response in patients and improve immune function.[3] Often, after a long day at the office, unwinding to music can often have a much more relaxing and rejuvenating effect than turning on the TV. In contrast, of course, listening to the news or honking horns can negatively affect our physiology.

According to the ancient Vedas, it's not just sound vibrations that affect our physiology and psychology. Thoughts are also vibrational in nature, similar to sound waves, and these thought waves have a physiological impact that affects our emotions and well-being. Vishvketu teaches that the first vibration we create, even before we make any sound, is that of our thoughts. They can be measured along with their frequencies and amplitudes similar to sound measurement. Sensors can measure and process these invisible brain wave frequencies and determine the cognitive state you are in—asleep, meditating, awake, happy, sad, and much more. Researchers today are still working to prove that humans can feel or sense thought waves from others, but the Vedic wisdom is firm: With the right processing capability, we can sense thoughts.

Therefore, when we sense "good vibes" or "bad vibes," "good mojo" or "bad mojo," we are receiving and interpreting thought waves. (Some might think of this as acute intuition, but the vibrational quality is essential in the yogic framework.) In business, when I observe that a person's "vibe" doesn't match their apparent mannerisms, it alerts me to proceed cautiously. For instance, someone who is very polite and charming may give off a vibration that indicates nefarious intentions. This sensitivity, if well cultivated through Vedic practices, can save us in many a challenging situation. Vishvketu's sensitivity to thought waves is why he can sense if his students have been doing their yoga practice or not; advanced yogis can sense if someone's thought waves are coherent (meaning they are meditating regularly) or scattered from the stresses of life. He explains that a similar phenomenon takes place when a mother is tuned in to her child's thoughts; this sense is much stronger than logical deduction. Receiving and processing thought waves is also a probable explanation for the phenomenon of telepathy, which has been proven to actually be possible. A 2014 study exhibited accurate mind-to-mind communication of a simple thought using a machine as the go-between (i.e., capturing electromagnetic waves from the brains of one group, then generating those waves back to another group). The Vedas knew innately that thoughts can be felt by us, and while the scientific community continues to work, you can benefit from that wisdom today.[4]

HEALING THROUGH VIBRATIONS

In the yoga tradition, the whole body is seen as a series of oscillations and vibrations down to our cellular level. As thoughts and sounds generate waves, those waves generate cellular-level vibrations, which elicit emotions on the mental level. This is what the "mind-body connection" means, from a yogic perspective: that our thought patterns have a distinct influence on our physical cells. The same principle, then, applies to sounds and vibrations from the outside world: In our daily lives, we are bombarded with sound frequencies and thought waves all day. Imagine for a moment the sound of a jackhammer on a sidewalk. Now imagine the sound of a trickling stream in the forest. Even just the simple visualization elicits two opposing reactions in our physiology. If sounds and people that cause irritation, fear, and anxiety surround us all day (just consider our news consumption), we'll feel anxious, stressed, or drained. The body and mind can recover balance from low doses of negative vibrations, but after enough consistent negative input, the body loses the ability to relax and self-heal, leading to physical and mental imbalance that manifests as anxiety, fear, irritability, depression, exhaustion, or physical ailments and trouble healing.

Just as a well-maintained radio with a clean antenna and functioning circuitry can tune in to silent radio waves and process them into sounds, so too can a clean physiology. If we are fatigued and desensitized, we are like a malfunctioning radio hearing static all the time. We can't see the signs of our road ahead, nor sense clues about what the right choices are for us. Our sensitivity and reception to positivity in life starts to degrade. As we cleanse our instrument and improve its reception, we start to tune in better to the right opportunities and the right choices that naturally amplify our success forward. Investing time in these practices pay massive dividends since you start to see more clearly the most efficient and multiplicative choices toward your well-being and success. You receive better signals from your own intuition. This "antenna polishing" begins with some lifestyle changes and ends with more clarity around one's life purpose.

The first step to improving our radio reception is to understand what positive and negative influences hurt or enhance our life experience. Take serious stock of who you surround yourself with, what media you consume, and what sounds are prominent in your life. Assess what effect these waves might be having on your psychology and physiology. Evaluate whether you are so used to a negative vibration that it doesn't bother you anymore; you may be tuning out positive vibrations or information that is important to our success and well-being. We must take time on a regular basis to heal from contracting sounds and thought waves.

COMMUNITY VIBRATIONS

The yogis felt intuitively that the community you surround yourself with has a vibratory effect on your own thought waves and on your actual physiology. The Sanskrit concept of *sangha* describes the gathering of like-minded, positive people who are living life toward their purpose. Regularly spending time with your "tribe" generates positivity that the ancient yogis identified as thought-wave influence. Such an environment can be found in many monasteries, ashrams, temples, mosques, churches, synagogues, and other such spiritual centers and communities. Vishvketu explains how in his ashram, after years of spiritual seekers staying, gathering, and practicing yoga together, the place has a special positive vibration. When I visit, I feel immediately enveloped with positive energy and love—a feeling of home—even if the ashram is full of people I do not know.

Practicing yoga and meditation in groups also generates these powerful thought-wave vibrations. When a group of people meditate together, they feel a deeper sense of connectedness in their meditation; this is known as *coherence*. In this silent activity, a harmonization of brain waves deeply penetrates the entire being of the group. Again, positive thoughts generate positive waves, which generate positive feelings that permeate our entire physiology.

A similar effect occurs in groups of people praying together. Studies on the power of prayer in healing, though early and not wholly conclusive, suggest that prayer leads to shorter hospital stays, improved immune function, and reduced anxiety.[5] From a yoga viewpoint, the positive thought waves generated by prayer improve the harmonization of the healing cells in the sick person's body. For those of us who don't attend churches, temples, mosques, or synagogues, just being around positive community has a similar effect. The positive psychology movement has correlated positive thinking with more well-being and happiness, and research suggests that just surrounding yourself with happier people improves your well-being. For instance, one study involving over four thousand participants over twenty years showed that just having a happy friend living within a mile's radius could increase happiness by 25 percent.[6] Dan Buettner's work on Blue Zones and the principles for longevity reinforce this principle, showing that associating with the "right tribe" of positive, like-minded people is one of the key factors of happiness and well-being.[7] The Vedic explanation for this phenomenon is that the positive thought waves around you make your own thoughts vibrate more positively, which in turn delivers more positive vibrations to your physiology.

MUSICAL VIBRATIONS

In addition to surrounding ourselves with positive community, we can use music as a source of vibration to cultivate more joy and expansion in our lives. We can use sound as a practice just by listening to music that brings us joy. Positive sound vibrations from music that you love can infuse your body with happiness and joy and lift up your psychology. I advise my clients to listen to music they love or indulge in singing or dancing on a daily basis. The important thing is to lose yourself completely in the joy of the sound-based activity. This can have a powerful harmonizing effect and slough off the burden of the day's negative sounds and influences. You should feel some kind of devotion, expansion, and happiness. Combine the positive vibrations of community and music by practicing music with others, perhaps singing in a group; this can produce the same type of coherence that happens in group meditation or group prayer.

Many religious traditions combine sound work with positive community through group devotional practice such as song, music, dance, and chanting. *Bhakti yoga* is the school of yoga known as the path of devotion; it is the idea of surrendering to a higher power through selfless love, and it often involves sound, music, and community. (Other schools of yoga are *karma yoga*, the path of selfless work; *jnana yoga*, the path of study; and *raja yoga*, the path of practice found in this book.) Through the medium of music and singing, with others or on our own, we learn to let go of our attachment to stress and problems and feel a sense of bliss as the heart opens. Within the yoga tradition, specific devotional chants are targeted at unlocking inner joy, healing deeply, and cultivating connection with the self and a higher power. By combining powerful Sanskrit mantra, which has an activating effect on the physiology, with devotional rhythms and melody that open the heart, these yogic chants (*kirtan*) are a potent tool for sound-based balancing work. These specific devotional chants are part of the everyday culture in India, but they can have powerful effects on any of us.

I experienced the power of devotional chanting when my elderly mother was in the intensive care unit after open-heart surgery. She had become dependent on the ventilator, no longer able to breathe by herself, and we had to decide whether to pull her off life support. As I sat by her bedside listening to the beeps of the machines and the air rushing in and out of the ventilator, processing this grave decision, I started to sing a Krishna Das kirtan chant that I often listened to (often to quell my stress in LA traffic). Instead of debating what to do next, which would be my tendency, I just let go and sang. As I chanted, lost in the obscure Sanskrit hymns, I became oblivious to the hospital setting and felt a sense of opening in my heart. For a moment, I forgot where I was and the serious situation I was in. I just felt incredible love and connection and noticed that tears had been streaming down my face onto my mother's bedside. I am not sure what happened in that moment; perhaps she felt my love and found strength, or perhaps the music infused in her physiology to counter her illness as the Vedas would believe. But when the doctor returned for my decision, my mother was breathing through her own power. We slowly pulled her off the ventilator, and she remained able to breathe on her own. She has been living many years since that moment. If nothing else, I am grateful that chanting and music helped me find love and connection in overwhelmingly difficult circumstances.

For a long time, as a left-brained engineer, I didn't relate to all this singing and dancing bhakti yogis do. My experience with my mother was my first clue that I didn't have the world figured out quite right. The next was a few years later in India at Vishvketu's ashram, where everyone else seems to really get this idea. It was a morning gathering down in the courtyard area, on a cool day, with a group of yogis bundled up in shawls and knitted caps, playing drums and cymbals and singing some devotional chants. They were blissfully swaying away to the music, and smiling so broadly, I figured they were all faking it. People don't smile like that. But I took a seat and started singing along, pretending to smile just like the others. Inside, however, I was sending out all kinds of negative thought waves: *This isn't for me, this isn't working, I am not a bhakti yogi, I can't keep tune, I don't have rhythm, why are they all still smiling so much?* (The same mental chatter as when we meditate.) Then I glimpsed the expression of a statue I had seen many times before. But this time, all of a sudden, it had a profound effect on me. I felt a surge of expansion, and I started feeling those tears again, streaming down my cheeks. I felt completely connected and overwhelmingly inspired by everyone and everything around me—in short, I felt intoxicated with joy. I noticed myself, like I was watching myself, singing loud in tune and in rhythm, with a massive smile on my face, one with the group. Go figure. This is when I learned that faking it till you make it really works when it comes to devotional practice. For some people, the idea of surrendering and devotion through music is second nature. For others like myself, who are overly logical and a lot more skeptical, it takes a bit of time just going through the motions, before I actually reach the feeling of devoted connectedness.

Devotional music targets the opening of the heart and trains us in the art and power of surrender. Sound-based devotional practice has a powerful healing and heart-opening effect and should be practiced on a regular basis—I recommend at least weekly—to help us get out of our heads and into our hearts and allow the divine potential in us to help us on our paths. Vishvketu explains that chanting puts us into a trance and releases us from our mental and logical minds, landing us right into our hearts. Sri Ramakrishna, a learned saint in the Vedic tradition, refers to this state of pure connectedness to the divine as *God intoxication.*

As an entry-level approach, we can just listen to music that makes us smile with joy. A step deeper is to sing along with that music we love. Then, we can try listening to devotional music, from any tradition, that resonates with us and makes us feel connected. An even deeper experience comes when we listen to music and sing along with others, similar to an experience at a concert, or what I experienced at the ashram. If there is a religious or spiritual tradition that you resonate with, try deeply listening and experiencing some surrender as you listen to music from that tradition, or join with others in enjoying a live experience. See if you are able to bring yourself to an emotional place as a way to connect to your deeper being. By chanting ourselves along with the devotional music, we can deepen the feeling of sound-vibration healing taking place in our physiology. In times of trouble, I tend to turn on devotional music that I know the words to and then chant along or sing along to it. Pick whatever music reminds you of divine connection, and as you listen and sign along, it will open that connection in you. Devotional music from any tradition achieves similar healing

and empowering effects. My personal favorites span multiple traditions: Sanskrit call-and-response kirtan music, Hindu devotional
songs (*bhajans*), Qawwali music of the Sufi Islamic tradition,
Gregorian chants of the Catholic tradition, Christian hymns, and
Tibetan Buddhist chants. Listening to these types of music live with
other people can be an ecstatic experience. Explore different styles,
and find which has the most powerful effect on you. Even just singing along without knowing why will eventually open something up
in you—fake it till you make it.

MANTRAS

The next level of advancement in sound work is to use specific
mantras of the Vedic knowledge system as tools to harmonize the
instrument of our body and mind. Based in Sanskrit, they are like
codes for unlocking specific energies in your body. In Western culture, the word *mantra* has come to reference something we say
over and over to set an intention for ourselves. And this is a pretty
good definition, since mantras in the traditional sense are usually
repeated to effect some change in our lives. The word *mantra* is
divided into two parts: *Man* means "mind," and *tra* means "instrument." So *mantra* means "an instrument of the mind." Mantras
are used as a way to help our mind effect certain outcomes. You
can almost think of a mantra as a tuning fork that helps us tune
our being in a very deep and specific way for better performance.

In the Vedic tradition, there are mantras for everything,
and they range from single syllables, single words, and names
to complex constructs with particular meter and tonality. There
are specific mantras for birth, marriage, eating, bathing, sleeping, dying—anything you can imagine. Each produces a specific
combination of energetic vibrational sounds that release specific

energy to enhance the particular activity or intention. Often the vibratory quality of the sound is more important than any understanding of the meaning of the mantra.

While positive vibrations are about whole-body healing, and devotional chanting is targeted at opening the heart and surrendering to a higher power, mantras take a much more mathematical and specialized approach that targets specific energy centers beyond the heart. Mantras in the Vedic tradition are in the Sanskrit language, which is also the language of the ancient Vedic texts. Sanskrit is the ancient Indo-Aryan language used thousands of years ago in the ancient Vedic culture. One of the oldest languages known to humankind, it influenced the development of Greek and Latin. Scholars often call it the mother of all tongues because it influenced Latin, which in turn influenced the modern romance languages.[8] Vishvketu teaches that Sanskrit is unique because it is based on specific vibrations that communicate both inward and outward relative to our being. Just the sounds alone communicate subtleties beyond the mundane literal meaning. Therefore, it is important for practitioners of yoga to know and use Sanskrit terms. English translations cannot fully convey the full meaning and its subtle, nonintellectual elements.

The ancient yogis believed that these specific sounds had a profound effect on the mental, physical, and spiritual levels and could activate specific physio-energetic locations in our being. They developed a system of both physical anatomy, which mapped the physical organs and tissues of the body, and subtle anatomy, which mapped various energetic systems and centers related to our being. The energetic systems are very complex and consist of numerous channels and nodes. Each of the fifty unique sounds in the Sanskrit alphabet is said to correlate to specific energy centers in this subtle anatomy system.[9] The ancient yogis were able to tune in to these specific locations and decipher the vibratory sound of each location, and the collection of sounds that comprised the most important energy locations of the body became the Sanskrit alphabet. So, as each letter of the Sanskrit alphabet is pronounced, its vibration activates specific energy centers that create specific physiological and psychological effects. And the combined vibrations of Sanskrit words activate synergistic energy centers. A Sanskrit mantra, therefore, is a tuning instrument created by a specific combination of root sounds that synergistically activate and tune energetic centers within us. In essence, mantras are sounds designed to effect specific outcomes in the instrument of your physiology.

A Sanskrit word communicates meaning at the intellectual level and at the subtle body level, into your physiology and your mental state. Mantras can thus change mood, emotions, mental states, and physiological states. The ancient yogis believed that sounds found in nature and the resonant sounds of our energy centers are healing and can reverse the effects of the negative sounds we might encounter as part of daily life. We can use sounds of nature for healing or use the Sanskrit language—the energetic language of our body—in a more targeted way to unlock specific energies that transcend our physical, mental, and subtle bodies.

Vishvketu refers to a mantra as a frequency-based antibiotic. Depending on the affliction that has entered your body or mind, a specific mantra can be prescribed as an antidote. In the West, this concept takes the form of mantra healing, sound healing, crystal healing, or music therapy. Many of the specific approaches using mantras have been lost in antiquity, and Vedic scholars are continually interpreting new findings from the ancient texts. But even today, an Ayurvedic physician may prescribe specific mantras along with herbal remedies and lifestyle changes to target your particular imbalance. The Vedic astrology tradition uses mantras as a way to manifest planetary archetypes or energies in our being; for instance, a mantra for the planet Mars would give us some more fiery pitta qualities or enhance our warrior spirit, while a mantra to the Moon might give us some calming, tranquil kapha energy and enhance our mental equanimity.

CHAKRAS

In the yogic model, the energetic centers that mantras activate are known as chakras. Our subtle anatomy consists of thousands of energetic channels known as *nadis*, which carry and distribute our prana throughout our being, like a complex, intersecting series of railway lines. The major junction points of nadis form the main energetic distribution centers of the body: the chakras (wheels). These energetic junction points are like busy train stations, where many channels pass through and meet. If everything is flowing well, the trains run on time without collision and deliver energy to all the parts of our being where it needs to go. If there is imbalance, the train station jams up with delays, collisions, and confusion. But playing the right sound through the loudspeakers of the station returns balance: The trains run on time, stop colliding, and smoothly carry their precious energy cargo to the right places. In other words, sound—specific sounds coded to specific vibrations—is what heals and balances our energy centers, our chakras.

Each of the chakras has a vibratory quality that is related to a specific area of our life. To tune these chakras is to help improve their vibration to better flow energy to an area of our life. There are different ways to think about how this process works. In *Eastern Body, Western Mind*, which correlates the chakra system to Western psychology, author Anodea Judith describes a chakra as "a center of organization that receives, assimilates, and expresses life force energy." Vishvketu refers to chakras as magnets that receive frequencies of sound and thoughts. I like the analogy that they are like radio stations that can tune in to very subtle waves in our environment—what we think of as gut feelings and instincts. If a chakra is imbalanced, it acts like a malfunctioning radio, hearing static instead of the subtle vibrations around us. A healthy chakra can tune in to find more harmony in our lives. If we examine our life and see imbalance in a certain area, we can work on tuning that specific chakra with specific sounds—specific vibrations. As it comes into harmony, we start to make better intuitive choices in that area of our life. (People sometimes incorrectly call a chakra *blocked*, but it would be more accurate to say *out of tune*.)

The health of our chakras also affects what we sense about others. If your chakras are tuned and healthy, you sense both love and danger better—both good vibes and bad vibes. If they are out of tune, you have to rely solely on intellect to make judgment calls. I find the best decisions in business come from gut backed up with some analytics. The gut feeling is tuned in to the information in your chakra system. Tuning your chakra system through yoga asanas and mantras improves your gut feel and helps you read others and yourself better. As I mentioned earlier, regular yoga techniques helped me read the reactions of expressionless investors, and chakra tuning helped improve my sensitivity to others' energies.

For everyday students of yoga, the primary seven chakras are the ones we need to know about. Each of these chakras has a specific location in the body, and though they are part of the subtle anatomy, they each correlate to particular sets of organs, glands, and psycho-emotional areas of our life. So, we can send positive energy to specific parts of our physical anatomy as well as to specific areas of our life. For instance, when I was feeling strongly about switching to executive coaching, I had a tremendous amount of passion, but I didn't know how to start manifesting this new life. I started a sound practice to develop the energy flow in my solar plexus chakra, which correlates with manifesting things. Tuning this chakra supercharged the goals, visions, and action steps I was developing.

As we know, sound is the most powerful and primary tuning mechanism of chakras; healers use sound bowls and gongs in addition to mantras. But the sound work is enhanced through yoga asanas. Poses correlate to various chakras, working as a preparatory step in activating the chakras. When you perform a yoga pose, you are working your physical anatomy and your subtle anatomy simultaneously, exercising and preparing those nadi channels and chakra junction points for tuning. It is like warming up the strings before you begin to tune an instrument, or ensuring proper connection to all the speakers in the train station before you play harmonizing music to get the trains running efficiently. Once the physical and subtle preparation is done through yoga asanas, the specific mantra sounds for each chakra can then be used to more effectively tune and harmonize the particular chakra.

CHAKRA MANTRAS

The following is a listing of the seven major chakras, with their locations, the physical systems they affect, their energetic influences on various aspects of your life, and the specific tuning mantra that works on that chakra. Ideally, at the end of your yoga asana practice, you will focus on each anatomical area of a particular chakra and chant the corresponding mantra. If a specific issue you are having is described under a specific chakra, likely there are some train delays happening in that particular train station, and the right energies are not flowing smoothly in that part of your life—in other words, that chakra might be out of tune. If you are having specific issues in an area of your life, you can use a *japa* practice, repetition of a mantra, to work more deeply on improving energy flow through that chakra: While focusing on that chakra's location in your body, chant its specific mantra out loud 108 times daily for thirty days, using a 108-bead *mala* (garland) to count the repetitions with your fingers. (Note that malas typically contain 108 beads plus a main pendant bead, known as the guru bead, which you don't count in japa practice.) The number 108 carries strong significance in the Vedic tradition (as well as other traditions such as Buddhism and Jainism), with connections to astronomy and Vedic astrology.[10] To align with natural cycles, start the practice on a new moon and continue until the next new moon.

As you tackle challenges in the physical realm, trust that we are complex beings, and a more esoteric angle like this can be just as important to your holistic health and growth as the more concrete elements of your practice.

CHAKRAS

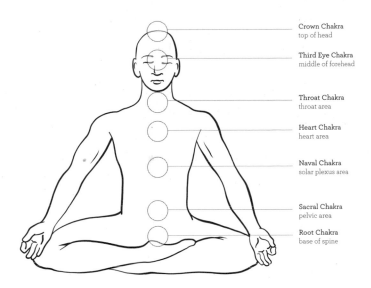

Crown Chakra
top of head

Third Eye Chakra
middle of forehead

Throat Chakra
throat area

Heart Chakra
heart area

Naval Chakra
solar plexus area

Sacral Chakra
pelvic area

Root Chakra
base of spine

Root chakra *(muladhara chakra)*

> **Key Word:** Grounding
> **Location:** Base of spine, near rectal area
> **Mantra:** Lum (rhymes with gum)
> **Life Areas:**
> - Feeling grounded and stable
> - Sense of security and survival instincts
> - Connection to ancestors and family
> - Financial stability and security
> - Commitment and lasting partnerships
> - Physical body health, particularly bones and muscles

Sacral chakra *(swadhisthana chakra)*

> **Key Word:** Creativity
> **Location:** Sacrum, pelvic area, between navel and reproductive organs

Mantra: Vum (rhymes with gum)
Life Areas:

- Creativity and birthing of ideas
- Rejuvenation, renewal
- Desire, sensory pleasures, food, sex, indulgence
- Clarity of direction and purpose
- Busyness (Vishvketu calls this the "teenager chakra," being busy without clear direction)
- Circulation and regulation of body fluids such as blood, hormones, and reproductive fluids

Navel chakra (*manipura chakra*)

Key Word: Manifestation
Location: Just above navel, solar plexus area
Mantra: Rum (rhymes with gum)
Life Areas:

- Fear, judgment, jealousy
- Manifestation and execution of ideas (very important for business)
- Action, making things happen, vitality
- Energy, motivation, confidence, willpower
- Transforming, releasing negativity
- Digestion, homeostasis, and overall health

Heart chakra (*anahata chakra*)

Key Word: Love
Location: Heart area
Mantra: Yum (rhymes with gum)
Life Areas:

- Love, compassion, kindness, happiness, and contentment
- Connection with others
- Letting go and surrendering to a higher power

- Nurturing, devotion, giving and receiving of love
- Letting go of emotions
- Physical and emotional issues with the heart

Throat chakra *(vishuddha chakra)*

Key Word: Communication and expression
Location: Throat
Mantra: Hum (rhymes with gum)
Life Areas:
- Saying the right thing at the right time
- Communication and expressing yourself, speaking, singing
- Regulation of input and output, or what you take into your body and what you express
- Sharing at a deep and honest level
- Release of repressive emotions through words (If you do a lot of heart chakra work and release many emotions, they still need to be expressed via throat chakra work. This is why talk therapy can be helpful, but only if the heart-level work is released first.)
- Thyroid and parathyroid glands

Third-eye chakra *(ajna chakra)*

Key Word: Intuition
Location: Middle of forehead just above eyes
Mantra: Om
Life Areas:
- Concentration, intuition, gut feeling, psychic powers
- Awareness in life
- Beyond the mind (In Hindi there is a saying, *"Man banau, dhyan se karo,"* which means use your mind to set your intention, then execute with awareness—by letting go

of the mind. Once you set your clear goal, the third-eye chakra is where you cultivate awareness beyond the mind to execute the goal.)

- Becoming sensible with your powers of sensitivity (gained through yoga practices)
- Inner guidance and power of discriminatory thought (knowing what is right and wrong)
- Pituitary gland (known as the master gland)

Crown chakra *(sahasrara chakra)*

> **Key Word:** Spirituality
> **Location:** Crown of the head
> **Mantra:** Sohum
> **Life Areas:**
> - Spiritual evolution

After your yoga asanas, which open and prepare the chakras for tuning, sit upright, with your eyes closed, and visualize the location of each chakra in your body one by one. As you visualize the chakra location, take a deep, long inhale, then chant the specific chakra's mantra out loud during a full and complete exhale. Go through each chakra one by one. Completing the seven mantra-chakra visualizations is a nice daily tuning that helps energy continue to flow positively to all areas of your life.

Enjoy experimenting with the chakra mantras and the visualization and activation of your chakra system. Start to observe whether challenge areas of your life seem to group within a particular chakra area. Problems that seem disconnected may have a relationship to one chakra, so by practicing the mantra for that chakra, you can overcome multiple issues simultaneously.

SEED MANTRAS

Even simpler than the chakra mantras are *bija*, or seed mantras. There are very simple but highly effective sounds derived from the Sanskrit alphabet and also sometimes from sounds in nature. They activate a specific area of the physiology or energetic system. A seed mantra carries no meaning but is just a root sound that, when combined with others, makes a mantra with meaning.

The following three seed mantra sounds are very powerful for opening up the vocal cords if your career involves a lot of speaking or other vocal work—especially if you are in a role of persuading others through talking. Three seed mantras we recommend are:

aa (pronounced ahh with the mouth open)
ee (pronounced eee as in the word cheese)
uu (pronounced ooo as in the word crew)

While these may seem like simple sounds, they are very significant because they form the first three vowels of the Sanskrit alphabet. They are known as the primal vowels. The *aa* sound vibrates the upper body organs, while the *ee* sound vibrates the head area and the *uu* sound vibrates the face.[11] The brain, the lungs and rib cage of the upper body, the mouth, and the face are our tools for verbal expression. By specifically vibrating and tuning these areas of our body, we can thus tune our speaking abilities. Along with yoga asanas and pranayama techniques, where we improve the flexibility of the diaphragm, rib cage, and lungs, vocal exercises also open and loosen all the physiological systems involved in improving our speaking. The system together is like a supercharged version of vocal warm-ups and practice.

To practice this technique, inhale deeply then chant out loud *aaa* until your breath is fully expelled. Do the same for *eee* and for *uuu*. Repeat as many times as you wish for vocal toning—at least five to seven rounds. Make sure you are making the sounds from deep in your belly so that you are using the whole of the lungs to make the sounds and tone the vocal cords.

OM: THE PRIMORDIAL SOUND

Finally, one of the most powerful mantras in the Vedic tradition is *om*, a word that has now permeated popular culture. The practice of saying *om* on a regular basis has many healing effects, such as calming stress and balancing emotions, and therefore, we recommend chanting it at least once at the end of every yoga practice, or up to three times. It sounds similar to the word *home*, without the *h*. Ideally, as you articulate the sound, you spend equal time on all three components of the sound: the *ahh* that initiates the sound, the *ohh* that forms the middle, and the *mmm* that completes the sound. You should take a deep inhale and chant the sound over the course of a complete exhale. *Om* can also be followed by saying the mantra *shanti* three times, which translates as "deep peace." The first *shanti* sets an intention for peace for yourself, the second asks for peace for those close to you in your life, and the third sets an intention for peace for all living beings. So, in combination, you would say out loud, "Om, shanti, shanti, shanti," at the end of your yoga practice.

If you want to go deeper, chanting *om* 108 times out loud can be a full practice by itself and can elicit very powerful changes in your being. *Om* is considered to be the primordial sound of the universe, and by chanting it 108 times—a count that is astronomically connected to our universe—you improve its potency.[12] At the surface, it can help calm you and restore balance in stressful times. On a deeper level, it can help harmonize your energy channels and help you move through challenges. Try it at least once to see if you want to make it a weekly practice. A seated position with eyes closed is ideal for any japa practice, but anywhere you feel comfortable, even a noisy environment, can work because the sound you are making helps you focus. (You can also use a mala as described earlier to count out the 108.) Practice it weekly or any time you feel you need it as a complement to your regular formal meditation practice. The *om* practice can be thought of as the catchall, super mantra that can be used for any purpose. Even if you just set an intention to overcome something that is troubling you and then complete an *om* chanting practice, you may find some positive change.

OTHER MANTRA PRACTICES

Stemming from the wisdom surrounding vibrations and the energetic body, mantras are used throughout the Vedic tradition for healing and transformation. There are thousands of mantras, ranging from single syllables to complex stanzas. You can attend Vedic fire rituals at various ashrams and yoga centers to experience longer mantra practice, and you can explore books on mantras. Recitations of mantras are also available online and in recordings that you can look up. A common mantra used by yogis is the *gayatri* mantra, an incantation that seeks to lead us to light. Another one that I use often is the *mahamrityunjaya* mantra, which sets an intention for powerful healing. Both Vishvketu and I chant these two mantras on a daily basis in the morning as an opening to yoga practice. There are many more complex mantras in the yoga tradition that can be used in different ways to elicit powerful changes in your life. It is beyond the scope and medium of this book to effectively teach complex mantra practices, but if you are interested, be sure to find a qualified and knowledgeable teacher to train in mantra work. Also be sure to notice any other mantras that appear in your life from your interactions and new-found awareness that might be useful to incorporate into your daily practice; as with every part of the Vedic tradition, listen to yourself and what works for you. If a friend is inspired by a particular mantra and mentions it to you, experiment with it and see if it has any effects for you.

Through vibrational awareness, sound work (including devotional music), and mantra practice, you can deepen the benefits of the rest of the Vedic knowledge system and grow further in your pursuit of self-awareness, balance, and spiritual growth. Find music that inspires you, attend concerts that touch your soul, and experiment with different sound techniques. Spend time in nature and notice the primordial sounds all around you, see if you can decipher the repeated mantras of nature. Explore the complex world of Sanskrit mantras and see what literally resonates with you. As you incorporate the techniques in this closing chapter, you will enhance the mind-body energetic work that you are doing through yoga and Ayurveda practices. Sound vibrations will serve to heal and realign you at many levels and positively align you toward better mental and physical health. The sound layer of your practice will serve as that extra edge that enables you to stay better tuned to the world around you, enjoy better health, and more effectively accomplish your work.

NOTES

1. Maryann Mott, "Did Animals Sense Tsumani Was Coming?," *National Geographic*, Jan. 4, 2005, https://www.nationalgeographic.com /animals/2005/01/news-animals-tsunami-sense-coming/.
2. Diana O. Neal and Linda L. Lindeke, "Music as a Nursing Intervention for Preterm Infants in the NICU," *Neonatal Network*, 2008, 27(5), 319–327, doi: 10.1891/0730-0832.27.5.319.
3. Amy Novotney, "Music as Medicine," *Science Watch*, Nov. 2013, 44(10), https://www.apa.org/monitor/2013/11/music.aspx.
4. Eric Haseltine, "Mental Telepathy Is Real," *Psychology Today*, Mar. 6, 2015, https://www.psychologytoday.com/us/blog/long -fuse-big-bang/201503/mental-telepathy-is-real.
5. B. Coruh, H. Ayele, M. Pugh, and T. Mulligan, "Does Religious Activity Improve Health Outcomes?: A Critical Review of the Recent Literature," PubMed.gov, May 2005, 1(3), 186–191, doi: 10.1016 /j.explore.2005.02.001.
6. James H. Fowler and Nicholas A. Christakis, "Dynamic Spread of Happiness in a Large Social Network: Longitudinal Analysis Over 20 Years in the Framingham Heart Study," *British Medical Journal*, 337(a2338), 1–9, https://doi.org/10.1136/bmj.a2338.
7. Dan Buettner, "POWER 9®: Reverse Engineering Longevity," Blue Zones, https://www.bluezones.com/2016/11/power-9/.
8. Thomas Ashley-Farrand, *Healing Mantras: Using Sound Affirmations for Personal Power, Creativity, and Healing* (New York: Ballantine Wellspring, 1999).
9. Ibid.
10. The number 108 is significant in the yoga tradition and is considered the ideal number of repetitions of any mantra used for healing. The number is also significant in astronomy since the distance between the Earth and the sun (our giver of life) is 108 times the diameter of the sun. This same ratio applies to the moon (a symbol of our mind in the Vedic tradition), where the distance between the Earth and the moon is 108 moon diameters. Also in the ancient Vedic astrology system, the moon has 108 specific locations from which it is measured, each with its own unique mental influence.
11. David Frawley, *Mantra Yoga and Primal Sound: Secrets of Seed (Bija) Mantras* (Twin Lakes, WI: Lotus Press, 2010).
12. See note 10 above.

SELF-REFLECTION QUESTIONS

1. Have you met people who gave off good vibes or bad vibes? What is it about them that gave you this feeling? Do you have a sense of where inside you this feeling came from?

2. How would you improve the vibes you are surrounded by in your life?

3. How would being more sensitive to people's vibes help you in your work and personal life?

4. What type of music moves you emotionally, and how often do you indulge in it? Are there any religious or spiritual traditions whose music you have wanted to explore?

5. What areas of life do you have the most challenges in currently? Do they relate to the areas covered by the chakras? Which chakra areas?

6. What sound practices will you incorporate into your life?

CONCLUSION

We hope the teachings in this book—from the most concrete diet and lifestyle coaching to the more abstract role of mantras and chakras—give you much strength, resilience, and happiness in life. As you integrate the different parts of this book into your life, we hope you find a much more powerful and fulfilling existence in your work and career, abundant joy and success in your personal life, and harmony between the two.

As you continue on your journey of learning and self-improvement, we invite you to notice the correlations between the ancient teachings of the Vedas and those of other traditions, as well as connections to modern self-help approaches. There is space within the Vedic system for any practice that brings you health, balance, and joy. You may be surprised where you see correlations, and it is okay to continue to explore various traditions and methodologies and adopt the teachings that benefit you the most. But we encourage you to consider the Vedic knowledge system as your foundation—your primary lifestyle framework. Based on our personal life experiences, our many observations of others in our lives, and the growing body of scientific evidence, it will lead you to your fullest potential of success and happiness, and that is what we want for you. We see it as the most elaborate and sophisticated system in human existence, with a truly holistic approach in understanding and harmonizing our relationship to the universe.

As you continue your practice of yoga and experience the ways it can improve your life, you might also be interested in exploring deeper areas of the Vedic tradition. Many of the references in this book can be used for deeper study in any areas of life management or your yoga journey. Attend discourses by learned teachers and inspiring people or consider a stay at a spiritual retreat or take a course on meditation, yoga, Vedic wisdom, or Ayurveda. With your growing self-knowledge and awareness, built through your continual processing and rebalancing practices, you will have the ability to easily recognize what best serves you throughout your life.

Remember that, as often as we look to the outside world for teachers, the ultimate teacher is within us. The Vedic system describes a *guru* as a dispeller of darkness, so anything or anyone in your life that sheds light on who you are acts as a guru, be it a friend, a child, a spouse, a teacher, or even an inanimate object, such as a mountain or river, that serves to inspire you. The same tradition, however, recognizes that the guru *within* us is the highest teacher of all, and that any guru, teacher, or enlightened saint only serves to connect us to the teacher within. So for instructor-led yoga classes or any kind of spiritual learning, be sure to connect to your inner teacher—it will take you to a deeper and more effective practice or understanding. In the words of Ramana Maharshi, "The Guru is none other than the Self. As the seeker's mind is bent outward, the Self takes a human shape as a Guru, to help drive it inward."

Above all, live with a clear sense of purpose, honor that purpose on a regular basis, and make sure you eat, sleep, work, and exercise in a thoughtful and balanced way. Look for help when you need it, and tune in to what you truly need, not based on what others tell you but based on your own powerful intuition coupled with your newfound knowledge. Do something to connect to your deeper power—to honor your higher nature—on a regular and consistent basis. Keep exploring your existence; be a "yogi scientist," as Vishvketu says.

We hope you find a deep, meaningful connection with yourself through your exploration of the wisdom of the Vedic knowledge system and use your new knowledge and power to do good and fulfilling work in this world, and live a life of happiness, harmony, and success.

SELF-REFLECTION QUESTIONS

1. What areas of further study into the Vedic tradition are interesting to you?

2. What other life-management tools would you like to explore further in conjunction with the Vedic framework?

ACKNOWLEDGMENTS

We are grateful for the knowledge of the Vedic tradition and for the opportunity to spread these teachings. We would like to thank all of our teachers from various knowledge approaches, both Eastern and Western, who have imparted so much wisdom to us.

We would like to thank our parents for honoring our interests and encouraging us to be true and authentic to our nature. We would also like to thank our family and friends who have supported us in our growth and our students and clients from whom we continue to learn so much.

We would like to specially acknowledge Baba Premnath, teacher to Yogrishi Vishvketu, through whom his wisdom continues to flow.

Vish would like to specially thank his wife, Kari, for the love and light that she emanates and the nourishing support she has provided throughout.

Finally, we would like to thank the Mandala Publishing team for the tremendous effort in bringing this project to light. Thank you to Robbie for sparking us to put words on paper, to Phillip for his spiritual support and belief in our message, to Tessa, Anna, and Rachel for their tireless editing to ensure our voices shine through, and to the design team for the art that communicates beyond words.

APPENDIX

Business Casual Yogi

Work Plan

CHAPTER ONE: LIFE OUT OF BALANCE

Through the methodology of *The Business Casual Yogi*, my vision is to _____.

_____ is a key factor holding me back from this vision.

CHAPTER TWO: YOGA BEYOND THE MAT

	Great	Needs Work	How I Will Improve
Yamas			
Non-violence			
Truthfulness			
Non-stealing			
Healthy sexuality			
Non-attached			
Niyamas			
Clean and tidy			
Contentment			
Discipline			
Introspection			
Surrender to higher power			

CHAPTER THREE: WHY ARE WE HERE? THE AIMS OF LIFE

	1	2	3	4	5
I live with a clear sense of purpose					
I earn financially in a healthy, balanced way					
I have fun in a healthy, balanced way					
I have regular spiritual practices					

I will bring more balance across my aims in life by:

_____

List of 10 mundane pleasures that I will draw from regularly each week.

1.
2.
3.
4.
5.
6.
7.
8.
9.
10.

CHAPTER FOUR: YOUR PURPOSE: WHERE ARE YOU HEADED?

My life purpose statement:

_____

CHAPTER FIVE: YOUR NATURE: WHO ARE YOU?

My primary and secondary doshas are:

_____   _____

CHAPTER SIX: BRINGING BALANCE TO YOUR LIFE

My ideal healthy daily routine:

Wake up at:

Morning activities:

Breakfast at:

Nature of morning work tasks:

Lunch at:

Nature of afternoon work tasks:

End work at:

Evening activities:

Dinner at:

Pre-bedtime activities:

In bed at:

Lights out at:

CHAPTER SEVEN: EATING FOR BALANCE

Types of foods I will reduce:

_____

Types of foods I will increase:

_____

Mindful eating habits I will cultivate:

_____

Fasting level:

I	II	III	IV	V

Every _____ months

CHAPTER EIGHT: TAKE A BREATH

Daily breathing exercises

		Number of Times	Number of Rounds
Full yogic breath:	☐		
Purification breath:	☐		
Alternate nostril breathing:	☐		
Ocean breath:	☐		
Honey bee breath	☐		
Cooling breath	☐		

CHAPTER NINE: MOVE YOUR BODY

Yoga asana sequence: | I | II | III |

Number of times per week: _____

Session length: _____

Custom routine:

CHAPTER TEN: MEDITATION: TRANSCEND YOUR LIMITATIONS

Meditation time per sitting: _____

Frequency per day: _____

CHAPTER ELEVEN: TUNING YOUR SYSTEM THROUGH SOUND

Specific chakra areas out of balance:

_____

Mantra practices (techniques, number of repetitions, number of times per week):

_____

_____

Other tools to incorporate into your life:

_____

_____

_____

PRONUNCIATION OF SANSKRIT TERMS

n this guide, long vowels are indicated using uppercase letters, and short vowels using lowercase letters.

A

ahimsa [a-him-sA]
ajna chakra [aj-nA chuk-ra]
ama [a-mA]
anahata chakra [a-nA-ha-tA
   chuk-ra]
anuloma viloma
   [anU-lomA-vI-lO-mA]
aparigraha [a-pa-rI-grA-ha]
ardhachandrasana
   [ar-dhA-chun-drA-sa-na]
artha [ar-thA]
asana [A-sa-na]
ashtanga [ash-tAn-gA]
asteya [A-stay-ya]
atma dharma [at-ma dhar-ma]
atha yoga anushasanam
   [athA-yO-ga-anu-sha-san-aM]
Ayurveda [ai-yur-vay-dA]
ayus [ai-yUs]

B

balakasana [ba-la-kA-sa-na]
bhajan [bha-jan]
bhakti yoga [bh-ak-tI yO-ga]
bhujangasana [bhu-jun-gA-sa-na]
brahmacharya [brha-ma-cha-ri-yA]
brahmari pranayama [brha-ma-rI
   prA-nA-yA-mA]

C

chakra [chuk-ra]
chandrasana [chun-drA-sa-na]
chetakasana [chay-tuck-A-sa-na]

D

dandasana [dun-dA-sa-na]
dharana [dhA-ra-na]
dharma [dhar-ma]
dhruvasana [droo-vA-sa-na]

dhyana [dhyA-na]
dosha [dO-shA]
dirgha [dir-gA]
dirgha pranayama [dir-gA
  prA-nA-yA-mA]

G
gayatri mantra [gA-yat-trI mun-tra]
guru [gu-ru]

I
ishvar pranidhan [ish-wa-ra
  prA-ni-dAn]

J
jal neti [jul nay-tI]
janusirsasana [jA-nu-shirs-A-sa-na]
japa [ja-puh]
jivanmukta [jI-vun mUk-tI]
jnana yoga [jyAn-a yO-ga]

K
kama [ka-ma]
kapalabhati [ka-pa-la-bhA-ti]
kapha [ka-fA]
karma yoga [kar-mA yO-ga]
kirtan [kir-tun]
klesha [klay-shA]
kriya [krI-yA]

M
mahamrityunjaya mantra [ma-hA-
  mrt-yun-ja-yA mun-tra]
mahaveerabhadrasana
  [ma-hA-vI-rA-bhad-rA-sa-na]
mala [ma-la]
malasana [mal-A-sa-na]
manipura chakra [ma-ni-pU-ra
  chuk-ra]
mantra [mun-tra]

marjariasana [mar-ja-rI-A-sa-na]
matsyasana [ma-tsyA-sa-na]
moksha [mOhk-sha]
muladhara chakra [mU-lA-dhA-ra
  chuk-ra]

N
nadi [na-dI]
nirakaar dhyan [nI-rA-kAAr
  di-hyA-n]
niyama [ni-ya-mA]

O
om [O-m]

P
panchakarma [punch-a-kar-mA]
pariwari dharma [pa-ri-wa-ri
  dhar-mA]
parvatasana [par-va-tA-sa-na]
paschimottasana
  [pa-shE-mO-ttA-nA-sa-na]
pavanamuktasana
  [pa-va-na-muk-ttA-sa-na]
pitta [pit-tA]
prana [prA-nA]
pranayama [prA-nA-yA-mA]
pratyahara [pra-tyA-hA-ra]
prsthauttanasana
  [prish-tha-Uta-nA-sa-na]
purushartas [pU-rU-shar-tAs]
purvottanasana
  [pUr-vO-ttAn-Asa-nA]

R
raja yoga [rA-ja yO-ga]

S
sahasrara chakra [sa-hes-rA
  chuk-ra]

sakaar dhyan [sa-kAr di-hyA-n]
samadhi [sa-mA-dhi]
samvega [sum-vay-gA]
sangha [sun-ghA]
sankalpa shakti [sun-kul-pa shuk-tI]
santosha [sun-tO-sha]
sarvangasana [sar-vAn-gA-sa-na]
satya [sut-ya]
saucha [shO-chA]
savasana [sa-vA-sa-na]
shakti [shuk-tI]
shanti [sh-An-tI]
sharir dharma [shA-rI-r dhar-ma]
shitali [si-tA-lI]
sohum [sO-huM]
sthira sukhum asanam
 [stI-ra-sU-kum-asA-nuM]
swadhisthana chakra [swA-dI-
 stA-nA chuk-ra]
swadhyaya [swAd-hai-yA]

T
tadasana [tA-dA-sa-na]
tapas [ta-pas]
tapasya [ta-pa-syA]
trikonasana [tri-kO-nA-sa-na]

U
ujjai [Uj-jA-yi]
ujaii pranayama [Uj-jA-yi
 prA-nA-yA-mA
utkatasana [Ut-kut-tA-sa-na]

V
vata [vA-ttA]
veda [vay-dA]
veerabhadrasana
 [vI-ra-bha-drA-sa-na]
vishuddha chakra [vi-shu-ddha
 chuk-ra]
vkrsasana [vk-rA-sa-na]

Y
yama [yA-ma]
yoga [yO-ga]
yoga nidra [yO-ga nid-rA]
yogas chitta vritti nirodha
 [yO-gus-chiT-tA-vrit-tI-nir-Od-hA]

INDEX

THE AUTHORS

VISH CHATTERJI, MBA

Vish Chatterji is an accomplished business leader turned executive coach with a track record spanning the automotive and technology industries. He has launched new businesses in hardware, software, and cloud products across global markets. He is recognized for his rapid-growth innovation strategies and his blend of creative thinking and operational skills.

Throughout his twenty-year career in corporate America, Vish maintained a diligent yoga and meditation practice as a way to ground and tackle the challenges of executive life. This practice started just after college during a backpacking trip through India to discover his roots. After months of adventures, riding on the roofs of buses, sleeping on dusty railway platforms, and sipping tea in remote villages, he decided his ultimate challenge would be to truly find himself by taking a solo spiritual trek through the Himalayas. A few days in, he hit some heavy snow and was forced to turn back. With a disappointed heart, as he descended below the tree line, he lost his bearings, mistakenly wandered down an animal trail, and ended up panicked and unsure of where he was.

In his effort to "find himself," he had found himself lost. Trying to stay calm, he made his way down the path of a mountain stream to find help. During that descent, he fell and hurt his ankle. Now lost, injured, and scared, he crawled the next several hours until he reached a village. The villagers took him in and nursed him until he was well enough to be carried out by donkey, jeep, and then bus, where he journeyed to the town of Rishikesh, the world capital of yoga. It was the town the Beatles went to during their self-seeking period, so Vish figured it would be a good place to recuperate.

There at the famous Yoga Niketan Ashram in Rishikesh, he met his dear lifelong friend and teacher, Yogrishi Vishvketu. The connection was instantaneous. Vishvketu spoke only a few words of English, while Vish spoke only a few words of Hindi. Though they shared the same name and same heritage, they were cultural opposites. Vishvketu a traditional Himalayan yogi who was celibate at the time, and Vish a former fraternity president who loved to party somehow connected and laughed away the next few weeks.

Over the next twenty years, they become close friends, advising each other through life, marriage, parenting, grief, and business. Vish became Vishvketu's business advisor through his growth from India to North America and helped build an internationally recognized yoga teacher training school and found and run an ashram in Rishikesh. Vishvketu became Vish's spiritual advisor and yoga teacher, advising him through his leadership journey in the corporate world and helping him to see and connect to his deeper and broader potential in being a coach and teacher.

During the intense funding negotiations of Vish's start-up, he escaped to one of Vishvketu's retreats in the Laurentian mountains of Canada, and during a forest walk, Vish lamented about his painful business challenges, and Vishvketu cryptically responded, "Vishwajeet [his Indian name], you do more yoga business, your business will be okay."

These words soon materialized into a major change in life direction for Vish. Almost serendipitously he started being asked by former colleagues for coaching help. Gladly accepting these timely opportunities, Vish soon had an organically growing coaching business in the midst of a collapsing start-up. He decided to formally exit the start-up in 2016 and honor his inner calling, blending the wisdom traditions of his ancestry with his professional experiences in the business world as a coach, teacher, and author.

Vish now resides in Los Angeles with his wife and three children and runs his coaching practice, Head & Heart Insights LLC, where he coaches, trains, and facilitates senior corporate executives to manifest the fullest of who they are in their life and work. He works with bright, self-aware leaders from big companies to small business owners by helping them clarify and execute their vision and strategy, both from a Western business perspective and through the tools of the Eastern traditions of yoga, Ayurveda, meditation, Vedic philosophy, and Vedic astrology. He speaks on the intersection of business and yoga and teaches meditation, yoga, and Ayurveda. He sits on the boards of several companies, serves as a trustee of Anand Prakash Ashram, serves on the board of counselors at the University of Southern California Masters of Business for Veterans program, and was elected to public office as a Board Director of the Beach Cities Health District in Los Angeles, focused on community preventative health programs. When he is not working, he can usually be found gardening, tinkering on projects around the house, cycling, cheering on his kids at soccer games and dance recitals, or playing with his family in the oceans and mountains of Southern California. Vish holds a bachelor's degree in mechanical engineering from Northwestern University and a master's of business administration from the University of Michigan's Stephen M. Ross School of Business. Vish is a certified executive coach, yoga teacher, meditation instructor, and Vedic counselor.

YOGRISHI VISHVKETU, PHD

Yogrishi Vishvketu grew up in a simple farmhouse surrounded by sugarcane fields in a rural area of northern India. He was quiet and contemplative as a child, but he had a mischievous streak. At age six, he snuck out of his home and ran as fast as he could to the nearest temple in the next village. Somehow, he navigated the ten miles to the temple and approached a monk, asking for his orange robes, the garb of a spiritual renunciate. The monk explained that Vishvketu was too young but gave him a written mantra to practice. When he returned home, to his parents' relief, he continued a normal childhood playing in the fields. But in the early mornings, before the family awoke, he would practice his mantra.

It wasn't even a couple of years later that his mother discovered a mountain of notebooks in his closet filled with the same mantra written over and over. She was naturally dismayed at her child's inability to let go of this spiritual penchant. He was now eight years old and stubborn and insistent. He begged her to let him leave home and go live in a traditional yoga school, known as a gurukul. So she made a pact: *If he washed and folded his clothes himself for one month, she would send him to the gurukul.* This was no challenge for Vishvketu, and by the month's end, he was enrolled in a jungle gurukul, Gurukul Mahavidyale Kanvashram, where he began his formal studies in the yoga tradition.

It was years later, while studying yoga and sports medicine at university, that he met Baba Premnath, a young ascetic from Rajasthan who used to dry his six-foot dreadlocks by dangling them from the second story of an ashram near the university. Baba Premnath's energy was immediate and wide open, and Vishvketu felt something shift in his consciousness upon meeting him. Baba Premnath began to teach the subtler, more esoteric aspects of yoga beyond the physical education Vishvketu was receiving. Baba Premnath initiated him with the name Vishvketu, meaning "the bridge that connects all worlds." This set Yogrishi Vishvketu on a journey of teaching others to bridge the realms of our human experience.

As Vishvketu neared graduation, eager to find a yoga teaching job, Baba Premnath prophesized, "You will not get a job from anyone; you will create jobs for others." As any college grad can attest, this would be disconcerting news to hear during recruiting season. True to the prophecy, a job did not materialize for Vishvketu, and so he went on to study yoga deeper.

After earning his doctoral degree in yoga, Vishvketu moved to the renowned Yoga Niketan Ashram in Rishikesh at the foothills of the Himalayas. There he sought advanced teachings in pranayama and yoga while teaching residential students from around the world. It was at this time that Vishvketu resolved to leave society and live the life of an ascetic in the forests and caves of the Himalayas. He wanted to go deeper into his spiritual practice and renounce the world, as many yogis before him had done. With some despondency around his life direction, he retreated into a three-month vow of silence and intensified his yogic practices to discover himself more deeply. During this time, his teacher appeared to him in a vision with a message Vishvketu did not want to hear: Baba Premnath said, "You will be a teacher of teachers."

Emerging from his isolation, he honored his teacher's words and started to manifest this destiny through the help of the Yoga Niketan Ashram and the support of the international students who had begun to follow him. He began to be known for his infectious laughter, deep wisdom, and delightful teaching stories. It was in the days after his solitude that his coauthor and friend Vish landed at the Yoga Niketan Ashram, and a close lifelong friendship developed.

Vishvketu then moved on to Canada, where he founded Akhanda Yoga Teacher Training, and in 2007, he cofounded the Anand Prakash Yoga Ashram in Rishikesh, where he continues to manifest his destiny of training yoga teachers from around the world. He also founded a charitable school, the Sansar Gyaan Pathshala, a free school for over two hundred fifty underserved children in rural Uttar Pradesh, India.

Vishvketu currently spends half the year at Anand Prakash teaching and the other half traveling across Europe, Asia, and North America teaching at yoga workshops and conferences. He is known for his authentic teachings and genuine lineage in the yoga tradition of the Himalayas, and he is called by those that know him the "yogi who laughs a lot." His deepest aim is to inspire people to connect to their true nature, one that is fearless, expansive, joyful, and playful. He is the author of *Yogasana: The Encyclopedia of Yoga Poses*, for which he researched, compiled, named, and photographed over eight hundred yoga poses. He is also the father of two young children who live in Ottawa, Canada. Vishvketu holds a bachelor's degree in yoga and sports medicine from Haryana Agricultural University and a master's and doctorate in yoga philosophy from Gurukul Kangri at the University of Haridwar.